Chicken Soup for the Soul®

Dads & Daughters

Our
101
BEST
STORIES

Chicken Soup for the Soul® Our 101 Best Stories:
Dads & Daughters; Stories about the Special Relationship between Fathers and Daughters by
Jack Canfield, Mark Victor Hansen & Amy Newmark

Published by Chicken Soup for the Soul Publishing, LLC   www.chickensoup.com

The publisher gratefully acknowledges the many publishers and individuals who
granted Chicken Soup for the Soul permission to reprint the cited material.

Cover photos courtesy of © Radius Images/Alamy, iStockphotos.com/sunnyfrog. Interior
illustration courtesy of iStockphoto.com/Vjom

Cover and Interior Design & Layout by Pneuma Books, LLC
For more info on Pneuma Books, visit www.pneumabooks.com

Distributed to the booktrade by Simon & Schuster. SAN: 200-2442

Publisher's Cataloging-in-Publication Data
(Prepared by The Donohue Group)

Chicken soup for the soul. Selections.
    Chicken soup for the soul : dads & daughters : stories about the special
relationship between fathers and daughters / [compiled by] Jack Canfield
[and] Mark Victor Hansen ; [edited by] Amy Newmark.

    p. ; cm. -- (Our 101 best stories)

    ISBN-13: 978-1-935096-19-1
    ISBN-10: 1-935096-19-2

1. Fathers and daughters--Literary collections. 2. Fathers--Literary collections. 3.
Daughters--Literary collections. 4. Fathers and daughters--Conduct of life--Anecdotes.
I. Canfield, Jack, 1944- II. Hansen, Mark Victor. III. Newmark, Amy. IV. Title.

PN6071.F3 C484 2008
810.8/03520431   2008932007

PRINTED IN THE UNITED STATES OF AMERICA
on acid∞free paper
16 15 14 13 12 10 09 08   01 02 03 04 05 06 07 08

Chicken Soup for the Soul

Our 101 BEST STORIES

Dads & Daughters

Stories about the
Special Relationship between
Fathers and Daughters

Jack Canfield
Mark Victor Hansen
Amy Newmark

CSS

Chicken Soup for the Soul Publishing, LLC
Cos Cob, CT

Chicken Soup for the Soul

Contents

A Special Foreword by Jack and Mark xi

❶
~No Better Way to Say I Love You~

1. The Wedding, *John P. Walker* 1
2. Love in a Box, *Nancy Julien Kopp* 5
3. You Did Good, *Carla Riehl* 8
4. The Look, *Patty Swyden Sullivan* 12
5. Daddy's Gift, *Shirley Garrett* 15
6. The Best One, *Michelle Marullo* 18
7. The Painted Tractor, *Bobbie Wilkinson* 20
8. Let Us Be United, *Kimi Beaven* 23
9. Daddy's Best Birthday, *Nita Sue Kent* 27
10. Beacon of Faith, *Margot Brown McWilliams* 30

❷
~Daddy's Little Girl~

11. The Dad He Planned to Be, *Stephanie Welcher Thompson* 37
12. Baby's First Words, *Sarah Monagle* 40
13. Long Distance Vitamins, *Emily Chase* 42
14. Gone Fishin', *David Clinton Matz* 44
15. Becoming a Jock Dad, *Andy Smith* 46
16. A Snow Cloud's Silver Lining, *Annmarie B. Tait* 49
17. A Special Bond, *Ed Mickus* 52
18. To Any Service Member, *Nick Hill* 55
19. The Trellis, *Daniel Schantz* 57
20. Wedding Day, *Pamela G. Smith* 60
21. My Traveling Companion, *Edmund W. Boyle* 62
22. Questions, *Danny Dugan* 65

❸
~"Step"ping Up to the Plate~

23. My Daughter, Once Removed, *William Jelani Cobb*..............71
24. Step-Babies, *Christie Craig* 75
25. The Unconditional Step, *Donald R. Novakovich* 79
26. Father Christmas, *Steven H. Manchester* 82
27. He Completed Us, *Michelle Lawson* 86
28. She Calls Me Daddy, *John Cox*....................................88
29. A Tale of Two Fathers, *Kimberly Ripley* 90

❹
~Gratitude~

30. Memorial Day Flags, *Arthur B. Wiknik Jr.*........................97
31. A Daughter's Letter, *Rani Nicola* 100
32. Trust Me, *Lanny Zechar*..103
33. A Bouquet to Remember, *Cindy L. Lassalle*.......................105
34. The Best "Father-Daughter Date" Ever!
    Carol McClain Bassett 108
35. Batter Up, Dad, *Anne Carter* 112
36. The Camping Trip, *Laura M. Stack*...............................115
37. The Visit, *Tre' M. Barron*......................................118
38. Softball People, *Stacey Becker*................................120
39. A Tribute to Gramps, *Dana O'Connor and Melissa Levin*......125

❺
~ Through the Eyes of a Child~

40. God's Hands, *Shirley Pope Waite*................................131
41. The Little Broom, *Bruce Porter* 132
42. A Garden So Rich, *Christie Craig*...............................136
43. Anna's First Cubs Game, *Louis Schutz* 139
44. A New Strength, *Kara L. Dutchover*..............................141
45. Moonshine, *Debra Ann Pawlak* 144

46. You Can Share My Daddy, *Linda L. Kerby*............................147
47. On the Nose, *D. B. Zane* 149
48. The Best Game I Never Saw, *Darrel Radford* 152
49. Just a Walk in the Park, *Steven H. Manchester* 155

❻

~Learning from Each Other~

50. What Do You Have to Say for Yourself? *Kate Rowinski*........163
51. Refresher Lesson from Dad, *Pamela Bumpus*.......................166
52. Honest Mike, *Marilyn Diephuis Sweeney* 168
53. Ghost Mother, *Michele Bender* 170
54. A Practice Round for Life, *Debra Moss* 174
55. Mollie's Moment, *Bill Shore* 178
56. Given Away, *Renata Waldrop* 181
57. The Gag Gift, *George Parler* 184
58. Only One, *J. G. Nursall*..187
59. Simple Wooden Boxes, *Martha Pendergrass Templeton*........192
60. Nonno Beppe's Gift, *Susanna Palomares* 195

❼

~Loss and Grieving~

61. A Surprise Gift for Mother, *Sarah A. Rivers* 201
62. Budding Hope, *Elaine G. Dumler* 204
63. The Ride, *Michelle Beaupre Matt*..207
64. The Smell of Grass, *Adelaide Isaac*.......................................210
65. Both Sides Now, *Bobbie Probstein*...212
66. Daddy's Garden, *Linda Swartz Bakkar* 215
67. Our Own Perfect Rainbow, *Liz Allison*...................................217
68. My Dad, *Brenda Gallardo* 219

❽

~The Power of Forgiveness~

69. Father Knows Best, *Abigail R. Gutierrez* 225
70. The Miracle of Forgiveness, *Karen Davis Lees* 228
71. Never Too Late, *Debra J. Schmidt* 231
72. The Haircut, *Margaret J. Wasilewski* 235
73. Behind the Mirror, *Laura Reilly* 239
74. Letter to a Stranger, *Karen L. Cooper* 242
75. A Dance with Dad, *Jean Jeffrey Gietzen* 247
76. Daddy's Story, *Ruth A. Hancock* 250

❾

~Treasured Moments~

77. I'm Daddy's Girl, *Becky Freeman* 257
78. The Day I Met The Splendid Splinter, *Ted Janse* 259
79. A Musical Eye-Opener, *Nancy B. Gibbs* 262
80. Daddy's Dance, *Louise Tucker Jones* 263
81. Turning Back the Clock, *Betty Cuniberti* 266
82. Naming Worms, *Allison McWood* 269
83. Who Giveth? *S. Maitland Schrecengost* 272
84. The Anniversary, *Ken Swarner* 274
85. Secret Ingredients, *Jane Zaffino* 276
86. One for the Books, *Becky Lee Weyrich* 279
87. We Are Dragon-Slayers, *Timothy P. Bete* 283
88. Summer Memories, *Harmony Zieman* 286
89. A Garden for Four, *Rayne Wolfe* 289
90. What's Up with Dads and Pork Chop Sandwiches?
     Angela Cervantes 292
91. Old Love Turned Brand New,
     Vicki Frizzell as told to Janet Matthews 296

⑩

~ I Will Always Be There for You~

92. Sand Castles, *Jennifer Reichert* 303
93. Just Between Us, *Janet Lynn Mitchell* 307
94. My Dad, My Source for Healing, *Kelsey Cameron* 310
95. I Love You, Pilgrim, *Aletheia Lee Butler* 312
96. The Promise, *Antonio Farias* 315
97. Run for Gold, *Ruth Barden* 319
98. Arm-in-Arm, *Michele Wallace Campanelli* 322
99. Secret Tears, *Nancy B. Gibbs* 325
100. Promises Kept, *Kristi Powers* 328
101. One More Cast, *Bruce Masterman* 331

MORE CHICKEN SOUP 334
WHO IS *JACK CANFIELD*? 343
WHO IS *MARK VICTOR HANSEN*? 345
WHO IS *AMY NEWMARK*? 347
ACKNOWLEDGMENTS 349

Chicken Soup for the Soul

A Special Foreword

by Jack and Mark

For us, 101 has always been a magical number. It was the number of stories in the first *Chicken Soup for the Soul* book, and it is the number of stories and poems we have always aimed for in our books. We love the number 101 because it signifies a beginning, not an end. After 100, we start anew with 101.

We hope that when you finish reading one of our books, it is only a beginning for you too—a new outlook on life, a renewed sense of purpose, a strengthened resolve to deal with an issue that has been bothering you. Perhaps you will pick up the phone and share one of the stories with a friend or a loved one. Perhaps you will turn to your keyboard and express yourself by writing a Chicken Soup story of your own, to share with other readers who are just like you.

This volume contains our 101 best stories and poems about fathers and their daughters. We share this with you at a very special time for us, the fifteenth anniversary of our *Chicken Soup for the Soul* series. When we published our first book in 1993, we never dreamed that we had started what became a publishing phenomenon, one of the best-selling series of books in history.

We did not set out to sell more than one hundred million books, or to publish more than 150 titles. We set out to touch the heart of one person at a time, hoping that person would in turn touch another person, and so on down the line. Fifteen years later, we know that it has worked. Your letters and stories have poured in by the hundreds of thousands, affirming our life's work, and inspiring us to continue to make a difference in your lives.

On our fifteenth anniversary, we have new energy, new resolve, and new dreams. We have recommitted to our goal of 101 stories or poems per book, we have refreshed our cover designs and our interior layouts, and we have grown the Chicken Soup for the Soul team, with new friends and partners across the country in New England.

In this new volume, we have selected our 101 best stories and poems about fathers and their daughters from our rich fifteen-year history. The stories that we have chosen were written by fathers about their daughters, and by daughters about their fathers. There is no denying the special bond between fathers and daughters as they move through life's phases, from birth to childhood, to those sometimes difficult teen years, to marriage and grandchildren, and to end-of-life issues.

We hope that you will enjoy reading these stories as much as we enjoyed selecting them for you, and that you will share them with your families and friends. We have identified the 35 *Chicken Soup for the Soul* books in which the stories originally appeared, in case you would like to continue reading about parenting and families among our other books. We hope you will also enjoy the additional books about parenting, sports, and life in general in "Our 101 Best Stories" series.

With our love, our thanks, and our respect,
~*Jack Canfield and Mark Victor Hansen*

Chapter 1

Dads & Daughters

No Better Way to Say I Love You

*Blessed indeed is the man
who hears many gentle voices call him father!
~Lydia M. Child*

The Wedding

*What lies behind us and what lies before us are tiny matters
compared to what lies within us.*
~Ralph Waldo Emerson

Jack and Jean were among our earliest friends when I began ministry in my very first church as full-time pastor. Their friendly faces and warm smiles were a great encouragement to a young preacher with the Sunday morning pulpit jitters. The smiles were genuine, and that was a surprise to me. They had been through more trials than almost anyone I'd known.

Jack had been a chemist with a successful company. Over a period of ten years, a diagnosis of severe rheumatoid arthritis took Jack from being a healthy workingman to someone confined to a wheelchair and living on a disability pension. By the time I met him, he could move himself from the wheelchair only with great difficulty, and then, only to shift to another chair, or to stand for a moment. Pain and effort showed in his face when making these transitions, which were usually few and far between.

He and Jean got around well in a new van, converted for the wheelchair. A small elevator installed in their townhouse moved Jack between the floors, and despite his misshapen, arthritis-bent fingers, he learned to use a computer and assisted us at the church with some of our financial work.

Through Jack and Jean, I came to know their now-adult daughters. When Susan, the eldest, arrived at my office to ask me to perform a wedding for her and her fiancé, Eric, it was no great surprise.

Her father had hinted only a few weeks earlier that this might be coming.

The counseling and the planning of the ceremony seemed to go by very quickly, and soon it was almost time for the wedding. One day Susan made an unscheduled stop at my office. From the look on her face, I knew that something was seriously wrong. She came straight to the point. "My dad wants to walk me down the aisle," she said, close to tears. "He really thinks he can do it. He absolutely insists on it."

"I'll practice until the wedding. I'm going to do this," he told me adamantly while we sat at his kitchen table drinking tea the next day. "Please pray for me!" I knew there was no changing his mind when he was determined to do something, and so I let the subject drop. I did, however, pray.

When the evening of the rehearsal arrived, we set up several scenarios which would allow Jack to "present" the bride. Only one of the three involved him walking, and we included it only to please Jack. A brief experiment that evening seemed to deflate Jack's determination as he only took a few steps before he had to sit back down. From the platform, I watched sadly as he hung his head where he sat. Again I prayed.

The wedding day arrived. Everything was going as planned. At the top of the hour, I found myself standing on the steps of the platform with groom and groomsmen awaiting the bridal party.

The music began playing and the bridesmaids proceeded down the aisle. Each paused and turned as she passed the front row of pews and took her place opposite the groomsmen. The maid of honor was last to walk, and as she turned in her appointed position, the music softly concluded.

After a brief pause, the organist played the dramatic opening notes of the wedding march. "Will you all please stand," I instructed.

I found myself thinking of Jack. He had been brought up the steps to the sanctuary earlier, and now waited in the wheelchair by the door. With the struggles of the previous evening still in mind, I was sure that Jack would not be walking the aisle today. I was disappointed for his sake, but I couldn't imagine his hurt. This had meant so much to him.

The doors to the church sanctuary opened to the side at the rear. This meant that the bride would have to walk behind the last row of pews before turning into the center aisle. I could just make out Susan's progress above the heads of the now standing congregation because of the puff of white taffeta that stood up from her veil.

I saw that puff of white stop, and then murmuring began near the back of the church. A moment later, the beautiful bride made her turn into the main aisle. It took a second to realize what was happening. Susan was being escorted by her father, and he was walking!

Slowly, and painfully, Jack took a few steps and then paused to catch his breath. With a cane in his left hand and her arm on his right, father and daughter moved toward me. It seemed as if the entire congregation was holding its collective breath, all of us fearing that the next step would be the last. I believe, in that moment, that we were all unified in prayer for Jack.

The organist looked at me with panic in her eyes as the music came close to its conclusion. I motioned for her to continue playing, and a few more minutes inched past before the bride and her father finally arrived at the front.

As the music concluded, I quickly gathered my thoughts. Still awestruck, I voiced a rather shaky introduction. I almost choked up when I asked, "Who presents this woman to be married to this man?" Jack's voice came back clear and strong, and not without some measure of pride: "Her mother and I do."

As Susan hugged her father and then took her place alongside her soon-to-be husband, I noticed that her face was wet with tears. I noticed my own face was wet. In fact, it seemed like the whole congregation had been deeply moved.

The wedding reception which followed was a wonderful affair. It was one of the grandest I had ever attended. But whatever the charm or excitement of the post-wedding celebration, the highlight of the day, in everyone's eyes, remained the miracle we had witnessed shortly before. The miracle of Jack, with determination born of love, and with faith in the living God, escorting his daughter down the aisle on her wedding day!

No truer words express the miracle of that day as those written in Mark 10:27: "With man this is impossible, but not with God; all things are possible with God."

~John P. Walker
Chicken Soup for the Christian Woman's Soul

Love in a Box

What we remember from childhood we remember forever—
permanent ghosts, stamped, inked, imprinted, eternally seen.
~Cynthia Ozick

When I was a little girl, I found love in a box all because of a class assignment. On a Friday night I made an announcement at the dinner table. The words bubbled out in a torrent of excitement I could no longer contain. "My teacher said we have to bring a box for our valentines on Monday. But it has to be a special box, all decorated."

Mother said, "We'll see," and she continued eating.

I wilted faster than a flower with no water. What did "We'll see" mean? I had to have that box or there would be no valentines for me. My second grade Valentine's Day would be a disaster. Maybe they didn't love me enough to help me with my project.

All day Saturday I waited, and I worried, but there was no mention of a valentine box. Sunday arrived, and my concern increased, but I knew an inquiry about the box might trigger anger and loud voices. I kept an anxious eye on both my parents all day. In 1947, in my house, children only asked once. More than that invited punitive measures.

Late Sunday afternoon, my father called me into our apartment's tiny kitchen. The table was covered with an assortment of white crepe paper, red construction paper, and bits and pieces of lace and ribbon from my mother's sewing basket. An empty shoebox rested on top of the paper. Relief flooded through me when Daddy said, "Let's get started on your project."

In the next hour my father transformed the empty shoebox into a valentine box I would never forget. Crepe paper covered the ugly cardboard. My father fashioned a wrinkled piece of the pliable paper and glued it around the middle. He cut a slot in the lid and covered it with more of the white paper. Next came red hearts attached in what I considered all the right places. He hummed a tune while he worked, and I kneeled on my chair witnessing the magical conversion of the shoebox and handing him the glue when he needed it. When he finished, my father's eyes sparkled, and a smile stretched across his thin face. "What do you think of that?"

My answer was a hug and a "Thank you, Daddy."

But inside, joy danced all the way to my heart. It was the first time that my father devoted so much time to me. His world consisted of working hard to support his family, adoring my mother, disciplining my brother and me, and listening to every sports event broadcast on the radio. Suddenly, a new door opened in my life. My father loved me.

Monday morning, my mother found a brown grocery sack to protect the beautiful box while I carried it to school. I barely felt the bitter cold of the February day as I held the precious treasure close to me. I would let no harm come to my beautiful valentine box.

My teacher cleared a space on a long, wide windowsill where the decorated boxes would stay until Valentine's Day. I studied each one as it was placed on the sill, and none compared with mine. Every time I peeked at my valentine box, I felt my father's love. My pride knew no bounds. There were moments when the box actually glowed in a spotlight all its own. No doubt I was the only one who witnessed that glow.

Every day some of my classmates brought valentine cards to school and slipped them into the slots of the special boxes. The holiday party arrived, and we brought our boxes to our desks to open the valentines. Frosted heart cookies, red punch, valentines and giggles filled our classroom. Chaos reigned until dismissal time arrived.

I carried my valentine box home proudly. It wasn't hidden in a grocery sack but held out for the world to admire. I showed it to the policeman who guided us across a busy city street. He patted me on the head and exclaimed about it. I made sure everyone along the way took note of my valentine box. My father had made it for me, and the love that filled it meant more to me than all the valentines nestled inside.

From that time on I never doubted my father's feelings for me. The valentine box became a symbol of his love that lasted through decades of other Valentine's Days. He gave me other gifts through the years, but none ever compared with the tender love I felt within the confines of the old, empty shoebox.

~Nancy Julien Kopp
Chicken Soup for the Father & Daughter Soul

You Did Good

Never part without loving words to think of during your absence.
It may be that you will not meet again in this life.
~Jean Paul Richter

My dad grew up during the Depression and later fought in World War II. When he was born, his own father was too old and tired to invest any time in his only child, so my dad learned early on how to work hard and make money. And no matter how bad things might be, my dad always knew how to look strong. In the postwar era, when everyone wanted to erase their horrifying memories and emotions, my father became a master at burying his feelings. After liberating the concentration camps and seeing the worst that any war had to offer, keeping his feelings inside was the only way my dad knew how to survive.

Without realizing it, my dad became domineering and controlling. As a parent, he did anything for his children and worked hard to provide the best for us. However, if he didn't agree with us about something, our feelings didn't interest him; his opinions always prevailed—"case closed." When it was time for emotional intimacy or vulnerability, my father played his cards close to his chest. He kept his feelings locked in a vault to which no one, including himself, had the combination.

Still, despite our being very different emotionally, my dad was my hero.

He was a world-class businessman, a marketing genius, an entrepreneur, a singer and a true visionary. When I was learning how to dream, he taught me how to dream big. "Broaden your horizons, sweetie," he used to say. "There's a whole world out there and nothing's stopping you." I emulated him, quoted him and listened for every nugget of wisdom I could glean from him.

I was a musician, actress and writer. Somehow, those occupations just didn't fit the bill with my father; what I did never seemed to meet his approval. Poetry and songwriting were intangible and involved an area unsafe for him: emotions.

"What are you doing out there in the backyard with your guitar and your journals, anyway?" he would ask me sarcastically when I was younger.

"I'm just writing songs," I answered, trying not to feel ashamed.

"Writing songs? How are you going to earn a living? What are you going to have to fall back on?" he demanded, exasperated.

There were things we could never talk about, things that were painfully left unsaid. I wanted with all my heart to tell my dad what a hero he was to me. I wanted him to understand who I really was. I began to wonder if the reason he couldn't approve of me was that he never really approved of himself. He was so hard on everybody, but he was the hardest and most unforgiving of himself. I tried to crack the door to his heart on many occasions. I tried so hard to share my feelings and create a bond of intimacy, but it was too awkward for him, too frightening. I often sent him sentimental cards and told him I loved him. He would hug me, but then crack a joke and cover it. There was so much that I needed to say to him, but I didn't know how to do it.

One Friday night I came home late for dinner and my son announced, "Grandpa's been trying to call you all day and is waiting for you to call him."

How strange, I thought. It was always my mom who did the long-distance calling while my dad sat in his recliner and read the paper, calling out things that she was supposed to remember to tell "the kids." Why would my dad be trying all day to reach me? I was tired and hungry and thought about calling him in the morning, but decided to dial him then. He answered right away and was relieved to hear from me.

"I've got a problem, sweetie," he said directly, "and I need your advice."

My advice? When had my father ever approached me as an adult for advice?

He was upset about some things going on among our relatives and actually wanted to confide in me about it. I was shocked. He was thoughtful and introspective and it drew me in.

"Oh, I probably shouldn't worry about them," he said trying to appear strong, "but it just drives me crazy."

We talked a long time and as he opened up to me, I felt that door to his heart crack open, something I had waited for my whole life. The more he shared his frustrations and reached out to me, the more I felt I could cross the line and tell him how I really felt.

"Dad," I began. "You know, you're not only a great person, you did a great job as a father. Did I ever tell you that?"

He didn't say anything, but I knew he was listening intently. "You did a great job," I exhorted. "I know you're upset now, but things will work out with everybody. The main thing I just want you to do is to give yourself credit—you never give yourself enough credit, Dad. You sent me to college, you gave me a vision, you supported me."

I'd finally said it.

He laughed good-naturedly. I continued, "I owe you a thank you, and I hope you realize how much you did for me as my dad."

I could almost hear him smiling on the other end. I knew he was touched and felt a little awkward. His voice sounded shaky. "Well, we got you educated," he said, laughing nervously.

"You did more than that," I said. "You did good."

"You like your house now, and your life?" he asked quietly, catching me off guard.

"Yeah, Dad, I'm happy. You don't have to worry—things are going great for us."

"That's good," he said, with a sigh of relief. "So everything's okay, then?" he asked, almost as if he were checking it all off a list that would allow him to rest easier.

"Everything's great, Dad."

I told him I loved him and he told me he loved me and I hung up the phone. As I got ready for bed, I thought about what an amazing conversation we had. I was high with the emotional intimacy, which had been long overdue.

Ten hours later, my mother called, waking me. I could hardly understand what she was trying to say.

"Your father's dead!" she screamed. "I found him lying on the dining room floor. He had just opened the drapes to let the sun in, and he fell over dead."

Suddenly I was standing straight up beside my bed, clinging to the phone and sobbing.

"Where are you right now, Mom?"

"I'm sitting here waiting for the police to come."

"Are you there alone?"

"Yes, but the neighbors are on their way over."

I was a thousand miles away. All I could think about was how many hours, minutes and seconds it would take me to jump on a plane and get there. I thought about my mother sitting there alone with my father, and I couldn't move fast enough.

The flight was long and painful, like a slow-motion dream. I had planned on going home to see my dad and mom in another month, and I wept aloud, thinking I was too late. Then I suddenly realized the incredible miracle of it all: I hadn't been late at all. Actually, everything had been right on time.

~Carla Riehl
Chicken Soup for the Christian Woman's Soul

The Look

He didn't tell me how to live; he lived, and let me watch him do it.
~Clarence Budington Kelland

We grew up viewing the documentation of our parents' love. Every year, on their anniversary, a white twin bed sheet pinned to brocade drapes served as our improvised movie screen. We sat mesmerized by the sight of their 1947 wedding. Live. On film.

I loved seeing Dad's thick wavy black hair and strong athletic build. Mom was more beautiful than Cinderella or Snow White, possessing the aura of a princess. They filled the screen with glamour, excitement and fairy-tale magic.

And then there was that look. The expression on Dad's face as he beheld his bride taught me to search a man's eyes for that same glowing reflection of devotion, awe and pride.

The images on our homemade screen reinforced in our minds the daily affection they demonstrated for us. The secret winks Dad sent Mom's way were intended to fly over our heads, but of course we always caught them, and they brought a sense of security. I identified his conspiratorial wink as a sign of their complete solidarity. They were an inseparable twosome moving through life as one.

So I began a quest for the real-life personification of the images I viewed on a plain bed sheet. My dream man was crystal clear in my mind. I wanted to find a husband to love me the way my dad loved my mom. I would recognize him by the look in his eye.

Of course, it is one thing to know what you are looking for; it is quite another to find it. But miracles do happen.

Like my parents, we met at a party. Bob spotted me — as the romantic cliché goes — across a crowded room, and asked his friend to introduce us. Frank dutifully steered me over. As soon as I saw him, my gaze locked with his. I was unaware of how gorgeous he was; I was far too distracted by his eyes boring into mine.

This look belonged to me.

If it was the look in his eyes that rocked me, it was learning about him and getting to know the depth of his character that steadied my feet. He was solid, loyal, witty, compassionate and charming. He was my dream come true.

I wanted desperately to introduce Bob to my parents — my role models for love. Unfortunately, by this time Dad was deeply immersed in his battle with Alzheimer's and was, for the most part, nonverbal. Locked away in his private world, he seldom even made eye contact.

But I needed him, in whatever limited capacity he could command, to meet and get to know Bob. I sought his approval for the biggest decision of my life. I knew Bob was the right man for me but I yearned for Dad's recognition, too.

The first time I introduced them, Dad cursed. His hand was caught between the edge of the kitchen table and the arm of his chair. It's funny how profanities survive in an otherwise frozen mind. I had hoped for a more tender meeting.

As we sat at the table, we watched for any sign of acknowledgement from Dad. He, however, was far too busy inspecting the tablecloth to notice us — absorbed, repeatedly rubbing his fingers along the stitched hem.

Bob said softly to me, "Honey, I think your dad may need his chin wiped clean."

I blotted Dad's chin with a soft cloth. His eyes lifted to rest briefly on mine and the gratitude in them squeezed my heart. In those precious fleeting seconds, I had my dad back. Then he cast his eyes downward and was gone again. I remember that moment precisely because the feeling was so overwhelming.

I was consumed with love and admiration for the indomitable, yet gentle, strength exuding from both sides of the table.

The second time Bob and I visited, we helped Mom put Dad to bed. As we lowered him down, he grabbed Bob's arm and in hushed, slurred words requested: "Come back." We were making progress.

The third time these two men of mine met, Dad sat in his usual silence. Not so usual was that Dad's eyes fixated on Bob with a calculated intensity. Then for the first time in longer than I could remember, my father spoke clearly and loudly.

"Marry her," he said to Bob. Bob was only too happy to comply.

My dad passed away shortly after speaking those words. Yet even though he was physically absent, I snatched glimpses of him at our wedding. In my mind, he was there at my mother's side gazing at her with love-filled eyes. And when I observed my new husband across a ballroom overflowing with family and friends, Bob gave me that look I so dearly remembered, and softly sealed it with a secret wink.

~Patty Swyden Sullivan
Chicken Soup for the Bride's Soul

Daddy's Gift

It's Christmas and I'm worn out. All the activities are draining, depleting me of energy, enthusiasm and confidence. Looking for a way to leave it behind, I wander outdoors and straddle my bicycle. It's a regular old bicycle, nothing fancy, but just the right vehicle to free my spirit. As I pedal up the driveway toward the street, I wander back in time.

It was 1955, on the eve of the first real Christmas my sister, Mary, and I ever had, and Daddy was determined that his two new daughters would find it filled with love and joy. I was four, Mary was two and the entire process of "coming to live with" Daddy, Mama and Lamar, a big brother, took place without their ever laying eyes on us. When asked how he could adopt two children sight unseen, Daddy answered, "It doesn't matter to me what they look like. If they need a home, we want 'em."

Our first two months with them were joyful, but expensive. We brought with us a lot of "needs"—tonsils to remove, medications to take, clothes to buy. But our greatest need was for emotional support and reassurance that this was indeed our home—for life. I knew there was a chance that our birth parents would reclaim us—a right they could exercise for up to a year.

The townspeople pitched in. Neighbors hosted a "children's shower," the local pharmacist donated the required medications and someone even provided a new tricycle for Santa to bring Mary. My little sister and I were so excited about our first Christmas. We learned about Jesus and how much He loved us. For the first time in our lives, we listened to Bible stories and sang "Jesus Loves Me." We learned to say the blessing and our prayers.

As the holidays approached, Aunt Florice secretly put the finishing touches on a set of matching mother-daughter dresses that Daddy knew would leave Mama in tears. Lamar, at fourteen, helped plan the details of how Santa would deliver the new baby dolls and the blocks that had been fashioned in the shop from leftover bits of wood.

Everything seemed to be in order for the wonderful Christmas celebration—yet Daddy was restless. He couldn't forget about the small blue bicycle Santa had been offered for just ten dollars, even though he and Mama had agreed they had spent enough.

On Christmas Eve, Daddy paced and thought, and thought and paced. He sensed that I had the most profound scars from our past. I was afraid of the dark, afraid of enclosed spaces, even afraid to go to the bathroom alone. In fact, I could not speak an intelligible sentence and often needed little Mary to interpret for me.

As dusk fell, he told Mama he had one last errand to run. On Christmas morning, my eyes grew wide when I saw the beautiful blue bicycle beside the tree. I couldn't wait to take it outside to the sidewalk. Daddy eagerly helped me learn and quickly recognized that I didn't need the training wheels after all. When they were removed, I pedaled and Daddy released his hold on the bicycle, sending me off for the first time on the road to freedom. But even as he let me go, he ran alongside me, there to help me if I wavered too far off course.

Now as I ride into the wind, calmed and recharged, I realize that long-ago bicycle trip had been the first of what would be a lifetime of send-offs. And with each one, whether I was attending my first day of school, learning to drive a car, heading off to college or landing my first real job, Daddy provided me with a way to soar along with the "training wheels" of a Christian home. And he and Mama were there, running alongside me whenever I questioned my course.

The melody plays in my head—"Jesus loves me, yes I know."

I enter a straightaway, rediscover my center of balance, release the handlebars and lift my hands to the sky in jubilant celebration and gratefulness for Daddy's gift.

~Shirley Garrett
Chicken Soup for the Christian Woman's Soul

The Best One

Always kiss your children goodnight—
even if they're already asleep.
~H. Jackson Brown, Jr.

When I was a little girl, my father had a time-honored tradition of tucking me into bed. Following my bedtime story, he would give me a nose kiss, tickle my stomach and whisper the most wonderful words into my ear.

"Michelle, of all the little girls in the whole wide world... " he would pause.

"Yes, Daddy?"

"How did your mommy and I get so lucky to get the best one?"

Before he had time to finish, I would say, "You got me!"

And then he would continue, "The best little girl in the whole wide world, and we got you."

"You got me!" I would scream and clap.

"Yes, you, Michelle, and we're so lucky." He would end with a bear hug and another kiss to my forehead.

Years passed and my father never missed a night, even when I thought he should have. After my basketball team was defeated, he came into my room.

"Michelle, of all the basketball players in the whole wide world," he paused.

"Yes, Daddy?" I stared at the floor.

"How did your mom and I get so lucky to get the best one?"

"You didn't."

"Of course we did, Michelle. We have you."

"But, Dad... "

"Yes, you, Michelle, and we're so lucky," he cheered, as he gave me a high five followed by a bear hug and a kiss to my forehead.

I thought becoming a teenager would end the ritual, but it didn't.

"Michelle, of all the teenagers in the whole wide world..." he would pause.

"Dad, I'm too old for this," I would sigh.

"How did your mother and I get so lucky to get the best one?"

"C'mon, Dad," I grunted.

"We have you, Michelle, and we're so lucky." Then the embarrassing hug and kiss.

Following college, I became engaged. My father never missed a night to call or leave a message reminding me how special I was to him. I even wondered if he would continue calling after I got married, but he didn't.

The daily calls I had taken for granted all my life ended the day he died from cancer, only weeks before my wedding.

I deeply missed sharing the day with my father. Standing behind the white church doors with my arm in my brother's, I waited for the wedding march to begin. Before we began our descent down the aisle, my brother reached inside his pocket and handed me an ivory napkin embroidered with pink ribbon. Inscribed were the words:

Of all the precious wives in the whole wide world, how did Mark get so lucky to marry the best one? He married you, Michelle, and he is so lucky! I am so proud of you, my little girl.

Love, Dad

Without a doubt, it was the best wedding gift I received. One I would never forget. My father showered me with his gifts every day of his life. How did I get so lucky?

~Michelle Marullo
Chicken Soup for the Bride's Soul

7

The Painted Tractor

The year was 1979, and my daughters were ages two, five and seven. Father's Day was approaching, and I was trying to come up with an original gift idea. Money was tight because we were in the process of renovating a barn into our home while we were living in it.

Suddenly, it hit me. "We'll paint his tractor!" It was Tom's first tractor, a used one he bought when we first moved to the northern Virginia countryside from Washington, D.C. "Yes, a new paint job for his tractor is what we'll give Daddy for Father's Day," I told my young daughters. They were delighted.

Off we went to the local hardware store in the nearest town. A salesman approached and asked if he could help me. "Yes," I said. "I'm looking for paint for my husband's tractor."

"What color do you have in mind?" the clerk asked.

I looked down at my daughters and asked each of them what color they wanted.

"I want pink," my oldest daughter said.

"I want yellow," my middle daughter said.

"I want blue," my youngest daughter said.

The salesman looked at me, barely able to hide his shock, and politely asked if my husband knew anything about what we were planning.

"No," I smiled. "We're surprising him for Father's Day. He's going to be thrilled!"

"I hope you have a strong marriage," the gentleman replied, genuinely flabbergasted.

We left the hardware store with several different colors of paint. I hired our favorite babysitter for a few consecutive afternoons after school to watch my youngest daughter while our masterpiece began. We started with the hubcaps. One soon had a big daisy in the center; another, a sunburst; the third, a smiley face; the fourth, a star.

We repainted the body of the tractor a pretty blue, and the head-lights resembled happy eyes. We painted "We love you!" on the hood facing his seat, which we emblazoned with a big red heart.

When our job was finished, we were all thrilled! Father's Day couldn't get here soon enough.

The big day finally arrived, and we sent Tom on a mini treasure hunt. We handed him a written clue, which led to a spot where he found another clue, and so forth, until he eventually wound up in his shed. There he discovered the newly painted tractor.

"Did you girls do this for me?" Tom asked with a huge smile on his face.

The girls jumped all over him, no longer able to contain their excitement.

Each of them then took turns showing their daddy which part of his tractor she had painted.

"Look at my star!" one chimed.

"And my daisy!" another squealed.

"I love it! I love it!" he laughed, hugging them all together. And he meant it. I knew he would.

We went back to the house together, and Tom put on his long-sleeve, black T-shirt designed to look like a tuxedo. He took an old top hat we'd stored away in the closet for who knows how long. "Can I have a picture taken with you girls?" he asked his daughters, now beaming with delight.

Tom drove his tractor closer to our house, and soon the girls were sitting on their father's lap or standing up next to him on his tractor. I snapped away with my camera.

The photo says it all: Tom, top hat, tuxedo, trio of daughters and a tractor, all saying, "We love you!"

~Bobbie Wilkinson
Chicken Soup for the Father & Daughter Soul

8

Let Us Be United

Give sorrow words;
the grief that does not speak whispers the o'er-fraught heart and bids it break.
~William Shakespeare

September 10, 2001, was our eighth wedding anniversary. My husband, Alan, was leaving the next day for a week back in California to try his last Clean Water Act case. He'd decided to give up a thriving environmental law practice for a year's sabbatical spending more time with family and offering volunteer work in India. We spent the day celebrating our love for each other, planning our future and counting the blessings in our lives. We were so grateful for our life together. Alan always said, "When we wake up each morning, we should feel gratitude for being alive." And we did.

Alan woke up at 4:30 on Tuesday for his morning flight to San Francisco. As he kissed our five-year-old daughter Sonali and me goodbye, I pulled him toward me, knocking him over. He laughed heartily and said, "I'll return with the pot of gold."

"You are my pot of gold, Alan," I said. "Come home safe and sound."

He assured me he would, and at 7:00 A.M., he called to say he had checked in, he loved us, and he'd be back by the weekend.

And then it all began.... The CNN announcer confirmed that Flight 93 bound for San Francisco had crashed in a field in Pennsylvania. In that instant, I felt a crushing blow. Devastated, with the wind knocked out of me, I could barely get a sound out as shock and disbelief poured through my veins. My heart literally stopped beating and I had to will myself to live. How could my husband, my best friend who I'd kissed goodbye hours earlier, be dead?

When Sonali came home from school, I let her play for an hour before I told her the news. I wanted to savor the innocence of her not knowing Daddy was dead. When she heard Alan's plane had crashed and he was not coming home, she wailed a cry so deep and heartbreaking, a cry I pray I will never hear again from any living being. She sobbed for an hour straight, and then she looked me in the eyes and said, "I am so sad. But I'm not the saddest girl in the world. Some children have lost their mommy and their daddy, and I still have you."

A few days after the crash, Sonali's brother Chris, concerned that Sonali might not understand what was really happening, asked her, "Do you know where Daddy is?"

"Yes, he's at work!"

Chris was wondering how to handle this, when she continued. "Silly, he's in court. Defending the angels."

Sonali's courage in the following weeks continued to amaze me and remind me of her dad. One of Alan's final contemplations was a sentence he'd heard in a recent workshop, Fear—Who Cares? I know these words helped guide him on September 11.

Sonali and I attended a memorial service at the crash site in Pennsylvania with her older brothers Chris and John. Standing at the fence, staring out at the field and the scorched trees, I couldn't help but notice what a beautiful place it was for him to die. Such an expansive countryside with golden red trees—this is where it all ended for Alan. Sonali picked up some dirt in her hands, folded her hands in prayer and began singing a beautiful hymn she learned in India the previous winter. Everyone stopped to listen to her. Then she held the dirt to her heart and threw it toward the plane.

As the sun peeked momentarily through the thick cloud cover, Sonali looked up and said, "There's Daddy!" She drew a heart in the gravel and asked for some flowers, which she arranged beautifully around the heart with one flower in the center for her daddy.

News of Sonali's courageous, sweet voice reached California, and we received a call from the governor's office. Would Sonali like to sing at California's Day of Remembrance?

"No, I don't think so. She just turned five a few weeks ago, and there will be too many people."

Sonali heard me and asked, "What am I too young to do?"

She listened to my reasons why not and simply said, "I want to do it." I agreed. And in the next few days, Sonali's repertoire of mostly Disney tunes expanded to include a beautiful prayer from the Rig Veda that we heard at the Siddha Yoga Meditation Ashram in New York where we were staying. Clearly, "Let Us Be United" was the perfect song for Sonali to sing:

> Let us be united;
> Let us speak in harmony;
> Let our minds apprehend alike;
> Common be our prayer;
> Common be our resolution;
> Alike be our feeling;
> Unified be our hearts;
> Perfect be our unity.

On the flight back to California, our flight attendant heard about where we were going and asked if Sonali wanted to sing her song for everyone on the plane.

A bit concerned, my mother asked Sonali, "Do you know how many people are on this plane?"

Sonali had no idea. So she took the flight attendant's hand, walked up and down the aisle, and then came back with her guess. "About a thousand," she said. "I can do that. I'll be fine."

In a clear, strong voice, Sonali sang to her fellow passengers. She then walked up and down the aisle with one of the crewmembers, receiving the smiles, thanks and love of all the United passengers. At the end of the flight, who stood on top of a box at the door with the flight attendant, thanking everyone and saying goodbye? Our Sonali!

When Sonali sang on the steps of the state capitol, her voice was unbelievably strong. It was as though she wanted to fill the whole universe with this impassioned prayer so it would reach her daddy. As she sang, I felt it also become a pure prayer to everyone gathered—a prayer that painted a vision. I was delighted when she asked me if she could sing again, this time for Alan's memorial service at Grace Cathedral in San Francisco.

That wasn't Sonali's last singing prayer. When the Golden State Warriors awarded a check to the Beaven family at a fundraiser in their honor, guess who sang to thousands of people in their stadium? When asked how she was able to sing in front of so many people, Sonali said, "I wasn't afraid because Daddy was singing with me."

October 15th would have been Alan's forty-ninth birthday, and Sonali wanted to have a birthday party for him. "Daddy's favorite place is the ocean, so let's go to the beach and have a big fire. Everybody can write a prayer on a piece of wood and when we put the wood in the fire, the prayers will rise to Daddy in heaven."

And so we did. As sweetly as Sonali's voice reached the heavens and so many hearts, so, too, our love rose into the moonlit sky. Alan's courage and spirituality are so strongly reflected in Sonali's ability to rise above her own heartbreak and loss and uplift people. Just as Alan didn't sit back in his seat with shaking knees but rose fearlessly to help save thousands of people's lives, so, too, Sonali chose not to bury herself in grief, but to sing her dad's vision of love and courage. I am grateful for them both!

~Kimi Beaven
Chicken Soup for the Soul of America

Daddy's Best Birthday

Sometimes the poorest man leaves his children the richest inheritance.
~Ruth E. Renkel

My father died a few months before his thirty-eighth birthday. I was fifty-three at the time. How could I be fifteen years older than my own father? Because the most important birth date our family celebrated was Daddy's Alcoholics Anonymous birthday.

I have thought a lot about what it means to me to have grown up in a family that simply didn't work long before the term "dysfunctional family" was coined. When I was little, I learned lessons that helped me survive at the time. I am still unlearning some of those early lessons.

Last summer, while working in the garden, I shifted a large stepping stone over onto a patch of grass and forgot to return it to its place. When at last I remembered to move it, the grass underneath was sickly pale and stunted. The grass still lived, and with time, water and the sunlight it needed to survive, it grew healthy. Had I left the stone there, the grass would have died and been replaced by grubs, snails and bare earth.

Parts of me are like a lawn where stones have been scattered at random. Some patches didn't get what they needed to grow strong and healthy. While finding and moving those stones, I have often been resentful and angry. There are spots where grass will never grow. It hurts to admit there were things I just didn't get when I was a little kid.

But in the course of all that work, I have come to appreciate how much sunshine did fall on me, and even how to grow plants more exotic than grass in the bare spots. And for the first time in my life, I wish I could remember more.

I've tried to remember how I felt in 1958 when Daddy stopped drinking. Instead, I wasn't even aware of what was going on. And when I did begin to realize something unusual was happening, I was skeptical, even cynical. No expectations for me! I had been sadly disappointed too many times before. Even in the beginning, my family was wise enough to realize that stopping one particularly destructive behavior doesn't mean instant cures, only freedom to work on the deeper issues that inevitably underlie "The Problem." So nobody ever promised anything that I remember. I wouldn't have believed them if they had.

As months went by, I slowly suspected change was possible. Then one night, as my mother and I were driving home, we saw my father's beat-up old blue panel truck parked at the neighborhood bar. I knew it was all over. Mother said, "I have to go see." She parked the car and left me sitting outside while she went inside. Through a window I could see Daddy, leaning against the bar, a tall, amber-colored glass in his hand. Everything inside me went into a protective crouch — deep, dark and hidden away.

Mother came out of the bar with a strange new expression on her face. She climbed into the car and said, "He's drinking iced tea. He needed to check up on some of his old friends. He'll be home in a little while." Something inside me was able to relax a little.

After Daddy's best birthday, thank God, and Daddy's hard work, he never did "fall off the wagon." Following the Alcoholics Anonymous slogan "one day at a time," he and mother truly lived one day at a time, working on their problems and helping other people through A.A. and Al-Anon. Daddy never became financially successful, and sometimes he said how sorry he was that he had no inheritance to leave his children. But he didn't brood over lost opportunities. When he turned eighty, he joined a fitness club and worked out on the weight machines to improve his golf swing.

Then, at an A.A. retreat, he fell and broke his hip. He and Mother fought his deteriorating condition for three years. A big man, and always physically fit, Daddy hated the indignities of not being able to walk or care for himself. Slowly, slowly his body shut down, and with Mother and a few other family members by his bed, he died. Later, Mother said, "He can walk again. And I know he walked into heaven clean and sober."

At my parents' fiftieth wedding anniversary some years before his death, the reception hall was filled with children, grandchildren, great-grandchildren, nieces, nephews, cousins and hundreds of friends from A.A. and church. How clear that memory is. How different it would have been if he had not been brave enough in 1958 to ask for help.

Daddy was wrong to think he had nothing to leave his children. He gave us over thirty-seven years and nine months of sobriety—almost fourteen thousand days—one day at a time. His courage is his legacy, our inheritance.

~Nita Sue Kent
Chicken Soup for the Golden Soul

10

Beacon of Faith

Probably the biggest problem that Christmas poses to a six-teen-year-old girl is what to give her father. Mothers are easy; they always need everything. But there seem to be so few gift options for dads: ties, socks, a new belt....

As Robyn Stevens, of Hancock, Maine, pondered the dilemma of what to get her father for Christmas 1991, she thought about how her grandmother always talked about the usefulness of flashlights. "You should always have one in your car," her grandmother would say. "And you should always have a couple in the house—you just never know when you might need one."

It seemed to Robyn that she had her answer. So she bought a flash-light for her father, Arthur Stevens. It wasn't anything fancy—just an ordinary, three-cell, garden variety model she got at Sears. "I thought he'd really like it," she remembers, "because it was waterproof and he spends a lot of time on the water."

Arthur Stevens opened his present on Christmas morning, grinned at his daughter and asked, "How did you know that this was just what I needed?"

Neither Robyn nor Arthur knew just how much he would come to need his gift.

On January 16, Arthur was twenty-five miles out to sea in the Gulf of Maine, along with crew members Captain Rudy Musetti and Dwayne Cleaves, and they were bringing the tugboat Harkness home from a construction job.

About halfway through the journey, the Harkness and its crew found themselves sailing straight into a nightmare. It was approaching 6 P.M. and had been dark for about three hours. The temperature had dropped drastically. With the winds at twenty-five miles per hour, the wind chill factor was minus sixty degrees.

A little after 6 P.M., Captain Musetti checked the stern and saw, to his horror, that it was taking on water fast. He couldn't leave the safety of the pilothouse to see what was wrong because the tug was pitching violently and the decks were sheer ice. There was also sea smoke to contend with — six feet of impenetrable condensation above the ocean, caused by the temperature difference between ocean and air.

Captain Musetti radioed the Coast Guard station at Southwest Harbor: "We're going down."

As it happened, the Harkness was sinking just off Matinicus Island, where the few families who lived there during winter were just settling down for dinner. Vance Bunker heard the radio conversations between the Harkness and the Coast Guard and knew that the three men aboard didn't stand a chance if he didn't set out to rescue them himself. The tugboat was too far out for the Coast Guard to reach it in time.

He and two other lobstermen, Rick Kohls and Paul Murray, left their dinners and families behind and set out in the Jan Ellen, Vance's thirty-six-foot lobster boat. None of them was sure exactly where the sinking tug was, and because of the smoke and the iced-up windshield, they couldn't see anything. All they could do was forge ahead in the darkness to where they thought the tug might be.

At 7:01 P.M., the Jan Ellen heard what would be the last radio transmission from the Harkness:

"The water is up to our chests in the wheelhouse," Captain Musetti reported. "We're going into the water."

After that Vance and his crew heard nothing but the roar of the wind and the creaking of the boat as it crashed into the eight-foot waves. The certainty that three men had just drowned made Rick Kohls sick to his stomach. Just then, he saw a strange sight. Piercing the sea smoke was a thin beam light pointing straight up. Rick shouted to Vance, "Look — over there. Follow that light!"

Vance couldn't see through his windshield, but he followed Rick's directions until they came upon something that dumbfounded them all: There, half-dead in the icy water, were three men with arms hooked together — their clothes frozen to a ladder that had come loose from the Harkness as she went down.

Arthur Stevens, the thinnest of the three men and the closest to death, had long since lost his ability to grasp anything. But the freezing cold had done the men an odd turn: Frozen to the back of Dwayne Cleaves's glove was a small, simple, garden-variety, three-cell, waterproof flashlight. And the beam of that flashlight was pointing straight up to the sky — a beacon for those who'd had enough faith and courage to follow it.

~Margot Brown McWilliams
Chicken Soup for the Soul Christmas Treasury

Chapter 2

Dads & Daughters

Daddy's Little Girl

*A father: The first man in your life to give you unconditional love,
and the one who every man after is compared to.
~Becca Kaufman and Paula Ramsey,
creators of WeddingQuestions.com*

The Dad He Planned to Be

Every child born into the world is a new thought of God,
an ever-fresh and radiant possibility.
~Kate Douglas Wiggin

Michael was shocked when we watched a videotape of a baby's birth during childbirth classes. But I, like several classmates, got teary-eyed as the tiny miracle entered the world. Passing a box of tissues around the room, the instructor turned on the lights. My twenty-nine-year-old husband leaned over to me. "What have we done?" he whispered, his face pale with horror.

After seeing that tape, Michael was adamant about not viewing the birth of our baby. He conceded to coach breathing exercises during labor, but when it came time for the actual delivery, he envisioned himself seated in a chair at the head of the bed holding my hand.

"Delivery is the touchdown," joked our birthing coach. "You wouldn't sit through four quarters of the Super Bowl then go to the fridge if the score was tied, your team had the ball on the two-yard line and there was less than a minute left in the game, would you?"

Throughout my pregnancy, Michael was the "go-to guy." During the first and second trimesters, I felt too tired to do anything but work and sleep, so he did the grocery shopping, errands and household chores. Weekly, he read me excerpts about how both mother and fetus were changing. "Your body is growing precious cargo," he'd reassure me. "It's taking all your energy to make our baby."

When my back hurt, he rubbed it. When my feet ached, he massaged them. The first time we felt the baby move, he cupped his hands around his mouth and shouted at my bulging belly, "Hi, little girl. I'm your daddy!"

But incongruent as it seemed, Michael wanted to sit in the stands rather than be on the field during the actual birth. "In fact, I don't want to look at the baby until she's properly cleaned," he emphasized. "And changing a diaper is out of the question. I'll vomit." From my husband's comments and behavior, I knew he would love our child, but the hands-on care of the baby would be my job.

Finally, I was in labor—for twenty-three hours—and Michael was by my side the entire time. He coached my breathing and held my arm as we walked halls. When the time came for me to give birth, Michael walked over to the dry-erase board in the hospital room and wrote: "Happy Birthday, Micah." He then took his seat near the head of the bed and prepared to watch the labor-and-delivery team perform their magic.

A few minutes later, one of the nurses called to him, "Dad, we need your help with pushing." White-faced, Michael stood. A nurse positioned him at the edge of the bed, shoved my foot into his stomach and wrapped his hands around my shin. "There, now," she said enthusiastically. "This will give you a perfect view of the birth." Michael smiled weakly. I thought he might faint.

A few minutes later, Michael shouted excitedly, "I see black hair!" Our daughter, Micah, was born, and the doctor immediately handed the gooey baby to my husband. "Isn't she beautiful?" he gasped, cradling her tiny body in his strong arms. Tears of happiness pooled in his eyes. I began crying as well, not only because our baby was here, but because of the tender joy in my husband's face.

When the nurse wanted to put Micah under warming lights, he said, "Honey, I don't want to leave you, but I should go with the baby to make sure she's all right."

"Hey, there, little girl," I heard him coo from across the room. "It's okay. Daddy's here."

Moments later, our families came. Michael proudly displayed our newborn, even before she was bathed.

That night, a nurse took Micah to administer some tests, saying she'd be back with the baby in an hour. "Let me put on my shoes. I'll go with you," hollered my husband from the foldout couch.

"I'll change her diaper before you go," I said.

"No, Honey, you rest," said Michael. "I need to practice changing her."

I tried to look nonchalant as he gently lifted Micah's legs and fumbled to get the diaper around her six-pound body, but inside, I was amazed. He's a hands-on dad, after all, I thought.

Micah is now eighteen months old and the pride of her daddy's heart. She's baptized him in bodily fluids and blessed him with giggles. Michael's shared in the good (when Da Da was her first word), the bad (when, as a newborn, she had jaundice and had to be strapped to a light table for seventy-two hours) and the ugly (when six-month-old Micah caught a virus and vomited in Daddy's face) aspects of parenthood.

Michael admits there's a big discrepancy between the way he planned to be a father and the dad he's become. But daughters do that to daddies.

~Stephanie Welcher Thompson
Chicken Soup for the Father & Daughter Soul

Baby's First Words

Babies are such a nice way to start people.
~Don Herrold

How hard it must be to miss watching your baby grow up. My husband, a navy pilot, deployed when our daughter Claire was just eight months old. She hadn't yet crawled, gotten teeth or said her first word, and he had to get used to hearing stories about all her accomplishments.

I know he was afraid that she would forget him when he was gone, so I made it my personal mission to make sure she remembered him. I showed her pictures every day, set Daddy's face as the screen saver on our computer, even made a doll with Daddy's face on it. I also put together a video of clips of her with her dad. Claire loved to watch that video and would stare at the screen each time I put it on.

About two months after my husband left, he was able to hook up a videophone to a computer and call us. Claire was sitting in my lap when we began our online messenger chat. Suddenly, my husband's picture came up on our screen and we heard his voice saying, "Hi!" Claire climbed from my lap, leaned on the desk and reached up to the computer screen. She put both hands where her dad's face was and said, "Daddy!"

Six thousand miles away, he heard it over the videophone speakers and a huge smile came across his face. Despite the separation from our baby, she hadn't forgotten him at all. And, thanks to modern technology, he was with us as she spoke her first word.

~Sarah Monagle
Chicken Soup for the Military Wife's Soul

Long Distance Vitamins

You know quite well deep within you, that there is only a single magic,
a single power, a single salvation... and that is called loving.
~Herman Hesse

We arrived at the hospital to find Dad exhausted and weak, but his smile was as sure as ever. It was another bout of pneumonia. My husband and I stayed with him for the weekend but had to return to our jobs by Monday morning. Local relatives would see that Dad got home from the hospital and they would look in on him regularly and prepare his meals. They would make sure he got his daily medicine and take him to his doctor appointments. But I longed to be able to let him know that we cared too, even when we weren't with him.

Then I remembered a family tradition I initiated when our children were small. When leaving their grandparents' home after a visit, each child would hide a love note about the house for their grandfather or grandmother to find after we were gone. They hid notes in the cereal box, to be poured into their bowls the next morning. They'd tuck a note under a hairbrush, in a deck of cards, next to the phone or even in the microwave. For days after our departure, their grandparents would smile as they discovered these reminders of our love.

So as I tidied Dad's kitchen and made up a bed for him downstairs in the living room, I began writing notes. Some were practical. "Dad, I froze the casserole that was in the fridge so it wouldn't spoil." Some expressed my love. "Dad, I hope you sleep well in your new bed." Most notes were downstairs, where he would be confined for several weeks until he regained strength, but one note I hid upstairs under his pillow. "Dad, if you have found this note, you must be feeling better. We are so glad!"

While others cared for Dad's day-to-day needs, we, of course, would stay in touch by phone. But our notes were a tangible reminder of our love and concern for him during this recovery period. Just like his medicines boosted him physically, these "emotional vitamins" would boost his spiritual health.

Several weeks later, in one of our regular phone calls, I asked Dad how he was doing. He said, "I'll tell you how I'm doing. I just found your note under my upstairs pillow!"

~Emily Chase
Chicken Soup for the Caregiver's Soul

Gone Fishin'

I t was my third year of trying to create the perfect lawn.

I was doing quite well this summer. I'd reseeded the bare spots from winter's ravages. I'd found just the right grass seed for our soil conditions. I'd created a sprinkler system that worked well for both the lawn and for entertaining my four children.

All was going well, until one day I noticed several sprouting dandelions. No problem, I thought. I hurried to the store and bought an herbicide. I figured that by the next weekend, I'd have those yellow devils whipped.

But when I got home, I took a closer look at the instructions. Reading the cautionary statements made me shudder; we live in a rural area with a nearby pond and have cats and dogs and children. I didn't want to inflict toxic chemicals on any of them. So I made the mixture weaker than the directions called for. Weak and ineffective: By the next weekend, those tough little dandelions didn't have so much as a withered leaf.

I had promised my four-year-old daughter Kayla we'd go fishing on Saturday. Kayla loves to fish and is very good at it. But when Saturday arrived, I found the little yellow splotches in my lawn had multiplied.

I'll have to deal with the dandelions before we go fishing, I told myself. The lawn is less than half an acre; how long can it take?

With screwdriver and garbage sack in hand, I attacked the pesky weeds.

"Pickin' flowers, Daddy?" Kayla asked.

"Yes, dear," I said, digging furiously at a tough root.

"I'll help," she offered. "I'll give some to Mommy."

"Go ahead, sweetie," I answered. "There's plenty."

An hour passed, and yellow splotches still remained.

"You said we's going fishin' today," Kayla complained.

"Yes, I know, dear," I said. "Just a little more flower picking, okay?"

"I'll get the fish poles," Kayla announced.

I labored on, prying up one stubborn root after another.

"I found some worms under a rock, Daddy," Kayla piped up. "I put them in a cup. Are you ready?"

"Almost, honey."

More minutes dragged by.

"You picked 'nough flowers, Daddy," Kayla insisted impatiently.

"Okay, honey, just a few more," I promised. But I couldn't stop. The compulsion to finish the job was overwhelming.

A few minutes later, a tap came on my shoulder.

"Make a wish, Daddy!" Kayla chirped.

As I turned, Kayla took a big breath, puffed, and sent a thousand baby dandelion seeds into the air.

I picked her up and kissed her, and we headed for the fish pond.

~David Clinton Matz
Chicken Soup for the Gardener's Soul

15

Becoming a Jock Dad

To give vent now and then to his feelings, whether of pleasure or discontent,
is a great ease to a man's heart.
~Francesco Guicciardini

Being a man, there is always that dreaded macho stigma hanging over you that a real man never shows his true emotions. Being a father pretty much puts an end to such a silly notion. I have accepted the fact that I have never been, nor will I ever be, a real man.

I am a fraud of manhood. I should be banned from the brotherhood of male ego. I'm nothing but a softy. A disgrace to everything that manhood stands for.

Actually, I'm just a father. When it comes to my girls, a long time ago I gave up holding in my emotions like a true man. Be it a banquet, recital, athletic competition or cheerleading, I have long established myself as a blubbering father who is quite generous in shedding a few tears of pride on my girls' behalf.

I remember my oldest daughter's last high school cross-country meet, when she broke the school record. She had a room full of trophies, plaques, medals and certificates for her achievements over the past four years, but the one thing she didn't have, that she really wanted the most, was the school record. She wanted to leave her high school with her name up on the gym wall proclaiming her the best distance runner in her school's long history.

Last week, she had a great run, but came up four seconds shy of the school record. Today would be her last chance. There would be no more tomorrows.

I positioned myself away from the crowd, on the final bend where the runners come into view and head for the home stretch. If she wasn't going to break the record, it would break my heart. She had worked so hard and wanted it so badly. It was now or never, and a parent hates the emotional volcano rumbling inside, as you stand on the sidelines, unable to do anything but watch. Especially in a race that covers a little over three miles, lasts some nineteen minutes or more, and is run out of view of neurotic parents.

As the race began, things were looking fairly good for my daughter. She looked fresh and focused. Conditions were perfect for her. It was cloudy, cold, with snow flurries fluttering about. She always loved running when conditions were bad. She was my mudder.

The toughest part of the race for the parents was when the runners disappeared from our view for about a quarter of a mile, until they rounded the bend on the hill where I stood and headed for home. It was in this quarter mile where those who had it made their move, while those who didn't simply faded off.

As I anxiously waited at the bend, a few of the girls made the turn and headed for the finish line. These were the girls who always won, and today would be no different for them.

I continued to pace. I was a nervous wreck. I kept watching my time clock, then the corner. She still had plenty of time. She looked good throughout the race, but I didn't know if she had run out of gas while out of view or if she was making her move.

Then it happened.

Around the bend came the familiar green and white that I had been following for the past four years. It was her! I frantically looked at my clock and absolutely fell apart. She could pretty much walk the rest of the way and still beat the school record!

I started jumping and running alongside of her, screaming and yelling with excitement, as she tried to remain focused on her race and ignoring the fool running next to her. I'm sure that she told everyone at the finish line that she had no idea who that lunatic was up at the bend, but I'm sure they all knew. Only a father would behave like that in public, and only a father like me would do so without any apologies.

You hope in a race like this that you might be able to beat the record by one or two seconds. Today, my daughter beat the school record by a whopping twelve seconds! Of course, unofficially, I smashed the world's record for the high jump of fatherhood.

As her coach, teammates and friends all celebrated with her down at the finish line, I laid on the ground alone, up by the bend, crying buckets of tears of joy for what my daughter had accomplished. She had worked so hard for this moment, and there was no one more thrilled than her father.

So, maybe I'm not a macho, cool and collected kind of real man. Fatherhood has always taken a priority in my heart. If that makes me more a lunatic than a man, so be it. My daughter had just presented her high school with an impressive new record in cross-country for young ladies to strive for in years to come. In a few months, she would graduate from her school as the greatest distance runner the school has ever had.

My daughter had become a champion because she applied her God-given talents to a sport that she really enjoyed.

I had become a champion jock dad because I set aside the macho images of manhood that a boy always has to grow up with, and simply learned to enjoy watching my daughter do what she loves to do. My only concern was not in what people were thinking about me, but thinking that the temperature might be cold enough to freeze my proud tears to the ground below me.

~Andy Smith
Chicken Soup for the Father's Soul

16

A Snow Cloud's Silver Lining

A father is always making his baby into a little woman.
And when she is a woman he turns her back again.
~Enid Bagnold

I t snowed like crazy on our wedding day. Not a piling up, traffic-paralyzing kind of snow, but the kind that leaves the trees sparkling and the streets looking like a river of licorice slush.

My mother closed all the drapes as if blocking the view would somehow force an end to it. But it didn't work. By the time my father and I were ready to leave for the church, the driveway and street were slathered with a generous portion of semi-frozen grayish sludge.

My father had cleared a path in front of the house but when it was time to go, Mom still insisted I wear plastic bags over my shoes to protect them "just in case." As luck would have it, the only two plastic bags in the house were empty bread bags.

Somehow my little-girl dreams of this day never included parading to the church with bread bags peaking out beneath the hem of the gown I'd waited my whole life to wear. Still, snowflakes continued swirling down and no alternate plan prevailed. So, on went the bread bags over my shoes, and off we went.

Carefully we made our way out the front door and to the rented silver Mercedes waiting to take us to the church. Ed, the driver, never said a word, but the look on his face was priceless as he watched me approach with blue-and-yellow-plastic-polka-dot clown feet.

As we started out of the driveway, I realized that never before in my life had I taken a ride with my dad without him driving. Gripped by this moment of truth, I turned my head to look through the back window and watched our house—and my childhood—shrink slowly out of sight.

One lone tear trickled down my cheek while Dad sat quietly beside me. Then I felt him reach over and take my hand. This small, quiet gesture spoke volumes of what he, too, must have been feeling—but never said.

The freshly fallen snow transformed a relatively short ride into a slow and cautious journey through the landmarks of my youth. As we passed the playground, the schoolyard and even the corner candy store, each seemed to call my name and whisper goodbye.

As much as I looked forward to all the future held for my husband and me, this intense feeling of ending my girlhood pierced my heart. Sensing this, my father squeezed my hand and drew me close to his side. His warm embrace assured me everything would be all right.

While Ed parked the car at the church, Dad and I simultaneously looked at each other, then cast our eyes down to the polka-dot Wonder Bread "booties," which by now had taken on a role of their own and seemed to be staring back at us.

My father turned to me and said, "Do you really want to step out of this car with clown feet?"

"Well, not really, but what else can I do?"

The street and sidewalk surrounding the church had been on the receiving end of a barrage of galoshes, snow tires and shovels since early that morning. What started as a pristine blanket of white now appeared to be nothing more than a dirty mess that threatened to ruin my shoes, as well as whatever part of the dress and train that would end up getting dragged through it.

"Lose the boots," Dad said. With those words he got out of the car and walked around to the door on my side.

I leaned forward and slipped the bags off my feet to reveal lovely white satin ballet slippers with the pale pink satin ribbons that twirled about my ankles and came to rest in a delicate bow. I dreaded the thought of how they would look by the time I reached the church steps.

I methodically gathered up as much of the dress and train as I could, and stepped out of the car trying to keep it all from touching the ground. As I turned toward Dad, suddenly I felt my feet lift off the ground and in an instant I was swept into his arms. Just that quickly my dress and shoes were safely out of harm's way and my heart had wings to fly.

How many years had it been since Dad had carried me in his arms? How much like a princess I felt, and how appropriate it seemed to close the door on my childhood in such a poignant way.

Dad carried me from the sidewalk all the way up the steps and into the vestibule of the church where my mother and bridesmaids awaited our arrival. Setting me down in front of my mother, he kissed me on the cheek and said, "Now that was fun. Wasn't it?" To which I replied, "Let's do it again!" We all laughed and a few moments later he walked me down the aisle where I joyfully stepped forward into the future.

Dad faced his own moment of truth that day. My husband and I were married on my parents' thirty-sixth wedding anniversary. I imagine walking his last baby down the aisle on this day surely brought home to his heart that life was moving on; no turning back the clock.

My husband and I celebrated our twentieth wedding anniversary this year. Life moved on for us as it did for Dad—who now smiles on us from heaven.

The warm memories of our wedding day remain with me, but few are as tender as that precious moment when Daddy's little girl was swept off her feet one last time.

~Annmarie B. Tait
Chicken Soup for the Bride's Soul

17

A Special Bond

Seventeen hours of confinement inside the Boeing 747 provided endless opportunities for reflection, as well as anticipation of the most significant event of our lives. Susan, my wife of five years, sat beside me lost in the six-inch image of an in-flight movie. Outwardly she appeared unfazed by the fact that we were headed to central China, where in two short days we would be united with our first and only child: a little girl born in Anhui Province two years and four months earlier. The photos and bio forwarded to us by the Chinese government's adoption agency provided information such as height, weight, age and health status. But something more than simple images on paper had been given to us. In my heart the beginning of an incredible love was stirring, the likes of which I had never known before.

My reflections took me back to rural Long Island, where I grew up in a typical middle-class family. Who would have thought that at fifty-two years of age I'd become a global dad? I always was a late bloomer. With Navy, college, career and a string of unfulfilling relationships, the thought of children had always been a "someday" thing. Now, "someday" was rushing toward me at six hundred miles per hour, and I was scared to death.

Han Dong Cheng was scared, too. Her gut-wrenching screams echoed through the orphanage as she was handed over to this strange-looking couple. In time, she wore herself out and began surveying her new situation. She was a beautiful little girl with jet-black hair, bright brown eyes and, when it finally appeared, an incredible smile that lit up the room. Through the camera lens, I watched her and Susan share some playful moments. I was quite happy to just watch this exquisite little creature begin to open up and relax. But, while Jordyn Nicole (her American adoptive name) and her new mommy were beginning the bonding process, Daddy was persona non grata. She was extremely fearful of me and wouldn't allow me within arm's reach, turning away in tears whenever I approached. This heartbreaking sequence occurred several times over our remaining ten days in China. It tested the limits of my emotional strength and maturity to understand and accept it. I was only able to cope by telling myself things would be different once we got home — or so I thought.

Susan and I had been having marital difficulties for some time, and despite our best efforts, the marriage wasn't working. Truth be told, we should have been going to divorce court, not China. I now thank God every day that we chose China instead. For the time being, it was easy to put our personal issues aside as the presence of our new daughter provided a renewed sense of excitement in our otherwise unhappy marriage. This was tempered, however, by Jordyn's continuing negative reaction to me. It was many days before I could come close enough to touch her and attempt to hold her.

Days turned into weeks, and slowly but surely, I began building the relationship with my daughter that I had wanted for so long. Eventually, I could actually hold her, and I could tell she was beginning to accept my presence in her life. To my delight, Daddy became a jungle gym, a clown, a horsey — anything to strengthen our developing relationship. Her laughter began to fill our house and fill my heart. Even though I knew I was lagging behind Mommy, I felt a definite bond forming between us. She was turning into an extremely happy little girl, adapting to her new life in a way that indicated all would be fine if we just gave her lots of love and let it happen in God's own way.

Just as my relationship with Jordyn blossomed, my relationship with Susan withered. There were two camps: Mommy and Jordyn, and Daddy and Jordyn. As difficult as it was, we both placed Jordyn's well-being first and strove to never jeopardize her happiness or undermine her relationship with the other parent. We focused on our respective relationships with her, overcompensating with huge amounts of love and attention. Divorce was inevitable, but we stayed together long enough to cement my growing bond with our daughter.

Twenty months after the trip to China, our divorce was final. After much negotiating, we agreed on joint custody and to live close enough to each other for frequent visitation. We were able to agree on nearly all issues, and I realized what a welcome relief a divorce could be for an unhappy marriage.

Over the following months, my relationship with Jordyn continued to grow. This little girl, who only two years before was a complete stranger, had become my daughter in the full sense of the word. The stirrings of love I felt those many months before had fully blossomed, and I knew I couldn't possibly love her more had she been my biological daughter.

Today, my six-year-old daughter and I share a special love and bond that has been strengthened by all the difficulties we went through. She taught me that patience, love and understanding can transcend all obstacles. We are one human race created by God, transcending borders and nationalities, colors and races, philosophies and religions. We can love one another, whether we live next door or halfway around the world.

Nearly every day, I hear the words that once seemed so elusive, and that still cause a catch in my throat each time I hear them: "I love you, Daddy."

~Ed Mickus
Chicken Soup for the Single Parent's Soul

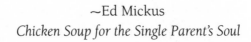

18

To Any Service Member

A block of granite which was an obstacle in the pathway of the weak
becomes a stepping stone in the pathway of the strong.
~Thomas Carlyle

During the Persian Gulf War, I was stationed aboard the naval amphibious ship USS Nassau. As a senior Marine intelligence analyst, my workdays were routinely twelve to sixteen hours long. Like all the veterans, we looked forward to receiving mail from home.

Unlike the Vietnam War, the Gulf War found support among most Americans. As a result, we soldiers received an enormous amount of "To any service member" mail from the States. I never took any of those letters, since I wrote to my wife and two children on a daily basis, as well as occasionally writing notes to my daughter's classroom, and I didn't feel I had time to write to anyone else.

After five or six months of hearing the mail orderly announcing the availability of "To any service member" mail, I decided to take a few of the letters. I planned, as time permitted, to drop them a line telling them "Thanks" for their support.

I picked up three letters, and placed them in my cargo pocket and proceeded back to work. Over the next week or so, I started responding to the letters. When it came time to answer the third letter, I noticed it had no return address, but a Colorado postmark, which made me think longingly of home. I had missed spending Thanksgiving, Christmas and New Year's with my family, and I was really lonesome for them.

I opened the card and started to read the letter enclosed. About the third or fourth sentence down, it read, "My daddy is a Marine over there, if you see him tell him hi and I love and miss him." This statement really touched me and made me miss my family even more. I looked down to the signature—and sat in stunned silence as tears filled my eyes.

My own daughter Chris had signed the letter.

~Nick Hill
Chicken Soup for the Veteran's Soul

The Trellis

Why is this so hard, I wonder. All I have to do is tack together a few sticks of wood and daub them with white paint, but I feel as if I'm making a cross for my own execution. Already I've gone through a tablet full of designs and a forest of pine lath. I want this to be right.

"I'd like a white trellis," was your modest request. "Something for a background at my wedding. Sarah Parkes will cover it with ivy. It will be beautiful, Daddy, a symbol of life."

I was glad you asked me to make the trellis because I wanted to have a part in the wedding. Seems like men are mostly in the way at such occasions—like chess pieces standing around, waiting to be "positioned." The groom himself would never be missed if he didn't show. They would just stand a cardboard cutout in his place and no one would be the wiser.

Weddings are of women, by women and for women. But with this trellis, I can have a part of the action.

If I can ever get it made.

I've made far more difficult things for you, like that colonial cradle for your doll, and that two-story dollhouse with handmade furnishings. And your desk, with all the drawers.

But this trellis!

Kneeling on the patio, I carefully weave the pine slats into a crosshatch, and a design slowly emerges. As I work, I ponder the way your life has woven itself into mine, and I wonder what I will be like without Natalie around the house.

Can we unweave twenty-one years of sharing? Can a father give away his daughter without coming a little unraveled himself?

It's not that I don't want you to marry. I do. When your dreams come true, so do mine. Matt is such a good choice. A gentle, handsome man, as devoted to you as your parents. "Nat and Matt" sounds right, like a little poem.

I can hardly see to drive these tiny nails. Allergies, probably. Or maybe it's the cool April breeze that keeps fogging my eyes. Or the smart scent of pine wood.

They will stand this trellis up on the stage at church. My job is to take you by the arm and gently lead you down the aisle to the trellis. Another man will help you up the next step of life. I'll sit there stoically with your mother, watching you embrace someone new. Your sister will sing your favorite songs. Your grandfathers will perform the ceremony. And God will come down to bless the union. Your mother has it all organized.

All I have to do is finish this simple trellis.

When the wedding is over, they will fold this ivy arbor and shove it into a dark storage room, where it will be forever forgotten. But memories of my little girl will vine themselves through the arbor of my heart for the rest of my years.

I stand the trellis up against the garage and slather it with bride-white paint—this fragrant veneer that covers the old, rugged tree with beauty and promise.

Painted, the trellis looks like two alabaster gates. Gates that lead to a future I may never see, if you move far away. Out there on the long road of daily living, who knows what will happen? There will be long days filled with sweet monotony. Bright moments of joy. And tedious hours of sorrow. I wish for you the full spectrum of life.

I rub the syrupy paint from my fingers with a rag that used to be your favorite T-shirt. Then I stand back to appraise my work.

Without the ivy it seems so empty and lonely.
It is, after all, just a simple trellis.
And it is finished.

But it's the hardest thing I've ever made.

~Daniel Schantz
A Second Chicken Soup for the Woman's Soul

Wedding Day

She slips toward him
all dressed in white.
Never before has he
beheld such a sight.
His throat closes tight,
not a word can he say,
to this precious daughter
on her wedding day.
She floats even nearer,
a smile on her face.
Her small, dainty hand
on his arm she does place.
The organ notes swell,
the doors opened wide,
he'll soon give away
this vision, this bride.
In step to the music
they head down the aisle.
Why does he sense
it's at least a mile?
He wants to go back
and run for the door,
to return to their life
as it was before.
She was his first-born,
the apple of his eye.

When had the years
so quickly passed by?
He looks straight ahead,
plants a smile on his face,
for the sake of the man
who will soon take his place.
The last steps approach,
he starts to pray,
"Lord give me strength
to give her away."
He kisses her hand
and squeezes her arm,
whispers to the groom,
"Protect her from harm."
The young man nods slowly,
tears fill his eyes,
as he receives the hand
of this treasured prize.

~Pamela G. Smith
Chicken Soup for the Father & Daughter Soul

21

Chicken Soup for the Soul

My Traveling Companion

A daughter may outgrow your lap, but she will never outgrow your heart.
~Author Unknown

I've spent most of my career as a traveling salesman, and I know that there's nothing lonelier than a bunch of salesmen eating their meals in a motel coffee shop.

One year, my five-year-old daughter pressed a gift into my hands. The wrapping paper was all twisted, and it was bound together into a shapeless mass by at least a mile of tape.

I gave her a big hug and sloppy kiss — the kind that all daddies give — and proceeded to unwrap the little package she had bestowed on me. The contents hidden within felt kind of soft, and I was very careful not to cause any damage. With excitement radiating from her face, little brown-eyed Jeanine stood attentively beside me in her too-small pajamas while I completed the process of unraveling my surprise.

A pair of black, beady eyes peeked out from their papery hiding place, then a yellow beak, a red bow tie and orange feet. It was a stuffed toy penguin that stood about five inches tall.

Attached to its right wing with still wet paste was a tiny, wooden sign, and a hand-painted declaration, "I Love My Dad!" Beneath it was a hand-drawn heart, colored with crayon.

Tears welled up in my eyes and immediately I gave it a special place on my dresser.

Seldom did much time pass before I had to leave on another business trip. One morning when I was packing, I tossed the penguin in my suitcase. That night when I called home, Jeanine was very upset that the penguin had disappeared. "Honey, it's here with me," I explained. "I brought it along."

After that day, she always helped me pack, and saw to it that the penguin went in along with my socks and shaving kit. Many years have gone by since then, and that little penguin has traveled hundreds of thousands of miles all across America and over to Europe. And we have made many friends along the way.

In Albuquerque, I checked into a hotel, dumped out my bag and dashed to a meeting. When I returned, I found the bed turned down and the penguin propped up on the pillow.

In Boston, upon returning to my room one evening, I saw that somebody had perched it in an empty drinking glass on the nightstand—it never did stand up that well. The next morning I left it sitting in a chair. Again that night it was in the glass.

Once, at New York's Kennedy airport, a customs inspector coolly asked that I open my bag. And right there, on top, was my little pal. Holding it up, the agent quipped, "That's about the most valuable thing I have seen in all my years on the job. Thank God we don't charge tax on love."

Late one night, after driving over a hundred miles from my previous hotel, I unpacked my luggage only to discover that the penguin was missing.

Frantically, I phoned the hotel. The clerk was incredulous and a bit aloof. He laughed, saying it hadn't been reported. Nonetheless, a half hour later, he called back to say that my penguin had been found.

The time was late, but not that late. I got back in my car and drove the couple of hours to retrieve my two-toned touring buddy, arriving near midnight.

The penguin was waiting at the front desk. In the lobby, tired business travelers looked on at the reunion—I think with a touch of envy. A few of them came out to shake my hand. One man told me that he had even volunteered to deliver it to me the very next day.

Jeanine is in college now and I don't travel as much anymore. The penguin spends most of its time sitting on my dresser—a reminder that love is the best traveling companion. All those years on the road, it was the one thing I never left home without.

~Edmund W. Boyle
Chicken Soup for the Traveler's Soul

22

Questions

I've always loved to fish with my children. When I've been with them, especially my young daughter Stephanie, the sport has served mainly as a backdrop for an endless stream of questions she has asked me throughout the years.

I realized Stephanie had a penchant for off-the-wall questions when she was four and we took her to see Niagara Falls. After driving five hours and depositing our bags in our hotel, we walked to the falls and were mesmerized by their beauty. I asked Stephanie what she thought of one of nature's greatest views, and she replied, "Is this all we're gonna do, watch this water go over the hill?"

And so her inquiries would begin early on at the fishing hole. "Daddy, if you could be a bird, which one would you be? Daddy, if I catch a big fish, can I cut him open and get my worm back? Daddy, can I have a boa constrictor?" And on and on.

Stephanie's attention span wasn't very long, especially on our early trips. If she didn't catch a bluegill after ten minutes, she would wander away to the playground in the park where we fished. I would push her on the swings, then coax her back to the pond with vague promises of catching the Big One. And then, soon enough, the questions would come again. "Daddy, are there sharks in this pond? Daddy, how do tornadoes start up? Daddy, how old are you? Nine?"

These expeditions were precious moments in our relationship, for as she grew older, I felt things change too quickly. During these fishing excursions, I willed time to slow down so I could enjoy them all the more because I noticed the questions were changing, too.

"Dad, how come the boys in my class are so weird? Dad, does it hurt the worm when you cut it in half? Dad, can I be a storm chaser when I grow up? The rain doesn't bother me, just the lightning."

I was a police officer, and early one morning I was called to the bank of the Allegheny River near Pittsburgh for a DOA. The victim, an elderly man, had been found at a popular fishing spot by a fellow fisherman at around 6:30 A.M. The victim was lying face up on the bank, a rod and reel propped up on a rock with the line in the water and a bucket full of live minnows by his side. I secured the area after medics verified he had no vital signs.

I spent about twenty minutes alone with the victim until the coroner arrived. I took his wallet from the rear pocket of his fishing jeans—I knew these were his fishing jeans because there were stains on the upper thighs from years of him wiping his hands on them when no rag was available. From the looks of these jeans, he had been a fisherman for a long time. The contents of his wallet revealed the man was from Pittsburgh, right across the river.

As I bent down to replace the wallet, I noticed a slight smile on his face as he stared up at me. I said a small prayer for him, glad that this elderly fellow passed away doing something it appeared he enjoyed. He had one last visit to his fishing spot, one last cast. A slight smile spread across my face.

In the past, I've been given sage advice from parents of preteens that I should appreciate these inquisitive fishing outings with my daughter while I'm still relevant in her grand scheme of the universe. In little ways, I've been feeling my importance slipping away already. I've given up answering the phone at home; it's Stephanie's hotline now, and friends call constantly to check up on what has happened since the last time they talked fifteen minutes earlier. I have to make an appointment a week in advance to get on the computer.

I recently took Stephanie fishing. Of course, as is our tradition, we had to stop at the grocery store to load up on fishing essentials such as bubble gum, SweeTarts, Pepsi and, yes, even bait. Sitting with her on the shore of the lake, I couldn't help but notice again how grown up she's becoming. In a lull of conversation, mostly one-sided with me doing the listening, I thought about the fisherman I found on the riverbank. I leaned back in my fishing chair and looked up, asking myself a question, Do you think he's up there, looking down with that smile of his? I answered my own question. Yeah, he's telling me to hold onto these fishing days with my daughter for as long as I can.

"Dad, do you, like, think I'd make a good veterinarian? Dad, don't you think *NSYNC are better than the Beatles? Dad, are we rich?"

Absolutely, Honey, beyond your wildest imagination.

~Danny Dugan
Chicken Soup for the Father & Daughter Soul

Dads & Daughters

"Step"ping Up to the Plate

Parenthood is a lot easier to get into than out of.
~Bruce Lansky

23

My Daughter, Once Removed

The family you come from isn't as important
as the family you're going to have.
~Ring Lardner

iesha is the first thing I think about when I wake up each morning. I haven't spoken to her in a month, but all her messages are still saved on my answering machine. A T-shirt lies in the exact spot where she left it during her last visit three months ago. I still tell her that she is my favorite person. Aiesha is eight, spoiling for nine. She is my daughter, once removed.

In my wide-eyed youth, I subscribed to such naive notions as "love makes you a parent," and "twenty-three chromosomes don't make you a daddy." Now I believe that fatherhood is created every morning at six, when you creak out of bed to crack eggs, rattle pans and let yourself be hustled into granting your kid ten more minutes of sleep. I still believe that genes don't make the parent, but now I ask, "What does a voided wedding vow make me?"

I know Aiesha because her mother, Shana, was my college girl-friend. She was wild and beautiful; her ways the complete opposite of my self-conscious, bookish ones. I broke up with her and then, years later, found myself wishing for her again. We were only together again for less than six months, but we did stay in touch after our breakup. Five years later, I moved to New York for graduate school. When we threw a surprise party for my mother's fiftieth birthday, I invited Shana. She showed up with a buoyant two-year-old who had impossibly round cheeks and whose favorite response was "No!"—even to things like, "You are adorable."

Soon Shana and I were hanging out again, back to our old routines. At some point in those first months of being reunited, I realized that I loved Shana and that Aiesha had already chosen me as her father. Shana and I got married.

I think men secretly want to raise their daughters to be the kind of women who were out of their league when they were young. And so it was with Aiesha. But really, it was about the words, teaching her the words to old classics such as "Ain't No Sunshine" and giggling through the part where Bill Withers sings, "And I know, I know, I know, I know, I know...." Kids love repetition. She turned out volumes of poems, plays, songs and stories that were duly typed up and e-mailed to all my friends, co-workers and distant relatives as evidence of her burgeoning literary genius.

There were signs early on, now that I think of it, that the marriage was headed south. I saw in gradual degrees that my wife was less and less interested in our relationship and knew that I was at the point where many a man would have bailed. I chose to work harder. When the newspapers ranked Aiesha's public school at the bottom half of those in the city, I reduced my grad classes and worked part-time to send her to a private school. When Shana was stuck at work a few hours before her women's group meeting was to be held in our apartment, I came home early and surprised her by cleaning up and preparing the food. I was like an outfielder who knows that the ball is headed for the bleachers, but smashes face first into the wall trying to catch it anyway. In my world, there was no such thing as a warning track.

Here is a marital cliché: You're in the kitchen cooking dinner when your spouse returns home from a hard day at the office and announces it's over. Just like that. When she told Aiesha that I was leaving, Aiesha asked, "Does this mean I don't have a father anymore?"

Friends, mostly female, tell me, "Once a father, always a father." But experience tells me differently: I could just as easily be evicted again; Shana could remarry and leave me a parental second-string player. Experience has taught me that ex-stepfather does not exist as a census category; I no longer qualify for a Father's Day card.

I know that I deeply and profoundly love that little girl. I understand the weight of the bond between parent and child. I also know that I was trying to single-handedly undo the mythology of black men, that I wanted a family that would laugh past the bleak statistics and indictments of black male irresponsibility. When I married Shana, Aiesha had not seen her biological father in more than a year. As far as I know, she has not seen him since. I saw tragedy in her growing up as yet another fatherless black girl, another child whose father abandoned her in favor of emptier pursuits. I wanted to be like my old man, quietly heroic in raising my brother and sister, and never once letting on that they were not his biological kin. I wanted to be a keeper.

These days, I know that my relationship with Aiesha is unwieldy, sagging beneath the weight of its own ambiguity. Fatherhood is all about watching the daily changes, whether it is hearing the new word she learned or noticing that now she doesn't have to stand on a stool to reach her toothbrush. But I know that in a year or two, my work may require that I move to Texas or California or Alaska, and it's possible that I'll fade from her memory.

Christmas is a hard, bright day, and I wake up alone with my head heavy. Aiesha has left me a message saying that she has a gift for me, and could I please come today so she can give it to me. Her mother and I have lived apart for six months, and I don't know Aiesha as well as I did in June. In another six months, she'll be a different child altogether.

When I see her outside, riding her bike in the parking lot of her building, I think about how she has grown tall and slender as a reed. I bought her a watch, yellow and red, but with no cartoon characters because Aiesha fancies herself a sophisticate. The note says:

Dear Aiesha,

My father once told me that keeping track of time is the first step to becoming an adult. I hope you think of me when you wear this.

She gives me a gift card. Written in her best eight-year-old scrawl, it says simply, "I love you." She's telling me the plot points to her latest story, the one she wants to publish when she's twelve. A moment later, she wants me to toss her into the air. "One more time!" she pleads, again and again, until my deltoids are burning.

She still remembers most of the words to "Ain't No Sunshine." Today, she's my daughter. Today.

~William Jelani Cobb
Chicken Soup for the Single Parent's Soul

24

Step-Babies

I t had been scheduled. Muffie, our seven-month-old Lhasa Apso, was to be fixed. But as luck would have it, we didn't schedule it soon enough. Five months pregnant myself, I sat at the kitchen table staring at my beautiful pet and reprimanding myself for not doing something sooner.

My ten-year-old daughter walked into the room and saw me staring at Muffie. "What's wrong?" she asked.

I thought Nina, an animal lover, would be thrilled to have puppies in the house. And lately I'd noticed her mood had seemed a little down. But when I told her, she simply looked from Muffie to my protruding stomach and stated, "I don't know how I feel about babies right now."

My heart squeezed. "What do you mean? I thought you wanted a brother or sister."

The expression on her young face turned anguished, and deep down I sensed her fears. Steve and I had married when Nina was six years old and because her biological father had long since severed the ties, Steve had become the daddy she had always wanted.

"What if Daddy loves the baby best?" she asked and tears filled her brown eyes. "It will be his, you know. Not just some stepchild he got stuck with."

My own eyes grew moist, and I reassured her that Steve had enough love to share and he would love them the same. But I still saw the doubt in her watery eyes, and it broke my heart. It seemed nothing we said or did could convince her.

Two months later, Muffie had two beautiful puppies and although Nina was fascinated, and I'd occasionally find her visiting with the puppies, she still remained somewhat aloof about the whole "baby" situation.

Then one day I came in and found Nina crying as she stood over the puppies.

"What's wrong?" I asked.

Through her tears she told me about a friend who had found a stray pregnant dog. After a few days, the animal had gone into labor and after several hours they took the dog to the vet. The puppies were premature: Two were born dead, and the other two were sickly. It seemed the mother dog was too weak to feed the puppies. "The vet is giving the mother until this afternoon, and if her milk doesn't come in, he's going to... put the puppies down. That means he going to kill them, doesn't it?" she asked.

Heartbroken, I took Nina in my arms, "Oh baby, I'm so sorry."

"They can't do that, Mama. They just can't," she cried.

She allowed me to hold her a second then she pulled away. "So I've been thinking. Maybe Muffie will take them as her stepchildren."

I was shocked at her idea. I'd heard that sometimes whelping animals would take other young, but I also knew it wasn't a sure thing.

"But honey," I told her. "Muffie's puppies are almost four weeks. And you said the puppies were premature."

"So, you told me I was premature, too. They didn't kill me."

"But honey," I said, "What if... " What if she doesn't accept them, I almost said, but right then my mind played back what Nina had said, "Maybe Muffie would take the children as her stepchildren... I was premature." Somehow Nina related to this situation at a deeper level than I first guessed.

I stood there in a quandary. I wanted to say we'd try, but what if Muffie rejected the puppies? Would that send a message to my daughter? Yet would our not trying send a message? I thought of the puppies, the consequences, and then I met my daughter's pleading gaze. "I'll talk to the vet."

The vet was not reassuring. My Muffie could very likely reject the puppies.

Steve and I talked, and in the end we felt that not to try would be more damaging than to have tried and failed. We also discussed the possibility of attempting to save the puppies ourselves. But with our baby on the way and Steve's job situation, the round-the-clock care seemed too daunting. In spite of our doubts, the next morning Steve went to the vet and got the puppies.

Nina stayed home from school, and although we had explained to her that Muffie could very well reject the new additions, Steve and I both worried.

Removing a towel from Muffie's box, I placed the two new puppies on the towel in another box. Then I put the box in the middle of the kitchen, a room away from where Muffie was nursing her own litter.

When Muffie heard the new puppies' soft cries, she came bustling into the kitchen to investigate. She stared down in the box, and I can honestly say I've never seen a dog with a more befuddled expression. She ran back to her puppies and stared down in the box as if to count. Then she scurried back to the two other puppies and looked at us in total bewilderment. After a moment, she smelled them, nudged them with her nose, and then left the room as if to say, "These aren't mine."

I looked at my daughter. Her big brown eyes had begun to fill with tears. "She doesn't want them, does she?"

"Let's give her some time," I told her. We waited for fifteen minutes. The new puppies began to cry again, and I felt like joining in. The vet had said not to force Muffie to take them. It had to be her choice. Eventually, I took Nina's hand and Steve wrapped his arm around her shoulder.

"We tried," he told her. Then he looked at her, and I saw the beginning of tears in his eyes. "But hey," he said. "We can still try. We'll get those droppers. We can do this."

Nina looked up at him with love in her eyes, somehow sensing this was a sacrifice on his part. "Thank you," she said.

Sighing, he reached down to pick up one of the yelping puppies and when he did Muffie came running into the room. She barked at him. He quickly put the tiny newcomer down, and we stood back. Muffie jumped into the box and licked the puppies. We all started laughing and hugging. Then, with our arms around each other we watched as she carried her adopted family, one at a time, to her box.

Steve took Nina by the hand and led her to the puppies. "You gave Muffie something very special today. You gave her two more puppies to love. Just like your mother gave me you to love." In gentle words, he assured Nina one more time that she had a place in his heart, a place that couldn't be erased no matter how many brothers and sisters she had.

Nina looked up at Steve, and then down at Muffie, who was lying contentedly with all four of the puppies, and her face brightened, breaking into a radiant smile. As she returned his bear hug, I could see that her fears had finally melted away. In that happy moment, I knew our combined family was going to be just fine.

~Christie Craig
Chicken Soup for the Cat and Dog Lover's Soul

25

The Unconditional Step

To be trusted is a greater compliment than to be loved.
~James Ramsay MacDonald

I didn't just marry their mother. She had two young teenage daughters whom I loved dearly. For several years, I watched them grow from little girls into beautiful young ladies. We got along great, but I worried that things would change once I married their mom.

Having never been married before, with no children of my own, I was concerned about taking on the role of "father." I read several articles on the subject—all contradicting one another and leaving me nothing but confused. I don't think I ever made a conscious decision on just "what" to be to the girls. Luckily I didn't have to—they made that decision for me.

Something wonderful happened. Without any encouragement from my wife or myself, the girls began to call me "Dad." Such a simple word, but an unfamiliar one that filled my heart with even more love for these amazing girls. By them reaching out, I realized that they needed a dad in their lives. And so the decision was made—I would be "Dad."

Several years passed and we made it through life with no major catastrophes. My marriage to their mother was a happy one and I was delighted that the girls and I had a strong relationship.

The older of the two, Veneta, was now eighteen and legally old enough to make her own decisions—and a big one she made!

On my birthday she presented me with a beautiful frame. This wasn't a picture or a piece of art, but a legal document protected by a beautiful casing. Veneta had given me the most precious gift — she had changed her last name to mine.

She told me that something was missing when she heard her name being called at her high school graduation. "It wasn't my father's name," she explained.

She continued by promising that the next time I was in a room where her name was announced, that it would be mine. "Everyone will know you're my dad."

I know grown men aren't supposed to cry, but I'll admit I did that day. This wasn't the last time she would make me cry.

Veneta graduated college, and along the way fell in love with a great guy who would become her husband.

After months of planning, the big day arrived and I would walk her down the aisle. I couldn't have been more proud of my daughter, who looked radiant.

As the music started, Veneta took my arm. "Are you ready, Dad?" she asked with poise.

I looked at her, trying to smile but feeling like I needed to cry. My quivering lips struggled with a humble, "Yes."

I kissed the top of her head — right through the veil — smiled and walked her proudly down the aisle. The ceremony was perfect.

At the reception, I heard the DJ announce the infamous father-daughter dance. Dancing not being one of my better attributes, I became consumed with nervousness. Scared to death, I put on a brave face, took my daughter's hand and led her to the empty dance floor.

While preparing to relax by taking a deep breath, I noticed someone hand Veneta a microphone and something in a frame. Another framed gift? Is this déjà vu? Not knowing what she was up to, Veneta kissed me on the cheek and stepped back. In front of everyone, she began to read a touching poem she wrote about our relationship. She called it "Something Special," and something special it was.

As she continued, I tried to block out everyone around us so I could just listen to her. Tears filled my eyes when I heard her voice quiver:

"Daddy, it is because of you and your love that I have the confidence and courage to stand here today as Mrs. Jeremy Veneta Novakovich Leonard. I hope that as you look upon me at this moment, it is with the same pride and unconditional love that I have always felt for you. As I begin my new life as Jeremy's wife, I hope you will continue to hold my hand 'in your heart,' offer me your guidance and advice, and continue to be my best friend. I will always be your little girl—and in your heart is where I always want to be. I am proud to be your daughter."

Mrs. Veneta Novakovich Leonard—always a Novakovich, I thought.

When my daughter finished, I thought about her promise to me years before. Hearing my name next to her new name took away all my insecurities from the past.

Then she took my hand for our father-daughter dance, and I suddenly realized that my fear of dancing had disappeared. As we swayed to the music with Veneta in my arms, she laid her head on my chest in a childlike manner. I told her I loved her and she simply replied, "I love you, too, Daddy."

~Donald R. Novakovich
Chicken Soup for the Bride's Soul

26

Father Christmas

I didn't realize how much Carissa resented me until I became united with her mother. The sweet eleven-year-old did everything she could to sabotage my loving relationship with Paula. No matter what I tried, there were no signs of progress. Carissa would leave her bed at night, claiming bad dreams, and crawl in next to her mom. Each time, I was slowly pushed out, destined to sleep on the cold couch. It was the perfect metaphor for our struggling relationship.

I hung in there, though, doing all I could to stay nice and teach well. With Christmas quickly approaching, I knew I had the perfect opportunity to show Carissa an example of selfless love. I played Santa each year, the location depending on where I was needed most. On the eve of Christmas, without fail, I tore the red suit free from the dry cleaner's plastic wrap and fluffed up the white beard.

Through the years, I faced great criticism for interrupting my own holiday by doing volunteer work. "It's a night only to spend with family and close friends," some said. I chuckled silently. They didn't understand. Though I spent every spare moment I could with those I loved, Christmas Eve could not be any more magical when spent with children who believed in me, Santa. I was hardly being selfless. In fact, it was the opposite. It was a most selfish act. Yet, year after year, I allowed those who sighed heavily to believe I was giving something up. I never let them in on my secret. I never wanted it to end.

As fate would have it, I had two stops planned for this year and wanted to spend both with Carissa. Paula was more than accommodating and insisted on going along.

On our way, I told them about my secret love of playing the jolly fat man.

Our first stop was at a Grange Hall in the country. With a wolves' bite in the air, we hurried for the door. Before Carissa took the first step inside, Gene Autry's version of "Rudolph the Red-Nosed Reindeer" poured out. Paula turned to the fat man in the red suit and smiled. The entire night was going to be filled with magic. We could both feel it.

On the giant square-dance floor, a tight community of people celebrated the holiday the old-fashioned way. They strung popcorn and dried cranberries on a giant Christmas tree. Before anyone could spot me, I bellowed, "HO! HO! HO!" The children came running.

Paula and Carissa stood off to the side to watch. The excitement of the children was contagious and overwhelming. Carissa beamed with the joy, and Paula fought back the tears.

A kind-looking, heavyset woman approached and took my hand, leading me to a chair that had been decorated for Santa. Though the kids hadn't seen it, there was a bag of gifts already waiting to be handed out. I waved Carissa over, and with Paula's gentle prodding, she came. "Pretty girl, can you help Santa hand out the gifts?" I asked in my deep Santa voice.

With dozens of tiny eyes upon her, Carissa nodded and went to work. She handed me a present from the bag. I read out the name and then personally handed it over to the excited child it belonged to. Together, we handed out a bag full of wrapped presents. Toward the end, I caught Carissa staring at me. Seated by the frozen window, her heart was beginning to thaw. She actually smiled, and it made my eyes fill.

Santa and his helpers were invited to share dinner with the townsfolk, and they weren't about to take "no" for an answer. Even through the matted beard, I enjoyed the feast.

Just before I was about to pass out from the heat exhaustion I suffered in the thick suit, we bid our farewell. Walking out of the Grange Hall, the starry night ushered us back into the present. I hurried for the van and, under the cover of darkness, tore off my wig and beard. While Paula and Carissa giggled, I took in the fresh air.

Forty miles later, I donned my wig and beard again. We were in the city, at Santa's last stop of the night.

The snow-swept streets were alive with holiday magic as the three of us stepped out of the van. With the tall buildings blocking the wind, the night felt twenty degrees warmer. With Carissa by my side, we stepped into the Boys Club to meet another pack of under-privileged children. I laughed from my belly, listened to wishes and handed out presents. I looked up again to catch Carissa staring. I smiled, and to my surprise, she returned it. I'd finally made progress and gotten through to her. I wondered then if I'd ever make a real difference in her life.

Upon returning home from the incredible experience, I collapsed in the living room. While I wrestled the sweat-drenched outfit free, Carissa proceeded to the tree. Escorted by her mother's gentle eyes, she reached under the soft pine, grabbed a neatly wrapped present and handed it to me. "I wanted to give this to you tonight," she whispered before quickly leaving the room.

I pulled off the black boots, wiped my hands on my pants and tore through the wrapping to find a framed essay. Through shocked and misty eyes, I read:

The Person I Admire Most
by Carissa Kennedy

The person I admire most is Steven Manchester... he is very funny and most of all he teaches me a lot about life... he is a United States veteran... he stood tall and fought with honor... honor is one of the things he teaches me... he also teaches me about respect at home and I think that is pure love... Steve teaches me friendship... not just with me but with everyone around him....

I wiped my eyes. I had already made a difference in Carissa's life. I just needed to remember that such truths are usually left unsaid and are normally invisible to the eye.

~Steven H. Manchester
Chicken Soup for the Father & Daughter Soul

27

He Completed Us

The most important thing a father can do for his children
is to love their mother.
~Theodore Hesburgh

My daughter Alyssa was born in 1992. I had just turned nineteen and was left to raise a daughter on my own. I was young, alone and bitter that her father wanted no part of our life.

I had a few boyfriends who did not mind that I was a young single mother, but I could never bring myself to include Alyssa in those relationships. It wasn't that I was ashamed of having a daughter; she was the first person to show and teach me what true love really was. I just never trusted a man enough to include Alyssa. That is, until I met Travis.

Travis and I met in the summer of 2000 and I think I fell in love with him the first time we talked. We had one of those conversations that seems to last forever and everyone else in the room seems to disappear. It wasn't until we were together for a few months and we were talking about moving in together that I felt ready to include Alyssa.

From the beginning they got along—not that it surprised me. He was the first person who actually got her to swim and get over many of her fears. Alyssa's dad has never played a role in her life and it was like a breath of fresh air to see Alyssa with a father figure.

The three of us grew as a family over the next couple of years. Travis's family accepted Alyssa and me into their family as if we had always been there from the beginning. I finally had the life that I had always dreamed of, except that it was missing one thing. Marriage.

Travis proposed on Valentine's Day that year and I could not wait. I wanted everything to be perfect. I planned for over a year, until I was driving everyone crazy, including myself. The wedding became my weekend project, and I made sure I included Alyssa from the very beginning. I didn't want her to feel left out. I expressed this to Travis to make sure he included her in everything as well.

Then he made a suggestion that confirmed how much I loved him.

The day of my wedding came and the sun was out. The stress and whirlwind of getting ready for the wedding had everyone running around freaking out, but Alyssa was the perfect princess all morning.

The church was beautiful and the bridesmaids made their way down the aisle followed by Alyssa and then myself. Travis and I said our vows to each other. It was a wonderful moment.

Our Reverend then asked Alyssa to step forward. It was then that Travis made his vow to my daughter.

I Travis, choose you, Alyssa,
to be my family.
I promise to honor and respect you,
and to provide for you to the best of my ability.
I promise to make our home a haven,
where trust, love and laughter are abundant.
I make these promises lovingly, and freely,
and vow to honor them all the days of my life.

He then placed a beautiful gold locket around her neck and gave her a kiss.

At that moment all the planning and worrying about how I looked didn't matter. I knew that God had sent the perfect man, a man who taught me the meaning of unconditional love, of trust and renewed faith. A man who, on this day, completed us.

~Michelle Lawson
Chicken Soup for the Bride's Soul

She Calls Me Daddy

A daughter is a day brightener and a heart warmer.
~Author Unknown

Wendy and I had just started dating, and we were beginning to think that this could be "it." I was hesitant at first because Wendy had a daughter from a previous marriage, and I didn't know if I possessed the ability to love two people at the same time.

Shaina was two years old when Wendy and I first met, and her father had just been stabbed to death on a bus in San Francisco. I had been single for thirty-two years and was a bit frightened about my lack of ability to be a good father to this beautiful child whose father had just been taken from her.

The relationship between Wendy and I continued to deepen, and we set the wedding date. Even then I was still a bit frightened.

I was the youngest in my family by five years, and had never been around children, especially girls! The idea of becoming a husband and a dad on the same day had my heart conflicted between joy and excitement and fear and trepidation.

Wendy and I started spending even more time together and going to church. We noticed that Shaina was getting more comfortable with me in a paternal way. Wendy wanted to make sure that I would not feel unnecessary pressure, so she explained to Shaina that she should call me Johnny until the wedding, and then she could call me Daddy.

So, as the wedding day approached, I thought of ways to make Shaina feel a part. I had asked Wendy's father for permission to marry his daughter, so I thought it would be cute to ask for Shaina's permission to marry her mommy.

"No," Shania said.

Startled, I smiled and said, "Please?" But she was set on her answer.

"No."

My heart dropped, and all my fears and insecurities stuck in my throat, choking my words. I couldn't catch my breath. Wendy and I glanced at each other completely stunned and wondered together, "Oh my, now what?"

I finally spoke, "Why not?"

With a shy smile and a little embarrassment, she replied, "Because I want to marry you."

~John Cox
Chicken Soup for the Father & Daughter Soul

29

A Tale of Two Fathers

O ur parents divorced when Karen was a toddler, and a few years later we were blessed with the best of a complicated world—a father and a stepfather. The situation wound up a bit confusing later on down the road. Especially when it was time for Karen to get married.

As sometimes happened in those days, long before shared custody and divorce mediation, we didn't maintain much contact with our natural father. It was hoped that our new stepfather would grow to be the apple of our eyes.

Gordon was, in fact, a wonderful man. He accepted us as his children and went on to nurture, counsel and play a major part in the raising of my sister and me. He was the humor in an otherwise dry existence. He was the fun where there often wasn't any. And he was the true keeper of our hearts, with our best interests always at the center of his own.

I maintained ties with my natural father, too, although initially strained. I saw the situation for what it was and did my best to mend all wounds. Gordon supported this whole-heartedly. Karen, being years younger than me, grew up without really knowing our natural father.

When Karen was in high school and I was married, living far away from home, we went through a second divorce. This time, however, I was careful to maintain ties. Gordon remained the father figure he'd always been and even became "Grandpa Gordon" to my firstborn. Karen and Gordon grew apart some, but reestablished ties after graduation.

Gordon eventually remarried. Carol was ideally suited to him and understood the complications of our situation. When they both encouraged Karen to mend her severed ties with Dad, she bravely set about renewing a relationship she barely remembered.

Communication with Dad was, at its best, on the surface. We knew he loved us and he knew we loved him, but the words were seldom spoken aloud. And none of us ever mentioned our relationship with Gordon.

Before Karen announced her engagement, she voiced her concerns. "I want Gordon to give me away when I get married."

"Mm-hmm," I replied.

"But I want Dad to give me away, too. I don't want to hurt either one of them."

I knew Gordon would understand. My father, however, would be a little harder to convince. "Let me see what I can do."

A letter, I decided, felt right. Gordon, of course, was privy to my plan and supported it.

Dear Dad,

We were children when this all started, and the situation was completely out of our hands. As adults now, we need and want you to be our father. We love you and want you to be a part of our lives.

But Gordon is a part of our lives, too. He has been a good man, an honest man, and has done everything a father would do for his children.

Karen is getting married in a few months. It would mean the world to her, and to me, if you would walk her down the aisle — together with Gordon.

Loving Gordon doesn't mean in any way that we love you any less. There is plenty of room for two wonderful fathers in our lives. Gordon always encouraged contact with you, never spoke a word against you or undermined our feelings for you. We respect the fact that you never voiced negative feelings about Gordon.

Give this some thought. Remember both Karen and I love you and want our family ties to be restored. Remember that in your absence, we established strong family ties with Gordon, and it would be unfair to all of us to expect that to stop.

It would be a beautiful sight to watch Karen walking down the aisle on her wedding day, flanked by two wonderful fathers. It would be an answer to prayer.

I love you.
Kim

A couple of weeks later, Karen received a phone call from Dad.

"So where do I go to get measured for my tux?"

In late August, Karen walked down the aisle with a handsome father on each side of her. They wore identical tuxedos with matching smiles and radiated the same fatherly love and joy.

The blessing to Karen and me was twofold. In addition to ending years of confusion and estrangement, we learned to share the joy of being the proud daughters of two extraordinary fathers.

~Kimberly Ripley
Chicken Soup for the Bride's Soul

Dads & Daughters

Gratitude

We can do no great things—only small things with great love.
~Mother Teresa

Memorial Day Flags

After what I owe to God, nothing should be more dear or more sacred than
the love and respect I owe to my country.
~François Auguste de Thou

I served as a U.S. Army infantry squad leader during the Vietnam War. For many years the general perception of Vietnam veterans has been less-than-stellar, but I was always proud of my service and my three daughters knew it. Every year, I marched in the local Memorial Day parade in full dress uniform, and I also prominently display my military awards in our home. About fifteen years ago, I joined a group of local Vietnam-era veterans who had taken charge of our town's Memorial Day parade. Our committee took a firm stand to eliminate activities that were not in the spirit of honoring the lives that were lost or disrupted in service to our country.

Besides organizing the parade every year, our group also placed American flags at the graves of our deceased veterans. I thought this simple patriotic task was something my three daughters should be involved with, so each year I took one of them along to assist. When my oldest daughter became a teenager, she no longer wanted to participate because to her it wasn't cool to be searching for gravestones with a group of old veterans. So I began bringing my middle daughter, but when she reached the same teenage threshold, she no longer wanted to help either. Undaunted, the following year I enlisted the aid of Ashley, my youngest.

For whatever reason, eleven-year-old Ashley seemed fascinated by the experience. She asked dozens of questions that ranged from what happened to the buried veterans to what was it like for me during the war. Needless to say, I was pleasantly surprised by her unusual interest in the people who served our nation.

As the years went by, Ashley did not display the same teenage aversion that her sisters did and continued to help place the flags. One damp, foggy weekend, however, she questioned whether we should wait for a nicer day. I explained that it was our duty to honor veterans no matter what the weather conditions, because during war-time, soldiers were often stuck in the rain, snow or sweltering heat for several weeks and even months, with little or no relief. Ashley nodded knowingly and never complained about the weather again.

As my daughters were growing up, I began to give presentations about my Vietnam experiences to their schools and local civic groups. I also volunteered to be the main speaker for several Memorial Day and Veteran's Day ceremonies and was one of the founding members of our new veteran's museum. My continued dedication sparked something in Ashley—I could see that she had developed a genuine sense of appreciation for people who have served in the military. She made me feel proud because appreciation was the one thing that veterans covet the most, and it was especially gratifying that it came from one of my own children.

When Ashley was a college freshman, I thought her feelings might change somewhat, but surprisingly she still had more to offer. This past Memorial Day, our parade committee wanted to have a woman be the main speaker, but everyone we contacted declined. Then, from out of nowhere, eighteen-year-old Ashley asked if she could give the speech. Her request was very unusual because our speakers generally had a military background or were familiar long-time residents. However, Ashley insisted she wanted to do it, so we gave her the honor.

At the Memorial Day ceremony, I proudly watched Ashley walk to the podium and slowly adjust the microphone. She boldly faced the audience and began. "I'm reminded of a cold, foggy day when I was a little girl complaining about putting flags on veterans' graves." Ashley spoke with such confidence and clarity, as if public speaking was routine for her. "The one or two days a year that we honor deceased veterans cannot begin to compare to the absolute devotion of the Tomb Sentinels who guard the Tomb of the Unknown Soldier at Arlington National Cemetery. No matter what the weather, or if the nation is at war or enjoying peace, every minute of every day a guard is watching over soldiers who will never be identified."

To this proud father, that was the day my daughter became a true American patriot.

~Arthur B. Wiknik Jr.
Chicken Soup for the Father & Daughter Soul

A Daughter's Letter

Death is the end of a lifetime, not the end of a relationship.
~Mitch Albom

Dear Dad,

My trip to the Wall was something I'll never forget. When you wrote me and asked me to make rubbings of your fellow soldiers' names for you, I knew that it was going to be something special, both for you and for me. And doing it alone was important to me. No kids, no husband, not even a friend. I didn't want the distraction of having anyone else there needing my attention.

I waited for a nice, sunny day—not too hot—and packed a lunch and took off on the metro. I walked through the streets of D.C. thinking about my quest. I was hoping that I had the right paper and the right pencils, and that my camera wouldn't flake out on me. When I arrived, I went straight to the registry to look up the addresses of the crew, which were easy to find. Then I headed toward the Wall.

Several students on field trips were standing around. I thought that this would keep me from doing my job, but as I approached each panel of the Wall that held a name I wanted, people just moved out of my way. I'm not sure if I said anything to them. Maybe they saw a certain look in my eyes that said I was there for a specific person. They were right to think so.

I came to the first panel, where I would find Thomas A. Davis's name. I located it quickly, and I had to sit down to do the rubbing as it was near the bottom of the Wall. I was nervous when I started. I wasn't sure that I had the paper lined up right, but as I dragged the pencil across the page, his name began to appear. I was really concentrating on the action so I could get it right for the rest, and that distracted me from the unhappy meaning of what I was doing.

The next one wasn't so easy. I found Thomas Duer a few panels down. He was within my reach, and I could stand and look at his name as if he were standing right there in front of me. But as I began rubbing, a sadness came over me. I thought about his age, twenty-five, and about what I was doing when I was that age. It seemed to me that I was only a kid at twenty-five, yet these men whose names I touched on the Wall never got any older than that. Never had children. Or if they did, never saw them grow up. Their parents must've gone out of their minds with grief over losing their boys. As I moved from name to name, thoughts like these kept going through my head, and I could hear people behind me, next to me and around me, all sharing those same feelings with the other people with them.

When I went to 14-E, where your crew is, I suddenly panicked. I couldn't reach anyone; they were all too high. I looked around for a tall person, then stopped. There was no way I was going to let some stranger do this. I had to do it! Only I was too short.

I began to cry, thinking I had failed you, when I saw a man who had a ladder. I was saved. I asked him to let me use it to trace my names off the Wall. He said he could do the rubbings for me, but he couldn't allow me to use the ladder. At first I fought him. I told him about my daddy, who went to Vietnam and whose friends died there: classmates and crew. I told him that this was something I had to do for him because it was the only thing I could do for him — I couldn't take it all away, and I couldn't help him with the pain; I said there are no words that can erase what my daddy saw and what he has to endure.

The man was so sympathetic, and he assured me that it would be okay if he did it, that the important thing was that I was there. I pointed out the names and watched him like a hawk, making sure he was doing it right. Of course, he'd been doing it awhile, so his came out better than mine. That was okay by me; I wanted it to be perfect.

After he was finished, he asked me a couple of questions about you, and I told him that you were over there twice but that I didn't know much more than that, except the names that I had on my letter from you. He told me that I was very lucky that you came home.

I told him that the way I see it, luck had little to do with it. You had to come home; you had to take care of us. You were meant to be my daddy, and you were meant to be around a long, long time.

But as I left the Wall, I remember thanking God that you did come home. I couldn't have stood there making a rubbing of your name; I'm not that strong.

I'm writing all this because if I tried to tell you, I know it wouldn't come out the same. I'm always hesitant to bring up Vietnam because I think it hurts you too much. I just hope you know that I'm always here for you and that I am very proud of you. I am so honored that you asked me to do this very special project for you. I will never know what it's like for you really, but I do often try to imagine.

Thank you for your service to our country, and thank you for being my daddy.

All my love,
Rani

~Rani Nicola
Chicken Soup for the Veteran's Soul

Trust Me

I wasn't expecting the feeling of total panic that hit me as I watched my ten-year-old daughter walk alone to the microphone at the front of the stage.

She was running for student body president, which meant that she had to deliver a brief campaign speech during an assembly of the entire school. She was pretty, articulate, charming and poised. I knew she would speak well. What made me nervous was the audience. The principal had ordered that no one could applaud for any candidate until the very end of the program, and the students had reacted to the restriction with boredom and resentment. Several times the principal had returned to issue warnings to those too eager to shout insults at their peers onstage.

I hadn't panicked when she asked for my help with the speech two weeks before. I told her that if she really, really wanted to win the election, the only way was to make all the kids laugh. To do so, she'd have to do something unexpected. "Trust me," I told her, "if you follow what I tell you, I guarantee it will go over well and you'll win." She had chosen her words carefully and practiced often; yet, in that moment of silence before she began speaking, my heart stopped beating.

What if I was wrong? What if they didn't laugh at her jokes? What if they ridiculed her attempts at humor and put her down? How could I have violated her trust? I was sure that I had thrown my oldest child to the sharks and that her respect for her father would be lost forever. I knew if she flopped and lost the election, she'd never believe anything I told her again.

"My name is Brittany, and I'm running for president," she started calmly. "I think you should vote for me because..." She paused and looked around. My hand on the video camera shook with fear as I waited for her to deliver the punch line. She picked up a Tupperware bowl from a bag behind her and put it upside down on her head. She pinched her nose and spoke in a robotic voice. "...I am an alien. I came to your planet to eat your cafeteria food!"

The audience was caught completely off-guard and erupted with glee. It took several seconds before the laughter died down enough for her to go on.

"But don't take my word for it," she continued. "Ask someone who has the same birthday as me, George Washington." With that, she turned her back to her classmates and put a gray wig over her hair. By now the crowd was squirming with anticipation. "Oh, my gosh, am I sore!" she shouted in an old man's voice as she stretched. "I guess that comes from being dead for a couple of hundred years!"

The hall erupted again. I knew her humor had tamed the crowd and that the election would be hers in a landslide.

When she finished her speech, outlining her agenda if elected, screams and shouts of approval filled the air. The children stomped their feet and pounded their fists on the chairs. It was pointless to attempt to contain the applause, and the principal was too amused to try. With every clap and yell, I thought my heart would burst.

I held the camera to my face to hide my tears. I was filled with love and pride for the daughter who had given her father her complete trust—and relieved that I had been worthy of it.

~Lanny Zechar
Chicken Soup for the Father & Daughter Soul

33

Chicken Soup for the Soul

A Bouquet to Remember

Every day is an opportunity to make a new happy ending.
~Author Unknown

"Where are the flowers?" My sister panicked pacing the living room dressed in her wedding gown.

"I don't know, sweetie. They were supposed to be here an hour ago. But don't worry; I'm sure they'll be here promptly," my mother assured Kathy to calm her down.

"Oh, no, the photographer's here. He's early!" the bride yelled hysterically. "I need my bouquet for the pictures."

I was seventeen years old and the bridesmaid. As a girl who always planned on getting married one day, I considered my sister's wedding day a learning experience.

That morning, Kathy was a wreck. She had planned every detail of her wedding carefully. The invitations, personalized napkins and matches, the bouquet with white roses, calla lilies and baby's breath. All planned a year in advance. The one thing Kathy didn't plan was the fact that something could go wrong.

We waited and waited for the flowers to arrive. My sister looked enchanting with her classic fairy-tale gown and full skirt that gathered at the waistline. But for her, no flowers meant no sweet fragrance, no delicate decorations, no beautiful pictures, no mementos, no wedding.

The groom was often called "a romantic fool" in the good sense of the word. He was the kind of guy who would leave little notes saying "I love you" for no special reason. The night before the wedding, he gave my sister a bracelet proving he was a hopeless romantic.

But there was nothing romantic in the air the next day. Trapped in an apartment filled with desperation and nervousness, I noticed my father open a window to smoke. It was interesting to see how one stressful situation could drive a man who had quit two years before to suddenly go back to the habit.

The doorbell rang. The florists, I thought, running frantically to answer the door. Disappointed to find a young delivery boy, I asked in my annoyed voice, "May I help you?"

"It's a delivery for Kathy Lassalle from her future husband, Hernan," he said, trying to keep my attention.

He pulled out a huge floral bouquet of red roses. My father's lit cigarette fell to the ground. He immediately grabbed the bouquet and took off for the bedroom, leaving me at the door to sign the paper.

"Thanks a lot," I said to the delivery boy as I watched my father mysteriously disappear. "Dad, that's not for you. Give Kathy her gift!" I shouted down the hall, wondering what he was up to.

Minutes later, my father reappeared in the room where we all waited. He had a big smile on his face; his way of saying that things were going to be all right. He then presented to us three gorgeous bouquets he had arranged from the groom's beautiful red roses.

We couldn't believe it. Dad (and Hernan) had saved the day.

With little time to spare, the photographer took pictures of the bride, bridesmaid and flower girl as planned. Not with the wedding bouquets, however, but with bouquets made out of love, creativity and urgency!

The scheduled flowers finally arrived just before we entered the church. My sister was happy to have the bouquet she designed herself; and the flower girl had her basket of flowers. I, on the other hand, decided to keep my dad's lovely red-rose creation, giving my original white bouquet to my mother.

Ten years later, when we look at my sister's wedding pictures, we notice something that nobody else does. In fact, we think it's cute that some pictures show a red bouquet of flowers and others show a white one. But each time, we are taken back to that eventful day. A day of emotion and stress, but most importantly a day where a groom's romantic gesture and a father's hidden talent made a bouquet to remember.

~Cindy L. Lassalle
Chicken Soup for the Bride's Soul

34

The Best "Father-Daughter Date" Ever!

A truly rich man is one whose children run into his arms when his hands are empty.
~Author Unknown

In early May 1996, my twelve-year-old son, Bobby, and I took a two-week trip with my dad, Rev. Dale McClain. We drove from Venice, Florida, to Stone Mountain, Georgia, to visit my brother. I was recently divorced and considering a possible move to Georgia or North Carolina, depending on the outcome of several interviews I had scheduled during our time there.

What a trip that turned out to be! Bobby, Dad and I told jokes and funny stories all the way to Stone Mountain. I can't remember when I've laughed that much! Traveling with Dad was always a real treat. Unlike the stereotypical "man on a mission," Dad always took time to stop and enjoy the sights. A beautiful sunset? We'd pull over so we could really see it! If anyone even hinted at being hungry, Dad immediately found a place to eat. He could turn getting a cup of coffee into an event.

After a few days in Stone Mountain, Dad and I left for North Carolina, where I had an interview at Montreat College. Leaving Bobby with the family in Georgia, Dad and I took off for another wonderful adventure together, just the two of us on our "father-daughter date," as Dad always called them. Our dates had spanned the globe, from India to Hong Kong to America. Dad was there, enriching me in every phase of my metamorphosis from toddler to teen to woman.

Some missionary kids—or MKs as we are called—grow up feeling a constant lack of their father's attention. I was blessed as a child in that I didn't have that experience. Dad was the most sentimental man I've ever known. No matter how intense the schedule, somehow he always took time to be with his children and, often, with each of us individually. I never felt deprived. Dad could cram more love and fun into one game of Monopoly than many fathers do in an entire summer. He never communicated a sense of obligation as a parent; on the contrary, I knew Dad's greatest delight was to be with his family.

We shared memories like these and many more on the scenic drive to Montreat College. As we walked up a steep incline to the campus, Dad seemed very weak. I wondered if his pulmonary fibrosis was acting up. His lungs were damaged years earlier while ministering in the Philippines where the air was thick with volcanic ash. He had already lived about eight years longer than the doctors projected. They had been good, strong years for the most part. But on this day, he seemed especially weary, older than his seventy-four years.

On our way back to Stone Mountain, Dad and I stopped in at The Cove, Billy Graham's restful retreat tucked in the mountains near Asheville. We particularly wanted to see the prayer chapel, a beautiful two-story building built among tall pines and glassed in on the second floor. The receptionist told us it was almost closing time, but encouraged us to go upstairs and enjoy a few minutes together anyway.

We were the only ones in the chapel. A late afternoon sun bathed the quiet room in a warm, almost sacred glow. It was so peaceful. God's presence was there. As we walked hand in hand toward the front, we noticed a beautiful, old grand piano. Reading my thoughts Dad said, "Carol, I'm sure they wouldn't mind if you played something. It's just the two of us anyway."

That's all the encouragement I needed! The piano, shipped from Germany, was over one hundred years old. The wood was beautiful, as were the old ivory keys. It was almost surreal, playing that magnificent old piano for my dad in such a serene setting.

I deliberately played the hymns and choruses I knew he loved the most: "And Can It Be," "When I Survey the Wondrous Cross" and "So Send I You." When I looked out at Dad, my heart melted. He was sitting about four rows back, looking at me, tears streaming down his cheeks. Just then the receptionist came in the back and walked to join us.

"That is so beautiful, dear," she kindly said to me. "Where did you learn to play like that?"

"From her mother," Dad replied, with obvious pride. "Her mother plays like an angel and has blessed people all over the world with her gift. My daughter has it, too." Dad wiped the tears away.

"Would you mind if we sang a song together?" she asked me. "I love 'Amazing Grace.'"

And so the three of us sang all the stanzas of that great hymn. When the song ended, the presence of God was so real that we reverently left the chapel without speaking.

The rest of the drive blurs in my memory. I recall Dad holding my hand most of the time as I drove. But something he told me stands out as a bright jewel, a gift I will always cherish.

I said, "Dad, it was so touching for me to look up and see you crying. I knew you were missing Mother and remembering a lifetime of listening to her play the piano."

"Oh, no, Honey. That's not what I was thinking at all. While I was listening to you play, my mind traveled back over the years to the night I drove six hours from Ohio to Lexington, Kentucky." I knew this story well, but dearly loved hearing it again. "I had just preached the closing sermon in a week of meetings. Your dear mother insisted that I keep my speaking commitment, even though your birth was already two weeks late. A man walked up to me with a big grin, held his hand out, and said, 'Congratulations, Rev. McClain, you're a father!'"

Dad's hand covered mine as he continued. "I was remembering barging into the hospital where a very large nurse tried to catch me as

I raced down the hall. She said, 'Excuse me, sir! You can't just come in here in the middle of the night to visit your wife!' I told her, 'Well, I'm Rev. McClain. My daughter is three days old, and I haven't seen her yet!' And that nurse said, 'Oh! We've been waiting for you, Rev. McClain. Come right this way.'"

Now I was the one crying.

"I was thinking about you, and how I've loved being your daddy. You could not possibly have brought me more joy than you have, Carol."

Holding hands, we drove and hummed and prayed on what would be our last date. What a legacy for a father to give his daughter.

~Carol McClain Bassett
Chicken Soup for the Father & Daughter Soul

35

Batter Up, Dad

Memory is the diary that we all carry around with us.
~Oscar Wilde

My father was an avid baseball fan. I grew up in New York City and was able to see the greats play at the Polo Grounds, Ebbets Field and Yankee Stadium. Many a Saturday was spent with my dad cheering on our favorite team. As much as I loved the game of baseball, alas, I was born female at a time when girls watched more than they played. Whenever he could, Dad took me out to the park where the neighborhood Little League played and pitched balls for me to hit. We played together for hours, and baseball became a big part of my life.

One day at the park, a woman pushing a young boy in a wheelchair stopped to watch us play. My dad was over to them in a flash to ask if the child could join our game. The woman explained that the boy was her son and that he had polio and wouldn't be able to get out of the chair. That didn't stop my dad. He placed the bat in the youngster's hand, pushed him out to home plate and assisted him in holding the bat. Then he yelled out to me on the mound, "Anne, pitch one in to us."

I was nervous that I might hit the child but could see the delight in the boy's eyes, so I aimed at the bat and let the ball fly. The ball made contact with the bat with an assist from my dad and the child screamed with joy. The ball flew over my head and headed for right field. I ran to catch up with it and, as I turned, I heard my dad singing "Take Me Out to the Ball Game" while he pushed the wheelchair around the bases. The mother clapped and the boy begged to be allowed to continue the game.

An hour later we all left the field, very tired but very happy. The boy's mother had tears in her eyes when she thanked my father for making it such a special day for her son. Dad smiled that wonderful grin that I loved so much and told the mother to bring the boy back next Saturday and we would play another game.

Dad and I were at the field the next Saturday but the mother and son never came. I felt sad and wondered what had happened to change their mind about joining us. Dad and I played many more games of baseball but never saw the two again.

Twenty years passed and my beloved father died at the tender age of fifty-nine. With my dad gone, things changed so much that the family decided to move to Long Island. I had very mixed emotions about leaving the neighborhood where I had grown up.

I decided to take one last walk around the park where Dad and I had spent so many happy moments. I stopped at the baseball field where we played our Saturday games. Two Little League teams were on the field just about to start a game. I sat down to watch for awhile. I felt the sting of tears in my eyes as I watched the children play the game that I loved. I missed my dad so much.

"Jeff, protect your base," one coach yelled. I cheered the runner on when the ball was hit far into the outfield. One coach turned and smiled and said, "The kids sure love a rooting section, Miss." He continued, "I never thought I'd ever be a coach playing on this field. You see, I had polio as a child and was confined to a wheelchair. One day my mother pushed me to the park and a man was playing baseball with his daughter. He stopped when he saw us watching and asked my mother if I could join them in their game. He helped me to hold the bat and his daughter pitched to me. I was able to hit the ball with the man's assistance and he ran me around the bases in my wheelchair singing the song 'Take Me Out to the Ball Game.' I went home happier that night than I had been in years.

"I believe that experience gave me the desire to walk again. We moved to New Jersey the next day—that's why my mother had taken me to the park, so I could say goodbye to my friends. I never forgot that man and his daughter or that day. I dreamed about running around the bases on my own two feet and the dream, with a lot of hard work, came true. I moved back here last year, and I've been coaching Little League since then. I guess I hope that some day I'll look up in the stands and see that man and his daughter again. Who knows, I might find him on one of the fields pitching to one of his grandkids—a lot of years have come and gone. I sure would like to thank him."

As the tears ran down my face I knew that my dad had just been thanked and even more I knew every time I heard "Batter up!" my dad would be right beside me, no matter where life took me and the family. That simple act of kindness that spring day had changed a life forever, and now twenty years later the memory of that day had changed my life forever. "Batter up, Dad," I said as I left the field, "I know you're still playing the game we love—baseball!"

~Anne Carter
Chicken Soup for the Baseball Fan's Soul

36

The Camping Trip

I was an Air Force brat. I spent my youth at the U.S. Air Force Academy in Colorado Springs, which practically backs up to the base of Pikes Peak. My backyard was a forest. My parents, two brothers and I loved the outdoors because that's all there was—no malls, just trees and Pikes Peak.

Our home was just a few hours from several national parks and camping spots. We loved backpacking and fishing, and we did it the old-fashioned way. No RVs or fancy trailers for us; all we needed was a tent, a sleeping bag and a hole in the ground.

Our family roadster was a 1968 VW Bus. It was kind of a reddish, orange color. (Okay, it was white with a lot of rust.) Dad had specially modified it for our weekend camping adventures. He would take out the middle bench, leaving the back bench for the three kids to sit on. Then he bolted the big wooden toy box against the wall, the long way, opposite the sliding door. A portable refrigerator was secured behind Mom's seat.

Somehow, I always managed to get the not-so-prime seat—the one in the middle with no window, wedged between my two brothers—in front of the portable potty in the back. No, a toilet was not a manufacturer's option on the 1968 VW Van; it was one of Dad's add-ons. Basically, it was a plastic trash can with a ring on the top to sit on and a Hefty bag! We'd pray hard whenever Dad took a sharp corner.

These were the days before mandatory seat belts, so Dad rigged his own version. He suspended a large board over our laps and then bolted it to the sides of the van. It was like a combination child restraint/craft desk.

I clearly remember the excitement of taking off on those trips. Mom would be smiling and humming, and Dad would be singing (or trying to sing), "If I Were a Rich Man." And we didn't care that he wasn't.

It was wonderful knowing we had three whole days in the outdoors before we had to return to, well, okay, the outdoors. I can remember smiling up at my daddy and saying, "Daddy, this is the best day of my life," and how he looked back at me with love.

Before each trip, we would get a special toy to play with. One time we got a "Zip and Flip." It kept us quiet and occupied for moments at a time. If you don't remember, Zip and Flip was a plastic paddle that was smooth on one side and had a ridged maze on the other. You'd rip out the wand to set the top spinning, toss it up in the air, flip your paddle over, catch it on the other side and work it through the maze.

So there we were, driving down the highway. I was sitting there, Zippin' and a Flippin.' I flipped my top, and it zipped out the window! To this day my brothers swear that I rivaled the shower scream in *Psycho*!

My daddy stopped that van so fast that you would have thought someone tied a spring to the last guardrail. He threw the VW in reverse and backed up on the interstate to the place where he heard me do my Janet Leigh impression. Cars whizzed by and Mom complained, but that didn't faze my daddy. He jumped out of the van and tore through the jungle of roadside weeds, searching for my toy. My nose was pressed against the glass, watching him as tears streamed down my face.

Twenty minutes later, covered in mud, sweat and burrs, he broke through the weeds—and in his hand was my little red top. He had that same loving look on his face as he said, "Sweetie, let's keep the windows up next time, okay?"

That simple act of heroism may not seem like a big deal—it certainly wasn't a big deal to the rest of my family, who found it downright irritating—but it was a huge deal to me. In his special way, he had just told me that he loved me and would always protect me. He let me know I was the most special little girl in the whole world.

It really was one of the best days of my life.

~Laura M. Stack
Chicken Soup for the Father & Daughter Soul

The Visit

My dad, Angelo, was in the hospital in Tacoma, Washington. A former Marine and veteran of the Korean War, he was having his third knee-replacement surgery.

A long and very painful operation was going to be made even worse because Dad was going through it alone. There was no one to hold his hand, no familiar soft voices to reassure him. His wife was ill and unable to accompany him or even visit during his weeklong stay. My sisters and brother lived in California, and I lived even farther away, in Indiana. There wasn't even anyone to drive him to the hospital, so he had arrived that morning by cab. The thought of my dad lying there alone was more than I could stand. But what could I do from here?

I picked up the phone and called information for the Puyallup, Washington, Marine Corps recruiting station, where I joined the Marines ten years before. I thought that if I could talk to a Marine and explain the situation, maybe one of them would visit my dad.

I called the number. A man answered the phone and in a very confident voice said, "United States Marines, Sergeant Van-es. May I help you?"

Feeling just as certain, I replied, "Sergeant Van-es, you may find this request a little strange, but this is why I am calling..." I proceeded to tell him who I was and that my father was also a former Marine and one hundred percent disabled from the Korean War. I explained that he was in the hospital, alone, without anyone to visit and asked if Sergeant Van-es would please go and see him.

Without hesitation, he answered, "Absolutely."

Then I asked, "If I send flowers to the recruiting station, would you deliver them to my dad when you go to the hospital?"

"Ma'am, I will be happy to take the flowers to your dad. I'll give you my address. You send them, and I will make sure that he receives them," he replied.

The next morning, I sent the flowers to Sergeant Van-es's office just as we had planned. I went to work, and that evening, I returned home and phoned my dad to inquire about his surprise visitor.

If you have ever talked with a small child after that child has just seen Santa Claus, you will understand the glee I heard in my dad's voice. "I was just waking up when I thought I saw two Marines in their dress blue uniforms standing at the foot of my bed," he told me excitedly. "I thought I had died and gone to heaven. But they were really there!"

I began to laugh, partly at his excitement, but also because he didn't even mention his operation. He felt so honored: Two Marines he had never met took time out to visit an old Marine like him. He told me again and again how sharp they looked and how all the nurses thought he was so important. "But how did you ever get them to do that?" he asked me.

"It was easy. We are all Marines, Dad, past and present; it's the bond."

After hanging up with my dad, I called Sergeant Van-es to thank him for visiting my dad. And to thank him for the extra things he did to make it special: wearing his dress blue uniform, bringing another Marine along—he even took a digital camera with him. He had pictures taken of the two Marines with my dad right beside his bed. That evening, he emailed them to me so I could see for myself that my dad was not alone and that he was going to be okay.

As for the flowers, they hardly mattered, but I was glad for the opportunity to express my feelings. The card read:

Daddy, I didn't want just anyone bringing you flowers... so I sent the World's Finest. Semper Fi.

~Tre' M. Barron
Chicken Soup for the Veteran's Soul

38

Softball People

Participate with your child in sports.
Go to his games and help develop his skills. Showing him that you think what
he's doing is important will build his confidence.
~Lou Patton

First grade was more than just learning to read and write; it brought me other lifelong joys. That year I learned to play softball, and I got to know my father. On game days I went to school wearing a bright green uniform. I loved waiting at the office early in the morning to get an early dismissal for games. I loved walking through the hallways and seeing other teammates in matching attire. I loved carrying my glove with me, nodding matter-of-factly when the cute boys asked, "Are you a lefty?"

Toward the end of the school day, my teacher Ms. Capinagro always said, "Softball people, it's time." With that signal, seven of my classmates shut their books, shoved them into their small wooden desks and grabbed their bags. For the next ten minutes, the lesson was suspended while we noisily put on cleats, stirrups and caps. We left the room slowly, but once we hit the corner, the race was on. When we reached a doorway, we'd stop and walk softly, glancing at the students inside. Then we'd start up again. By the time we reached the main entrance of New City Elementary School, we were all pretty much out of breath. Yet at the sight of the maroon Chevy station wagon at the curb, we resumed our race.

"Okay, two in front, four in the back, and one on the roof," my father said, trying to guide us into his car. We all piled in, rejoicing.

Once again, we had gotten dismissed thirty minutes early! Coach Howie liked having a pre-game practice and we weren't about to argue with that.

At the field, everybody had to help carry equipment: balls, bases, bats, helmets, rope (to measure the distance from the pitcher's mound to home plate), ice packs and water coolers. The first order of business was batting order. Coach Howie used a void, blank check on which he wrote the numbers one through twelve. He ripped up the check, and placed the numbers in a hat. He always did the batting order like that, and somehow I always wound up last. As a six-year-old, it wasn't easy to take.

Once after Coach Howie had read the lineup, I marched up, pouting. "Dad, why am I always last?" I watched the arc of his bushy eyebrows tense up and form wrinkles of mild concern across his forehead. He looked so tall then, even though he wasn't more than five-six.

After a few seconds of silence, he crouched down on his knees with the smile I knew so well and he whispered into my ear, "We can't reveal our secret weapon too early in the lineup, can we?"

I nodded, and the game was underway. Our secret weapon? I would bat last any day to remain the secret weapon.

After the game, it was ice cream for everyone. Coach Howie congratulated each player on her performance while each player blushed and wiped a chocolate mustache from her tiny face. As we headed home, my father always went on about how great I had played. "And the way you fielded that misthrow at first base was incredible. You can't teach that, you know."

It was in this way that I learned to love softball. Our green "Bears" uniforms worn when the parents pitched to the players changed to blue "Angels" apparel once we reached second grade and a member of the team could handle pitching, but Coach Howie was still our leader. First grade through sixth, he didn't miss a single game. Players came and went, but everybody loved to play for Howie. Everybody fielded, and everybody batted. At the end of each season, he organized a parent-versus-child softball game. He would always get up to the plate, with ten bats in his arms, and pretend he forgot that first base and not third is where the runner had to go.

It was at the last one of these particular games, the spring of sixth grade, when I realized that my softball days under Coach Howie would soon be over. The players' parents had gotten together and collected money for a gift.

Nobody said anything, but we all knew that this was the last game that my father would ever coach. He unwrapped the gift, a plaque inscribed with all of our names and a huge, "Angels 1989." He read the top aloud: "To Coach Howie, a Little Guy with a Big Heart, We Thank You." With tears forming in his eyes, he could only say repeatedly, "This is so nice, thanks." Sitting on a checkered blanket, eating a hot dog and munching on some chips, a lump formed in the pit of my stomach. Little League had ended, and with it the days of playing for Coach Howie.

In ninth grade, when most people took the bus, I convinced my father that if he drove me, I could sleep a whole forty-five minutes later and therefore do better in school. When he'd pull up to school, some of his former softball players and some other friends would see my father and wave.

In high school, my interest in friends and boyfriends sometimes took priority over my family. My father always tried to include himself. It was amazing how much gossip he could pick up by reading *The New York Times* on the steps outside my room. My telephone rang nonstop and when I shut my door for privacy, he wouldn't leave me alone until I told him who it was.

"You're so nosy," I said. "Don't you have anything better to do?"

"No," he said. "Anyway, you're going to miss me when you go off to college. I've got to annoy you now as much as I can."

In senior year, major decisions had to be made. Where would I be going to college? The day I was accepted to the University of Pennsylvania, my father brought flowers to my softball game. I had never seen him speechless since the day he had accepted that plaque from our old team's parents. My heart pounded with joy at how proud he was of me. He drove me to meet the softball coach after I learned that they were recruiting me for softball. As we walked around the campus that day, I felt that something very secure and supporting was slipping away and an entirely new world was waiting for me to enter.

After weeks of debate, I chose to go to Emory, a smaller school with a more comfortable environment. My father had a difficult time understanding why I chose a school so far away.

"But Emory doesn't have a softball team," he pleaded one day. Once I had made my decision to go there, he said, "Maybe you can start one."

As a junior in college, I did manage to start a softball club after showing the administration that there was a high interest in fast-pitch softball.

Laws like Title IX, demanding equal numbers of varsity sports between men and women's teams, carved a path for me to push for an Emory team. I found many students who, like myself, craved to play.

With two practices a week and over twenty girls showing up each time, we competed in scrimmages. Then the campus sports office found a softball team from a neighboring college that was looking for an opponent. In the spring, the softball club played in the first-ever women's fast-pitch softball game at Emory. Packing up equipment in the dugout, I realized that out of the fifteen years I had been playing softball, that game was the first one my father had ever missed.

During my senior year at Emory University, I became captain of the first-ever women's Varsity Softball team. With a brand-new field, uniforms and seventeen teammates, it has been an exciting experience. There is nobody happier than my father.

"Just think, Stacey," he said. "You will be part of history."

Although I love softball, what I want more than anything is to have my father back.

"But Dad, it doesn't mean a thing to me if you can't be there," I said. I want to get picked up from school early and go run towards his car. I want to hear him outside my door asking me who is on the phone. I want to look over into the bleachers during a game and see his reassuring smile.

As for life after college, my father has informed me that whatever I do, I must do it closer to home. "Your mother won't be able to handle it if you're not around here," he said. "Maybe you can move back into your old room."

"Don't worry about it, Coach," I said. "I'll still call you all the time from wherever I am."

I hung up the phone and stared at a recent picture of my parents. My father looked older and a bit tired. His bushy eyebrows showed hints of gray and white. What stood out the most was his navy-blue sweatshirt with the letters EMORY across his chest. I put on my socks and metal-spiked cleats and got ready for practice. I have to work hard. After all, I'm not guaranteed even the last spot in the lineup anymore. I've come a long way since first grade, and I owe much of my success to Coach Howie. It's an extra blessing to know that although he's no longer my softball coach, he'll always be my dad.

~Stacey Becker
Chicken Soup for the Father's Soul

39

A Tribute to Gramps

The following letter about our grandfather, Harold Poster, was written by our mother, Patricia Levin. Our grandfather attended Harvard University. For his fiftieth reunion book, a form letter was sent out asking what official titles, achievements, awards, etcetera, people had received and what they had accomplished since leaving Harvard. Our mother was very upset about the way the letter was written, as it implied that unless you had achieved some higher goal, you were a failure.

As my mother's letter will attest, our grandfather was a wonderful man, whose goal was to keep his family happy. He succeeded 110 percent! Our grandpa passed away eight years ago, and not one day goes by that our hearts don't ache from missing him so much.

Dear Class Secretary of 1934,

I am answering this questionnaire on behalf of my father. My father suffered a stroke about four months ago. Although he understands mostly everything, he is not able to write or speak clearly.

You ask in your questionnaire for a list of offices held, honors and awards received, and I am at a loss to think of any official titles my father has held. However, this is not to say that he has led an uneventful or uncharitable life. If awards were to be given for "Wonderful Father," "Exceptional Grandfather" and "Devoted

Friend," then surely he would have won them all. Never in my memory has there not been time for my father to be with his children, never a problem too large that Grandpa couldn't solve it. And when his friends tell me what a fine person he is, what a devoted friend, what an understanding man, I want to tell them, "I know, I know, he's my father; I've always known this." So, although these honors were not gained by a higher education or written on diplomas or awards, they are nonetheless meaningful. They were acquired by living every day to its fullest and bringing happiness to his children, grandchildren and friends.

So, under the titles of honors on your questionnaire, the best honor of all, I suppose, is mine. I am honored to say Harold Poster is my father.

Sincerely,
Patricia Levin

The response to our mother's letter followed a few days later:

Dear Mrs. Levin:

As Secretary of the Class and Editor of the Fiftieth Report, I have the task of reviewing all of the questionnaire returns before they proceed to the printer. I say "task" but generally speaking, it usually is a pleasure. Of all those reviewed, I couldn't help but write you about the one I considered the most warm and satisfying contribution for our Fiftieth Report. I can tell you without reservation that it served to describe a person who has achieved honor and success in his life far exceeding the vast majority who have listed paragraph after paragraph of alleged honors and successes (financial, to be sure!).

My only regret is that I did not know your father in college and in the intervening years. Now I know what a truly fine man he

*is and a lucky person to have produced his replica in you. I do
hope he is well on the road to recovery.*

Many thanks for your wonderful reply!
Sincerely,
John M. Lockwood, Secretary
Class of 1934

~Dana O'Connor and Melissa Levin
A 5th Portion of Chicken Soup for the Soul

Dads & Daughters

Through the Eyes of a Child

Pretty much all the honest truth telling in the world today
is done by children.
~Oliver Wendell Holmes

God's Hands

ollowing her granddaughter's baptism, my friend asked the youngster, "Why don't you draw me a picture of what happened to you in church?"

Judy drew a large pair of hands with a child standing in the middle of them. Grandma was impressed.

"Oh, did they sing 'He's Got the Whole World in His Hands'?"

Judy shook her head seriously. "No, Grandma. That's a picture of what Daddy said to Mommy. 'Now that Judy is baptized, God is sure going to have his hands full!'"

~Shirley Pope Waite
Chicken Soup for the Grandma's Soul

The Little Broom

tanding in drizzling rain just yards from the "pile" at Ground Zero, I reflected on what was lost, and what was being found. The frustration of not finding anyone alive for the past several days had clearly demoralized everyone on-scene. Even the search-and-rescue dogs were becoming depressed, having been trained to find living victims.

I thought about all that had happened since I arrived at this horrible scene six days after the Twin Towers fell on 9/11. As a stress counselor and a chaplain in my local fire department, I had felt compelled to take the earliest flight possible from my home high in the mountains of Colorado to this smoking ruin. Upon arrival, what I found was far worse than I had imagined.

When I first walked up to the wreckage of the World Trade Center, I nearly staggered backward. The magnitude of the destruction was far worse than any televised images. My eyes could scarcely take it all in, let alone get my mind around it. I stood in shock at the base of the nearly five-story pile of grotesquely twisted steel girders, pipes, wires, metal ductwork and unidentifiable debris.

Acrid smoke and steam rose up from the bowels of the wreckage. The pervasive smell of burning metal, insulation, wires and aviation fuel emanating from the pile burned my nose and eyes. There was another clearly discernible smell, infinitely more disturbing. At times, I could detect an odor of burning flesh, and my heart and mind reeled at the thought of the thousands of people trapped in that hellish pyre.

Around me firefighters and policemen were fighting desperately against time to find someone, anyone, alive in the rubble. Some of these people had labored here since the first morning of the collapse, sleeping and eating only when they had to, refusing to leave the side of their buried sons, fathers and brothers.

Clad in my firefighter turnout gear, the rockers of my yellow helmet emblazoned with the word "Chaplain," I prayed that God would help me to somehow comfort them in this dark hour of grief.

Within a few days after the attack, a tent morgue was set up in front of the World Financial Center on Vesey Street. For several days I worked in the exam room, watching distraught firefighters bring in human remains discovered in the wreckage. I never saw a whole body brought in. As the medical examiners and forensic experts sought clues that might help identify these precious people, I was deeply moved by the tender care and profound respect everyone demonstrated. It was difficult and gruesome work, yet it was a labor of love done not only for the deceased, but also for their families and loved ones. A positive identification would bring eventual closure to their heartbreaking loss.

In a scene I witnessed many times, when the deceased was identified as a firefighter or police officer, an American flag would be unfolded and draped over the stretcher. Several of us in the room would spontaneously reach out our latex-gloved hands to help gently tuck the flag in around the edges. It vaguely reminded me of a mother or father gently tucking a beloved child into bed after a long, tiring day.

The doctors would then step back, look toward me and simply say, "Chaplain?" Stepping forward and placing my gloved hand upon the draped flag, I'd pray for the deceased's family and seek God's mercy on this precious, heroic soul. One could hear the mask-muffled sobs of doctors, police officers and firefighters as we prayed. There in that place of shared grief and sorrow, we were all brothers and sisters.

As darkness began to envelop Ground Zero, the clouds of smoke rising from the debris gave an eerie effect to the huge lights erected at the site. I stood watching the SAR dogs, firefighters and police officers searching through the rubble for any trace of the thousands of people yet missing. In the midst of this scene from hell, I heard the faint ringing of my cell phone inside my rain-drenched firefighting jacket.

Answering, I heard a small voice say, "What are you dooo-ing, Daddy?"

It was my five-year-old daughter, Hannah. Born in Nanchang, China, and abandoned by her parents at the tender age of four days old, her only crime was that of being born a girl. Left beside a lonely, dusty road, wrapped in her only earthly possession, a filthy rag of a blanket, she was found by passersby and brought to a government-operated nursery. The first thirteen months of her life were spent there, lying in a tiny crib with only one caretaker for her and the twenty-seven other little girls around her.

Hannah's sweet voice drew me back into a reality that almost seemed a dim memory. She was calling from her "normal" world, where her days were filled with Winnie the Pooh stories and the fascination of watching multi-colored birds visit the feeder on our deck, and I ached to be back in her world again.

How could I answer my little girl's question without alarming or spoiling, even in the slightest, her sweet innocence?

Over the blaring noises of Ground Zero I could hear her breathing into the phone, as small children often do, patiently waiting for my answer. My eyes swept over the smoldering wreckage just feet away, where thousands lay trapped. "Honey, some really mean bad guys made a big mess here in New York City, and I'm just helping to clean it up."

There was a pregnant pause. In her sweet, innocent voice, she replied, "Daddy, can I come with my little broom and help you?"

I plopped down in the mud as her words sank in. The effort to choke back sobs made it impossible to speak. Finally, I composed myself enough to mumble something about how important it was that she stay at home and help her mommy clean the messes there. Slipping the cell phone back in my field jacket, I began to cry. Little Hannah had just expressed exactly how I felt at that moment.

Whatever training and willingness to serve I possessed, all I had managed to bring to this horrendous disaster was a "little broom" to somehow help clean up the millions of tons of twisted wreckage, shattered dreams and broken hearts. It was as if a fissure in the rubble had opened up under me, and the pile was sucking me down into some dark void of helplessness.

The loud metallic clanking of one of the cranes dragging a huge chunk of twisted metal out of the rubble pulled my broken heart out of the wreckage of my own dark broodings. Scrambling to my feet, I wiped the tears with a grimy glove and slowly walked back to the makeshift morgue tent near the World Financial Center. The medical and support teams there were enduring the horrifying task of processing and cataloguing the thousands of body parts we were finding in the rubble. A weeping firefighter chaplain would once again take his "little broom" there for awhile, seeking to comfort and encourage, trying to sweep away a little of the filth of that horrible place from their souls. A "little broom" can do something useful and make a difference if made available. Even a little girl from China was smart enough to know that.

~Bruce Porter
Chicken Soup for the Christian Woman's Soul 2

A Garden So Rich

Life is a flower, of which love is the honey.
~Victor Hugo

I watched out the window as they started turning over the soil. Of course, my husband did most of the work, while our five-year-old son spent most of his energy fingering through the dirt looking for worms. Still, the sight of the two of them "working" side by side, preparing the ground for a spring garden, brought a smile to my face.

For just a moment, I considered joining them. Then I remembered the excitement I'd heard in my son's voice when he announced that Saturday morning, "Me and Daddy are going to plant a garden!"

I sipped my coffee, wondering if joining in on the fun would be interfering in a male-bonding project. Right then I heard my son call out, "Hey, Dad, bet you can't find a worm this fine."

"Oh, yeah? Look at this one," my husband countered.

I could see the two squirming creatures that dangled from their fingers in some sort of "fine" worm contest. For a second, I wondered how one went about qualifying a fine worm. Cringing, I made up my mind. This was definitely their project. I'd leave it to them. Besides, it might be more fun to stand back and simply see what grows out of this garden.

I watched as they poked the seeds into the black topsoil. They planted tomatoes, squash and green beans. I watched as they carefully transplanted the tomato plants into the ground. I listened to the spurts of laughter, the dialogue that passed back and forth.

"When will they grow, Daddy?"

"Soon," my husband replied.

"Tonight?"

"Not that soon."

"Tomorrow?" my son asked.

"In a few days. The seeds have to sprout, then grow."

"Then we'll have vegetables?"

"No, it takes a while."

"One day?" my son questioned.

"Longer," my husband replied.

"Two days?" his anxious young voice queried.

I saw the smile touch my husband's expression, and at that moment I knew I was already seeing the first of many fruits the garden would bring. My son would learn that some things in life aren't instant. My husband would learn how to better deal with a five-year-old's expectations and endless questions. Patience... what a wonderful fruit to grow.

In the evenings that followed, they knelt to the ground and looked for signs of new life. The sight of them, so close and with common goals, warmed my heart and made me happy I'd decided to watch from afar.

More days passed, and each afternoon I watched the two of them water their garden. My son always managed to get as wet as the garden, and, more times than not, even my husband came in drenched. The laughter that followed them in made the muddy tracks and extra laundry tolerable. Well, almost tolerable.

Finally, the plants appeared. From the distance I enjoyed my son's look of glee, as well as the look of wonder on my husband's face as he, too, watched our son. And like the tiny plants breaking through the earth, I saw fruit number two appear. Pride... what a wonderful fruit to grow.

The weeks passed; the garden grew. At the first fruit-bearing blossoms, I watched the two men in my life study and examine each plant. My son would ask questions and my husband did his best to explain.

"Why do they call squash, squash?" the smaller and dirtier gardener questioned.

"I don't know," came my husband's answer.

"I wonder how many worms live in this garden?" my son asked.

"I don't know," my husband replied.

"A million?"

"Probably," my husband said.

"Can we catch them?" Excitement radiated from his voice.

"I don't think so," my husband answered with a chuckle. "But look at this blossom."

"Will it really become a tomato?" came yet another question.

"It will." My husband smiled.

I smiled, too. For just as plants grow, I knew I was watching a relationship take root—watching cherished moments being framed for future memories.

They continued to water, to weed and to care for their small garden. And after all the work and effort, they proudly produced ten tomatoes, several medium-size squash and three pots of beans.

One afternoon, as he placed a few dusty tomatoes on the kitchen table, my husband shook his head ruefully and said, "We probably spent ten hours out there for each of these tomatoes. Was it worth it?"

Our smiles met at the same time. There was no need to answer. Relationships, memories, patience and pride. Who knew a garden could bear so much?

~Christie Craig
Chicken Soup for the Gardener's Soul

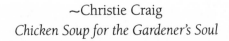

Anna's First Cubs Game

Youth comes but once in a lifetime.
~Henry Wadsworth Longfellow

I can still remember the first Major League Baseball game my father took me to as a child, so I wanted my five-year-old daughter Anna's first game to be just as memorable for her. Two weeks before the game, I purchased a kids' music tape filled with baseball songs. We endlessly learned the song "Take Me Out to the Ball Game" in anticipation of the famous seventh-inning stretch sung by Harry Carry and the Chicago Cubs' fans.

Decked out in her new official hat, shirt and oversized leather glove, we were ready for the game. Anna was enthralled with the field, players, game and happy fans surrounding us. Peanut, hot dog, popcorn and ice cream vendors filled her with treats, keeping her busy until the seventh-inning stretch. Suddenly, I had an idea. Turning to Anna, I asked her loudly, so everyone around us might catch on as well, if she would like everyone in the stadium to stand up and sing the song along with her.

Her eyes widened as she looked around and said, "You mean everyone will sing along with me? That's great, Dad!"

I answered, "No problem," and added that the man in the booth above us would not only join in, but he would help everyone as well.

Beckoning everyone to stand up and join us, Anna stood on her seat and sang as loud as she could. "Take me out to the ballgame..." We all joined her and cheered her on. She was beaming with pride, in love with the thought that the entire stadium was singing along with her.

When the song ended, we all applauded Anna and gave her high-fives. It was a magical moment; she was so happy. As I was about to sit back down, Anna had an even better idea. "Dad, make them do it again!"

People within earshot burst out laughing. Taking her hand, I said, "No problem, Anna. Next time we come, we can do it all again."

~Louis Schutz
Chicken Soup for the Father & Daughter Soul

44

A New Strength

"Whats wrong, Mommy?" One by one, three small figures straggled into my bedroom, navigating through the darkness to my side of the bed. The ringing of the phone and my crying had pulled them from their sleep in the few minutes before sunrise.

"Mommy's very sad right now," their daddy answered for me. "Mommy's sad because your Grandpa Bastien died early this morning."

All three climbed onto the bed and started stroking me, each trying to comfort a pain I thought they were too young to understand. Three sets of innocent eyes stared helplessly up at me, watching unfamiliar waves of grief ebb and flow.

They did not know their grandpa the way I had hoped they would. A gap of seven hundred miles saw to that. Their memories of Grandpa Bastien came from visits at Thanksgiving, long distance phone calls and pictures displayed in photo albums. They did not know the big, strong man I knew and loved so much. And for once, I was glad their little hearts were spared knowing him so they would not feel the depth of losing him.

None of them had ever seen or heard me cry so openly. Through tears I reassured them I would be all right but there was no way to explain the grief. There was no way to tell a four-, six- and eight-year-old how their mommy's life had changed. In an instant I had gone from having a father to having memories. At that moment, thirty-four years of memories and pictures seemed small and insignificant.

It would have been selfish to give words to my tears, explain to them that I would never again hear his voice, send him Father's Day cards or hold his hand. No, I knew it would be wrong to make them understand this grief, so I held back the words and released only the tears. They continued their vigil, sitting quietly, patting me tenderly with little hands.

As the first hint of morning light filtered through the blinds in the bedroom, they began to talk softly amongst themselves. One by one they hugged me and kissed me. One by one they scooted off the bed and left the room.

Off to play or watch cartoons, I presumed, and I was glad grief had not touched their innocence.

I felt helpless, though, watching them walk away. With one phone call, I had crossed this ominous bridge between my father's life and his death, and I didn't know how to return. I didn't know how I would learn to laugh or play or be the mother they needed me to be in the midst of this grief. After lying in bed for what seemed like an eternity, I dried my eyes and decided I'd try to explain my sadness to them in a way they could understand. While still formulating the words, they walked back into the room, each with knowing eyes.

"Here, Mommy," they whispered in unison. "We made this for you."

I took the little package from eager hands and carefully peeled away a layer of leftover Christmas wrapping paper. Inside I found a note written by my eight-year-old: "To Mommy: We love you. Love, Shae, Andrew and Annie."

"Thank you," I told them. "This is beautiful."

"No, Mommy, turn it over," one of them instructed me.

I turned over the note and on the other side discovered a paper frame, decorated with crayon lines and hearts, and inside the frame was a photograph of my dad, smiling his contented smile, hands folded across an ample belly. It was one of the last good pictures I had taken before he died, before sickness had taken the sparkle from his eye.

My well-planned speech fell away, and I knew no explanation

was needed. They understood my tears, and their handmade gift had given me new strength. As I looked at the picture, echoes of childhood memories flooded back, filling the emptiness. Yes, grief had touched my children, but they had their own special way of dealing with it. In their innocence, they taught me that the things I had thought insufficient, the memories and pictures, would be the very things to keep my dad alive.

~Kara L. Dutchover
Chicken Soup for the Grieving Soul

45

Moonshine

The night walked down the sky with the moon in her hand.
~Frederick L. Knowles

Long before life took over and complicated things, I was once a princess and my daddy was definitely the handsomest man in my four-year-old world. I especially liked the way he winked and his sense of fun. Sometimes, however, it got us both into a spot of trouble.

One unusually warm fall afternoon, we were out for a ride, just Daddy and me. In the days before air conditioning, seat belts and car seats, I sat alone in the back enjoying the breeze that swept through the car's open windows. At the same time, I found myself mesmerized by a mysterious glass jug sitting next to me. Fascinated by the reddish glow that sparkled in the sun, my fingers lightly played over the glass container, feeling the heat that seemed to come from inside it.

"Daddy, what's this?" I asked, my curiosity getting the better of me.

"Moonshine." He winked at me in the rearview mirror.

"Moonshine?" I repeated the word trying to comprehend what he meant exactly.

"Just for you," he added with a grin.

Moonshine, I thought to myself as I carefully looked over the amazing jar. It certainly looks like something that came from far away. Suddenly, it all made perfect sense. My daddy had gone up to the sky and caught some shine right from the moon. He put it in this jug and brought it back to Earth for me. I bet no other daddy had ever done that before! I was one lucky little girl.

Totally awestruck, I clutched the gallon jug, amazed by the magical substance inside. It seemed to glow even brighter, glistening in the afternoon sun. Just wait until everyone sees this! My very own moonshine in my very own glass jug!

Wrapped up in my imagination, I absently felt the car come to a stop. Looking up and through the windshield, I could see a red light dangling above us on a thick wire. I let my jug go long enough to climb onto my knees and peer out the open window on the passenger side.

Two policemen sat next to us in their patrol car, also with their windows rolled down. As we all waited for the red light to turn green, I couldn't contain my excitement for another second, so I hollered out to them: "My daddy's got moonshine in the back seat!"

They both turned to look at me, and then they looked at each other. The driver peered at my daddy. "Pull the car over, sir." He wasn't smiling.

"But officer...," my daddy tried.

"Just pull the car over, sir—now."

The two policemen parked directly behind us and asked my daddy and me to get out of the car. They then proceeded to search it, front seat, back seat and trunk. They even opened the hood.

"See, Daddy," I was hopping from one foot to the other, "the policemen want to see the moonshine, too!"

My daddy didn't say a word. He just closed his eyes and shook his head as we stood there waiting.

Finally, one of the officers held up my glass jug. "Sir, what's in here?"

"Just what the label says," Daddy sighed. "It's apple cider. Open it and have a taste if you want."

"But your daughter said..."

"I know. I told her it was moonshine," my dad admitted sheepishly. "She has no idea what that is."

Their serious faces suddenly turned into smiles and then peals of laughter followed. "Here you go, little lady." One of the officers held the door for me and helped me climb back into the car.

His partner handed over the glass bottle with a grin. "Take good care of your moonshine, Honey."

As we all drove away, I tightly held on to my bottle of moonshine. After all, it wasn't every princess whose daddy took a trip to the moon.

~Debra Ann Pawlak
Chicken Soup for the Father & Daughter Soul

46

You Can Share My Daddy

One can pay back the loan of gold,
but one dies forever in debt to those who are kind.
~Malayan Proverb

As I sat in the garden weeding, my four-year-old neighbor came over to the fence and settled down to supervise my activities. Since her mother had just had a baby the previous week, she was allowed more freedom to entertain herself and explore her world. She asked endless questions about what this was and why that was, and she finally asked about a metal object that had been fastened on the fence. I told her that I didn't know exactly what it was, but I thought it was something that my father had put there for some reason or another.

She looked around the yard carefully and said, "Where is your daddy? Is he at work?"

I explained to her that he had died several years ago, and that was how I came to live in the house.

She thought about this for a minute and then asked, "Well, then did you get a new daddy?"

I was not sure how to answer her, so I just went with the simple truth and said, "No, I didn't."

She thought about that for a moment, as if the prospect of not having a daddy was just too complex to embrace, and then she suddenly offered a solution that made sense to her. "You can share my daddy, if you want to. He is a very good daddy, and I don't think he would mind."

~Linda L. Kerby
Chicken Soup for the Father's Soul

On the Nose

Any man can be a father. It takes someone special to be a dad.
~Author Unknown

I will never forget the day I arrived home from kindergarten to find my dad opening the door for me. At first, I was elated. "Dad! You're home!" As a doctor in training, he was hardly ever home. Often, he had to spend nights at the hospital working thirty-six-hour shifts.

Dad did not waste any time with pleasantries. "Your mother has had an accident."

I dropped my school bag. Horrible visions swam across my eyes. Then my stomach lurched. I was sure I would throw up. Fighting back tears and swallowing hard, I hugged my dad. "What happened?" My need to know outweighed my fear of the answer.

"She was reaching for something in the closet, and her train case fell on her."

My mom had this small, hard suitcase that she always put her makeup in when she traveled. She never went anywhere by train, yet she called it her "train case."

"It broke her nose. I had to rush home to fix it."

"Oh." Good thing he was a doctor. "Where is she?"

Dad hugged me tight. "She's upstairs sleeping. Let her rest."

Was he kidding? For several seconds that felt like an eternity, I had thought that something horrible, something deadly, had happened to my mother. I had to see her.

I tried to get out of his grasp. "Please. I have to see she's okay."

Finally, Dad relented. "Just look. Don't wake her."

We tiptoed up the stairs. Dad opened the door so slowly I thought I'd die of anticipation. There she was, on her back under the covers, her nose and eyes covered with white bandages. Her always-perfect red hair stuck out in every direction. I watched her chest to be sure it was moving. It was.

Dad led me downstairs. "Well, it's just you and me, kiddo. Doesn't Mom give you a snack when you come home from school?"

"Yeah," I mumbled apprehensively, entering the kitchen. The table was set with two placemats complete with silverware, napkins and glasses.

"I've been getting it ready." Dad poured me a glass of milk. "There, nice and cold right out of the fridge like you like it." Then he added a large ice cube. I smiled, forgetting my mother's trauma for the moment. I didn't think Dad noticed these things. He actually knew I put ice in my milk—just one ice cube.

As the fear about my mother subsided, and the awe of my dad increased, my body returned to normal. My senses began working again. I inhaled deeply. "Mmmm." Something smelled good. Dad put on oven mitts and opened the oven door. "I hope you like it. Haven't made it since my college days. Don't know how to make anything chocolate."

He did it again. He knew that chocolate was one of my favorite things, especially with milk.

"Baked apples," Dad announced. He put one apple on each of the two plates that sat waiting and then brought them to the table. Dad sliced mine open for me and steam rose out, filling the air with the scent of apples, cinnamon and raisins. And nuts. I hesitated. Dad always told us about apples, raisins and walnuts. I did not like walnuts, only pecans.

"Careful, it's hot," he warned. "And don't worry. I used pecans."

"Pecans? Great."

"Well, let's see if this worked."

Dad scooted his chair close to mine as he moved toward the table. I leaned against him, and he managed to cut the apple with his arm wrapped around me. The warm snack heated my insides, and Dad's love filled me from the outside.

Sure Dad worked really hard and had to be away a lot. But he paid attention more than I knew. He cared. I was sorry that it took Mom breaking her nose for us to share this moment. So, even at age five, I was determined to pay more attention to the things he liked and steal more moments like these without waiting for something bad to happen.

~D. B. Zane
Chicken Soup for the Father & Daughter Soul

48

The Best Game I Never Saw

I t was supposed to be a perfect day. I had tickets to a Cincinnati Reds game in one hand and the hand of my five-year-old daughter, Molly, in the other. She had an excited little skip in her step as we walked up to the escalator that would take us to the stadium gates. What a treat this was going be!

As we walked, I envisioned all the neat father-daughter things we could share. Why, I could teach her the finer points of baseball. We could do the "wave" together. There would be fireworks because the Reds were bound to hit a few home runs and, of course, win the game.

I could tell her all about the famed "Big Red Machine" and how I had rooted for them when I was growing up. We would eat hot dogs and popcorn and sing "Take Me Out to the Ball Game" as we did the seventh-inning stretch. We would give each other high fives until our hands hurt as the Reds made big play after big play.

There was just one problem hovering over our heads. Rain clouds.

Oh, man, I thought. Not today. Please don't let it rain today, God. This is such a special occasion. All my life I've loved Cincinnati baseball. Never in my life did I imagine I'd have the opportunity to be a father and bring my little girl to a baseball game. It can't rain today. It just can't.

But it did. In fact, it poured. By the time we found our seats, the game had already started—and been stopped because of rain. The first thing my daughter saw in grand old Riverfront Stadium—the place where I had rooted for World Series champions and seen many dramatic victories—was the ground crew rolling a big tarp out on the field.

I was extremely disappointed. We had driven two hours to see this? It wasn't fair. Maybe, if we were lucky, the rain would stop at least long enough to see a couple of innings. Then I thought of Molly and how disappointed she must be.

But when I looked at her, I was surprised to see her smiling. Those trademark dimples of hers were in full bloom when she nudged me and pointed to the ground crew.

"Look at that, Daddy!" she said to the men working side-by-side pushing what looked like a big roll of carpet on the field. "Cool!"

I knew Pete Rose was "Charlie Hustle." I knew Joe Morgan could steal bases like no other and that Johnny Bench was the greatest catcher who had ever lived. But until Molly pointed it out to me, I honestly didn't know just how "cool" the ground crew was.

We watched together in amazement and amusement as they worked to roll that big tarp out on the field. I'd really never paid much attention to what an operation that was before Molly had pointed it out to me.

As the rain continued to fall, the jumbo TV screen in center field began to show highlights of all the great Reds teams in past years. Good, I thought. I could at least point out to her who some of my favorite players were. But just as I started to focus on the highlights, Molly nudged me again and said, "I'm hungry, Dad." I reluctantly got up and led her to the concession stand, frustrated all over again. I guess I wasn't supposed to see any baseball—live or taped—on this day.

The rain may have stopped the game, but it didn't stop the exuberance of little Molly. She had that explorer's look in her eye. As most of the fans headed for home, Molly and I headed for a most memorable adventure—the ramps surrounding the stadium.

After devouring a hot dog and some popcorn, Molly and I decided to walk around the stadium. We came to the first of many ramps that wind their way up, down and around that big sardine can of a ballpark. Then Molly's dimples popped out once again.

"Let's run, Daddy," she said.

My first instinct of caution gave way to the "oh, what the heck" spirit. So we ran down one ramp, Molly screaming in glee all the way.

Her spirit was contagious. As we reached the top of another one, no one else around, I decided to scream with her.

Inside the ballpark, those highlights I'd wanted to see were still rolling on the big screen. I could hear the voice of former play-by-play man Al Michaels screaming, "The Reds win the pennant! The Reds win the pennant!"

As Molly and I headed down another ramp, she screamed and I started yelling, "The Reds win the pennant! The Reds win the pennant!"

Up and down we went, ramp after ramp after ramp. Hand-in-hand we went. The rain fell. The crowd had left. The umpires and players were waiting for the official word that the game had been called. And underneath the stadium, Molly and I were having such fun.

It was a lousy day—weather-wise. There were no fireworks. The clouds covered the sky just like the tarp covered the field. But there was a great lesson in the silver linings of those clouds.

Fatherhood is grand, no matter what the weather. If you pay attention and are receptive to your children, it's an event that never gets postponed. Just when things are bad, there is a ramp right around the corner leading to a shining moment. World Series heroes are nothing compared to the magic found within your own children. All you have to do is just look.

I'll never forget that day with Molly. The day we went to my favorite ballpark and never sat in our seats. The day we went to see the Reds and watched the ground crew instead. The day when I didn't see a single inning of baseball but came away from the stadium more exhilarated than ever. Not because the Reds won, but because I was a dad.

It was the best game I never saw.

~Darrel Radford
Chicken Soup for the Baseball Fan's Soul

49

Just a Walk in the Park

The great man is he who does not lose his childlike heart.
~Mencius

She was the wisest person I'd ever met. With messy hair and tattered clothes, she never cared one bit about success or wealth. It seemed that her only job was to laugh all day, which kept her healthy. She listened well and, in her own innocent way, sought out the truth in everything. Her mind was a sponge in search of right. Her heart was pure, and she had no qualms about sharing it. In her eyes there was peace, while her mouth spouted the kindest words I'd ever heard. She was polite and good, trying desperately to choose right over wrong. In her smile there was forgiveness and healing, and she was an open book when it came to her feelings. The word "shame" was never affiliated with her true emotions. She worried so much less than most, and her sleep was sound. I often wondered if she'd found the secret to true joy. Her only possessions in the world were hope and love, and for that she thanked the Lord daily. I felt blessed she was my daughter; Aubrey was four years old, and I couldn't have loved her any more.

I remember that day when the trees were still bare, and we had to wear bulky winter jackets. As soon as we rounded the corner and saw the park, somehow, at that very moment, spring arrived. With shoes unlaced, only our noses could run faster than our feet. My best friend, Aubrey, beat me to the bottom of the hill. She was small, but she was quick.

First, we tackled the slides, but that was only a warm-up. From there, it was on to the real games. Like two wild gorillas we hit the jungle gym hard. Before long, our coats were unbuttoned, and the brisk air seemed hot. While playing hide-and-go-seek, either my big butt or her giggles gave us both away, so we decided on tag. That was the most fun. We laughed, really laughed, and meant every second of it. There were no adults there to tell us what we couldn't do. We were king and queen, and, knowing this, we quickly claimed our territory.

We built a fort under the jungle gym. Resting on a floor of dirt and wood chips, Aubrey made me a birthday cake out of mud. She sang out of tune as I blew out the candles. Then, to my surprise, she found it—a treasure, the most valuable thing on Earth—a bottle cap. Quietly digging a hole, we buried our treasure where nobody would ever find it. I marked the spot with a stick, and we promised each other that we would tell no one. It was our secret; something we could rediscover on our next visit to the park.

Covered in sweat and dirt, we shared a swing for the last time that day. Aubrey talked about her life, and I listened because that's what real dads do. Racing to the top of the hill I beat her home but, looking back one last time, I realized something: I had just enjoyed one of the best days of my entire life. There had been nothing but laughter, yet somewhere through it all, something very serious happened: I'd been reminded that I was still alive, alive to run and play and laugh. The simple experience was so profound, I was inspired to run home and pen several poems.

The truth is, although she was only four years old back then and twenty-five years younger than me, Aubrey taught me that I still had much to learn. In those days, I honestly think she knew more than me. And whenever I recall days like these, I'm sure of it.

Aubrey is an adolescent now, and I move a little slower, think more before speaking and take a little longer to do the same things I could when she was four.

Last week, she was asked to babysit our neighbor's five-year-old son, Ricky. When I heard she was planning to take him to the park, I asked if I could tag along and watch. Somewhere along life's way,

I'd become so busy with imaginary deadlines that I'd forgotten the blessings of innocent fun. It had been years since I'd gone to the park. Aubrey was thrilled to have me along.

Upon arrival, while Aubrey and Ricky headed for the swings, I said hello to the other adults on supervision patrol. Most offered a grin, a nod or heavy sigh, and then quickly returned to the army of small children on the jungle gym. I took a seat and tried to get comfortable on the hard, green bench, opting to do some people watching. In truth, I've made few choices in my life that turned out better. You see, as I sat on that bench and watched my daughter play with our neighbor's little boy, I realized something priceless: Through the years, all the times I thought my little girl wasn't looking, she had been. My examples had clearly paid off. Aubrey was a genuinely good person, the only perfect measurement of success for a father. I quietly wept tears of pure joy.

In time, Ricky approached. With his muddy face, he asked, "Will you play with me, too?"

"Geez, I don't know, Ricky. I'm getting a little old to be running around this park."

Little Ricky wouldn't hear it. As my daughter watched in amusement, he begged for me to play with him. I shook my head in disbelief. With all the kids running around, he actually wanted me to play with him. For the sake of not disappointing anyone, slowly, I stood and grabbed Ricky's hand.

As we stepped through the park, I peered down at him and saw the past return in one wonderful jolt. He was Aubrey, ten years earlier. His nose was running like a broken faucet, his shirt was untucked, and in his dirty face, there wasn't a worry in the world. Adopting his carelessness and surrendering to his imagination, I decided to forget myself and everything I knew as an adult. I still remembered the joy I'd shared with my daughter on a day no different from this. Now I'd been blessed with a second opportunity to view what was important, to be reminded of who I really was and what honestly meant anything in life.

The entire day was magical. Ricky told stories that made no sense.

The three of us ate fast-melting ice cream and danced under the sun. For Ricky and my entertainment, Aubrey described each person who passed with great fictitious detail. One was a real princess. Another was an astronaut.

We lay in the grass, rolled down a hill and looked up to watch big, puffy clouds float by. We took turns pointing out the obvious pictures painted above. Ricky then diverted our attention to a colony of ants that worked hard, marching in a straight row, each carrying his fair share. We played so many games that I had forgotten.

As the day wound down, Aubrey led us under the fort. With her bare hands she dug in the very area that had been our special hiding spot. My eyes filled from nostalgia and love that gushed for my daughter. Minutes later she held up the treasure. It was our secret bottle cap.

Little Ricky went wild. "It's a real treasure!" he squealed. "Let's bury it for some other lucky kids to find thousands of years from now. What a treasure!"

As he and Aubrey picked another spot to bury it, I decided then that everything worth knowing is learned young and understood by children. Lessons like playing fair, the reasons not to fight and sharing, for example, were really all anyone ever needed to know. In fact, anything more than that complicated and confused things.

I was so blessed for the sweet reminder, something everyone could use from time to time. I swear I'll never pass on the opportunity to take a walk through the park ever again. There are so many treasures that wait to be uncovered and rediscovered.

~Steven H. Manchester
Chicken Soup for the Father & Daughter Soul

Dads & Daughters

Learning from Each Other

A person's a person no matter how small.
~Theodor Geisel (Dr. Seuss)

What Do You Have to Say for Yourself?

Memory is more indelible than ink.
~Anita Loos

My dad died recently. I expected it; after all, he was eighty-six years old. He had emphysema and his heart was failing. His hands, ravaged by arthritis, could no longer grasp his coffee cup. I had not lived near him for over twenty-five years—I had my own life, four grown children, a busy career, a happy marriage, a house full of dogs.

I often heard friends talk about losing their parents. They talked about the pain of it, the loneliness, feelings of being lost without them. I thought that wouldn't be me. I knew I would miss him, and I would surely be sorry he was gone. But lost without him? After all, what did he really provide me these days in the way of guidance or support? I had been self-sufficient for a long time. Oh, I talked to him every week, but those calls were for his reassurance, to let him know we were fine. He hardly understood the world my brother and I live in. He couldn't understand our jobs, why we flew all over the world. It wasn't that he didn't know anything about the world. Even at his age, his eyes were good and his mind was sound. He read three papers a day. He knew the political landscape better than most anyone I knew. But his children's lives always seemed beyond his comprehension.

He would begin every Saturday's call with, "Well, what do you have to say for yourself?" And every Saturday, I would have to recount what I had done, what the kids had done, where I had traveled. I also had to be up on the latest in Washington politics, know whether the Green Bay Packers had won, and preferably, who they had recently traded. It would be helpful if I was up on all recent news events, and it would really be best if I had a strong opinion about something.

I'll admit it now, sometimes I found these calls exasperating. But I realize now that this question has been a part of my life since I could speak. I remember walking home from school, knowing my dad would be there, the question on his lips. And I would sometimes dawdle a little on the way, trying to think of an answer. Had I done something clever? Had I read something interesting?

Maybe the question was just a way to open a conversation. Maybe he just wanted to know how my day had gone. But now I realize it took on much greater meaning to me.

I felt that, every day, my dad was asking me to account for myself. What was I doing? And why was I doing it? Knowing this question was coming made me think more about what I did, what I wanted, what I cared about. Even his questions about our jobs now seem not a lack of understanding on his part, but rather an implicit question about whether this was really how we wanted to spend our time.

As I got older, there were times when my dad asked, "Well, what do you have to say for yourself?" and I would respond, "Nothing."

His eyebrows would shoot up and he would look at me over his reading glasses. Then he would say, "Nothing?"

And I would swallow hard, nod my head, and repeat, "Nothing."

He would look me up and down then respond with an exaggerated, "Mmmm... " Then he would shrug his shoulder in that big John Wayne-way of his and change the subject. But as he moved on to ask me about Jim's latest fishing trip or Jen's job or Brooke's college or Dan's girlfriend or Zach's latest book, I knew I had disappointed him. And that was hard to take.

Now there are no more phone calls. I am feeling a little lost. And

I am finding myself wanting to answer the question "What do you have to say for yourself?"

Today no one asks me to account for myself. Certainly not my husband, not my children. At the age of fifty, I can do what I want. There's no one there on Saturday to check on what I am up to, no one to wait for the answer on whether my latest book is done or why I haven't done that Habitat for Humanity work I said I would do. Not that Dad ever asked those things outright, either. But wrapped inside the "Big Question" were many implicit little ones.

Now, without my father acting as my compass in the world, I am faced with a greater test. I must go on, remembering that, though no one is asking, I must still account for myself and my actions. Will I become a slug without his weekly question? I hardly think so. But will an occasional Saturday go by when I feel I have been let off the hook, just a little? Probably.

So today, in honor of my dad, I would like to take another opportunity to account for myself.

What do I have to say for myself?

I say that I love deeply and am loved.

I know how to think clearly and act on what I believe.

I know how to set my priorities.

And when I see my children, I now always ask them, "Well, what do you have to say for yourself?"

Thanks, Dad.

~Kate Rowinski
Chicken Soup to Inspire a Woman's Soul

Refresher Lesson from Dad

If there is anything that we wish to change in the child,
we should first examine it and see whether it is not something that could
better be changed in ourselves.
~C.G. Jung, Integration of the Personality, 1939

It was a typical school morning. Ashley, our ten-year-old, finished homework during breakfast. Tiffany, who is nine, was told three times to finish up in the shower. The school menu sounded terrible, so lunches were packed. Finally, with only minutes to spare, we jumped into the car and were on our way.

One mile from school, Tiffany informed me from the backseat, "Mom, I must have left my book bag at Grandma and Grandpa's. It's not back here."

During planting season, when my husband Alan and I were busy in the fields, the girls went to my parents' house after school. I knew Alan was waiting for me then to work the ground ahead of the planter. So I launched into a lecture on responsibility. Even though Mom and Dad's house was only three blocks from the girls' school, I didn't want to waste time on an extra stop.

As I turned into their driveway, my plans changed.

There was Dad, leaning all of his weight on the handle of a jack, trying to lift his boat of a car off a flat rear tire. Sweat beaded his forehead, muscles knotted in his neck.

Dad suffered from hardening of the arteries and high blood pressure. Medication kept it in check, but after a slight stroke, his activities were limited. Changing a tire was not on the "okay to do" list.

"Dad, why didn't you call us or a garage? You shouldn't be doing this." Boy, I was in the lecture mode that morning. He smiled like a little boy caught doing something he knew he shouldn't.

"I knew you were busy," he explained.

Hurrying, I grabbed the tire iron and began loosening the lug nuts. Just like Dad taught me, I thought. That had been the rule—if I was driving, I had to be able to do simple repairs and maintenance: check the oil and battery, and change a flat.

As I removed Dad's damaged tire, memories of my first lesson flooded my mind. The warm autumn sun glistened off Dad's farmer-tanned arms, and muscles rippled under his blue denim work shirt as he single-handedly jacked up the rear of my car. Then his heavy work boots stomped down on the tire iron. I, a skinny sixteen-year-old girl, struggled to lift the tire, until I felt Dad's sturdy grasp along with mine. He smiled as he wiped his callused hands on the ever-present red bandanna. He reminded me, "Take your time, Sis. Anything worth doing is worth doing right and more likely to turn out that way if you take your time."

But now, Dad stood back, a little hunched over, smiling apologetically. Where had the time gone? When did we change places?

Tire changed, I loaded the kids back into the car—with the book bag. Dad repeated, "Thank you, Sis."

"Thank you, Dad," I choked back tears. "I was just remembering when you taught me how to take care of my car."

"Me, too," he said, his smile broadening.

We were late for school. Even a little later, because I took the time to apologize to Tiffany for being so impatient.

"You always say everything happens for a reason, Mom," Tiffany chided. "Maybe God knew that Grandpa needed you this morning."

Maybe so, Tiffany. And maybe He knew I needed a refresher lesson from my dad.

~Pamela Bumpus
Chicken Soup for the Christian Woman's Soul

Honest Mike

Honesty pays, but it don't seem to pay enough to suit some people.
~Frank McKinney "Kin" Hubbard

Everyone said my tall, thin dad looked like Abraham Lincoln. So when he started growing a beard and began looking for a tall top hat, everyone was sure he would win the prize for the best costume in our town's centennial celebration. But Daddy's resemblance to "Honest Abe" went much further than that.

As a teenager, Daddy had suffered from scarlet fever and rheumatic fever, leaving him with faulty heart valves and frail health. He had to drop out of high school because he couldn't climb the steep steps to his classes.

However, he was able to convince his doctor to let him do "light work," and he got a job as a timekeeper at a local factory.

As Daddy grew older, he found that the minimum wage he earned was not enough to support a family, but his heart condition and lack of education kept him from getting a better job. To stretch his income, he planted and tended a huge vegetable garden. Mom, my sister and I would help plant and harvest. We canned corn on the cob, shelled peas, picked raspberries and rooted in the soft soil for potatoes. Most of what we produced went into the cellar to feed us through the winter, and we sold the rest.

During the year of the centennial celebration, though, we weren't able to harvest our crop. A railroad track ran behind our property. A tanker car carrying a poisonous liquid sprang a leak and sprayed its contents on the vegetation all along that stretch of track. The railroad company issued a warning not to eat any of the produce from our gardens. They sent a notice to homeowners asking them to list the types and quantities of plants they had lost, so they could be reimbursed.

The day after we received our notice, we heard a knock on the door. Several neighbor men appeared, asking to talk to Daddy. They were afraid that the reimbursements would be far less than their actual losses, so they had decided to turn in claims three times bigger than they really were. These neighbors were aware of our financial situation and our dependence upon our garden. They had come to share their decision with Daddy, so he would not be left out.

That night, Mom and Daddy discussed the neighbors' suggestion. But even though Daddy did not know how we would survive without the garden, he was not able to lie to the railroad. On the insurance form, he honestly and accurately reported the plants he had lost. That decision left a huge burden hanging over my parents, yet Daddy had faith that honesty was always the best way.

And it was. I remember the excitement at our house the day the mailman delivered the check from the railroad company. Not only had we been paid for the cost of the seeds and plants we had purchased, but we were also paid for all the food we could possibly have harvested, plus a lot more.

As the town's centennial celebration drew closer, my dad began to look more and more like "Honest Abe." The neighbors who knew how he had refused to lie for his own gain began calling him "Honest Mike." But Daddy didn't live long enough to win that centennial costume prize. His injured heart gave out just a few weeks before the celebration. My sister and I, just eight and nine, cried as we buried Daddy with the candy bar and shaving cream we had planned to give him as birthday gifts.

But we did not bury his beliefs. To this day, whenever I am tempted to change the truth—even just a bit—I remember Daddy's garden and the seeds of honesty he planted there.

~Marilyn Diephuis Sweeney
Chicken Soup for the Gardener's Soul

Ghost Mother

If you don't like something change it;
if you can't change it, change the way you think about it.
~Mary Engelbreit

Six months before my thirteenth birthday, my parents gave my brother and me "the talk." The one about their loving us, but not each other and how much happier everyone would be if they separated. Yet, my parents rewrote the ending: "We think it would be best if you lived with your father." My mother was the one who said this, running her red nails through my hair. That moment has stayed in the center of my stomach since then, like a jagged stone rolling around.

Mothers are supposed to be that one person who represents home, who somehow makes everything okay when your world is shaking. A mother should be there for you no matter how many times you change your Halloween costume, how messy your room gets or what happens to her marriage. But mine saw motherhood as an optional endeavor, something she could easily discard like a sweater that no longer fit.

She quickly settled into her own life and her new apartment. Having married at twenty-one, this was the first time she was on her own. Her decorating business was growing, and she was more interested in catering to her clients than to two kids and a husband of fifteen years.

A few weeks after she moved out, she called on a Friday night. "Tomorrow, let's have lunch and then go shopping. Okay?" she asked.

I was so excited that I could hardly answer. That night I dreamed of riding beside my mom in the car. Saturday, I woke early, put on my favorite overalls and finished my homework in case she wanted to spend Sunday together, too. My friend Jennifer called. "Aren't you coming to the movies?" she asked. "Everyone's going."

"My mom and I have stuff to do. Shopping or something," I said, forcing my tone to be matter-of-fact. But morning turned into afternoon, and she didn't call. I spent the day by the phone pretending to read, playing solitaire and braiding my hair. I wouldn't eat anything because I thought at any minute she'd be there and want to take me out for lunch. And I didn't want my mom to have to eat alone. But she didn't call until after six o'clock. "Sorry, honey, I was working all day and not near a phone," she said quickly. "And now I'm so tired, I just need to take a nap. You understand, don't you?" No Mom, I didn't understand.

This same scenario happened many weekends for several years after she left. The rare times I did see her, she'd rent me four-hour movies like *Tess* and leave me alone to watch them. Or I'd go on her errands or to her office, never really with her, more like a balloon trailing after her. I'd sit alone at a desk in her office eating Chinese food from a paper carton while she worked or talked on the phone. But I never complained or stopped going. How could I when this was all I had of her?

Almost a year after she moved out, the clothes she didn't want remained in her walk-in closet. My father said he was too busy to pack them, but I think that—just as I did—he hoped it meant she wasn't gone for good. I used to sit in that closet, breathing in the lingering smell of her Ralph Lauren perfume. I'd wrap myself in her ivory cashmere cardigan and run my fingers along the beaded surface of a pink bag, remembering when she'd carried it with a chiffon dress. She had looked just like a princess. I'd rock the bag gently, feeling sorry for it that she had left it behind, too.

Living with my father and brother in their masculine world of boxer shorts and hockey games wasn't easy. Just when I should have been stepping out of my tomboy stage of wearing my brother's worn

Levi's and button-downs and starting to become a young woman, I was screaming at the basketball players on TV and munching on Doritos. Each of my friends watched her mother apply eyeliner and blush and practiced with her makeup while she was out. The only makeup I knew about was the black smudges under football players' eyes.

Growing up without my mother, I always had to carry myself to each new stage of life or get left behind. I wore the same clothes that my friends did, bought my first bra by myself and started shaving my legs when they did. But to me I was just following clumsily behind them, self-conscious that my motherlessness was showing. When I got my period, I huddled in my pink bathroom, feeling like a little girl at this sign of being a woman. Having to say, "I got my period, Dad," was mortifying. But the truth was, I felt more comfortable telling him than my mother. When she called the following week, she said, "Dad told me what happened, but he took care of it." This was a statement, not a question.

My mother became like a distant relative whom I saw several times a year, who sent a birthday card if she remembered and to whom I was stiffly polite and didn't curse in front of. The word "mom" was foreign to me. She never asked about my friends or school or seemed to notice that I was struggling to grow up without her. Each time I said goodbye, I knew it would be months before I saw her again.

Why didn't my mother want me? I wondered. Teachers and friends' parents always wore a look of pity when my father picked me up from parties, came alone to plays and parent-conference day and talked to them to arrange car pools. Hating their pity, I'd mix the few minutes my mother did give me with my imagination. Then I'd casually talk about her at lunch or at friends' houses so they wouldn't see that all I had was a ghost mother who touched my life only in memories.

Although it was tough at first, my father tried to do everything he could to fill the gaps my mother left. He put my brother and me first, at times sacrificing his own happiness for ours. Despite losing his wife and marriage, my father wore a smile on his face. After all, he was the person we looked toward to tell us everything was going to be okay, so we couldn't see him sad. He had no spouse to pick up where he left off or to help him with daily issues and unexpected situations. He took us to the doctor, listened to our problems and helped us with homework. He was there with treats when my friends slept over and told the kind of dumb fatherly jokes that made us laugh and roll our eyes. He was always at all my school plays and softball games. He never missed a gymnastics meet or recital. Most fathers never took off work to come to even one of these things; my father was at all of them.

Most of all, he was always conscious of my disappointments and tried to make a bad situation better. After a while, all the people who pitied me noticed my father's intense interest in my well-being and realized, as I did, that though my life was different, there was nothing wrong with it or me. In time, I adjusted to this. And though I never stopped wishing my mother were a more central part of my life, I saw the fact that she wasn't; she was just a part of who I am.

In recent years, I have become closer with her. I accept her for who she is, regardless of the fact that she wasn't always the mother I wanted her to be. As I have gotten older, I can look at what she did from a different perspective. And I think I've reached this point because my father taught me to be understanding of and sensitive to others. I've realized it's okay not to have a storybook home with a mom, dad, two kids and a dog. Who said that is the definition of family? My home may have been unique, but it had in it the same love and loyalty as other families.

~Michele Bender
Chicken Soup for the Teenage Soul III

54

A Practice Round for Life

The ball soared forward, arching away from its perch on the ladies tee without a trace of slice or hook, and landed with a solid "whump." I was too far away to see it a foot or so from the cup on the eighteenth green. Grinning from ear to ear, my father said, "You'll be back next week."

When you're a kid, it seems like your parents utter the same mantras over and over, day after day—"wash your hands, eat your peas." For my father, playing golf with me was his venue for spouting forth a barrage of maxims gleaned from a lifetime of living. Often, by the time we'd reached the eighteenth hole, I'd heard, "Never up, never in" at least four times. I was never sure if this phrase related wholly to golf, or had some deeper meaning in the overall scheme of existence. Still, I was only thirty-four and had a lot of learning yet to do.

"No way, Dad," I told him. "I hate this game."

He'd heard that one a few times, too. He ignored it, even though he knew, perhaps, it was the truth.

It was, almost. As a busy, career-minded, up-and-coming investment trader who hustled and clawed her way to the top of a demanding, frenetic field, I thought golf was a pointless, boring way to spend an afternoon. It just happened to be my father's favorite pastime since he'd grown a little too old to play tennis the way he was used to as a teaching pro. So now he loved playing golf with his coterie of cronies, but he loved playing golf with me, just the two of us, probably more than anything else in the world.

I was, of course, a very busy person, but I loved my dad and squeezed a round with him into my schedule whenever possible.

I drove the cart past the palms and pines lining the fairway. It was a glorious Florida afternoon with a slight breeze off the ocean and the songs of birds in stereo. My father could not have been happier. His grin would just not go away. I think this was years before the phrase "quality time" was coined, but that's what we were spending together. Since the time I was born, my dad sequestered every spare minute to spend time with me in active pursuits — tennis, of course, but also surfing, basketball, skating, building sand castles, gardening and just hanging together. Even when we puttered around, not a minute had been wasted, because the memories that remained were like splashes of molten gold. At the very least, I owed him this.

When we approached my ball, he patted me on the back, acknowledging, "You're really good at this game."

"Yeah. What about the last seventeen holes?" I had played dismally, but a father's love for a daughter is beyond reason or logic. He always, without fail, looked for the good in people and in life, and every round of golf was a good one.

"Don't worry about the past," he'd say. "It's the hole that lies ahead that matters." Another gem of unmitigated common sense I ignored, but which had somehow stubbornly insinuated its way by osmotic repetition into the web of my life.

Even though my ball was only inches from the cup, I missed the putt. I was thinking about the beer I would be having in the clubhouse instead of focusing on the moment. I slammed the head of my putter into the green, fully aware displays of impatient annoyance irked him, the quintessential sportsman who never showed his emotions during play.

He ignored my outburst as though it never happened. His shot from the edge of the green rolled smoothly into the hole, landing with that satisfying plunk of a golf ball coming home. We tallied our scores, and he had beaten me by a mere fifteen strokes.

I had never once bested my father in anything, much less golf.

He had innate athletic ability and his concentration and ability to focus were unmatched. Part of it was about being a female, about never being quite as good. When the frustration got to me at times, he would say patiently, "Don't ever let being a woman be an excuse." When he saw that one didn't work, he would fall back on the old standby, "Things will be better tomorrow." I loved that one. Never mind that he was right.

When my dad was diagnosed with cancer and the doctors said with grim finality that he would not recover, I took a leave of absence from my job. This was many years before the Family Medical Leave Act made this an acceptable and legal avenue. I didn't know how long he had to live and didn't care that I might lose my job and all the effort it had taken to get it. All of a sudden, those gems of thought, those words of wisdom I'd shoved to the hinterlands of my psyche took on a crystal clarity. I wanted to immerse myself in his wisdom, understanding, patience and all the other stable qualities he had demonstrated, but I had been too busy to care about, before they would be lost forever. It appeared to others as though I was making a sacrifice for him. But the truth was I needed him now, even though he had been there for me every day of my life. We played golf as much as we could, until he couldn't play anymore, and I soaked up his insights like a woman lost in the desert of life without water.

When he died, all of his golfing friends, most of whom I'd never met, came to the funeral. It made me sadly aware of how little I knew of his life outside our time together. It also became apparent, as they paid their respects in various ways, that he had bragged to them about what a great golfer I was. It was a ruse I tried to stifle, but I knew that even in death, he had used his love of golf in yet another way to profess his love and confidence in me.

I don't mean to imply my dad was perfect. He could sometimes be a bit inconsistent. Nonetheless, today, ten years later, I would give up every car, every house, every everything I have ever had for one round of golf with him, just for the simple pleasure of absorbing each link in his chain of pithy expressions: "Relax, it's just a game!" which he alternated to suit the occasion with, "Golf is much more than a game, sweetheart. It's a practice round for life!"

~Debra Moss
Chicken Soup for the Golfer's Soul

55

Mollie's Moment

Time is free, but it's priceless. You can't own it, but you can use it. You can't keep it, but you can send it. Once you've lost it, you can never get it back.
~Harvey Mackay

For years I worked in politics, a career choice that required long hours and a lot of traveling. When Senator Bob Kerrey ran for the U.S. presidency in 1992, for example, I helped on his campaign and ended up spending a great deal of time away from my wife, Bonnie, and our two young children, Zach and Mollie.

After the campaign, I came home to learn an important lesson about balancing career and family, about what kids really need from a dad — and about the building and dismantling of walls.

Shortly before Mollie's third birthday, I had just returned from a series of long trips with the senator, some of which had lasted six or seven days, with only a quick stop at home to change laundry.

Mollie and I were driving through our Silver Spring, Maryland, neighborhood on the way back from the grocery store when, from her car seat in the back, she said, "Dad, what street is your house on?"

"What?" I thought I hadn't heard correctly.

"What street is your house on?"

It was a telling moment. Although she knew I was her dad and she knew her mom and I were married, she did not know I lived in the same house that she did.

Though I was able to convince her that we resided at the same address, her uncertainty about my place in her life continued and manifested itself in many ways. A skinned knee sent her toppling towards Mom, not me. A question raised by something overheard at school would be saved for hours until Mom was around to ask.

I realized that not only did I have to spend more time with Mollie, I also had to spend it differently. The more I sensed her distance from me, the more goal-oriented things I tried to do with her—like going to the swimming pool or to the movies.

If Mollie and I didn't have some specifically scheduled activity, I would typically go and work on chores. For maximizing time and being productive, it made perfect sense.

When it was time to read a bedtime story, Bonnie would call me after the rest of the presleep routine had been completed, and I would walk into Mollie's room like a dentist who waited until the patient was prepped so he wouldn't have to waste a minute's time. It was the way I felt, and I'm sure now it was the way it made Mollie feel, too.

A turning point came one summer evening. Mollie was growing increasingly frustrated trying to build a secret hideout in the backyard. The sun was setting, and Mollie should have been winding down before bed, except that the thin slate tiles she tried to prop against one another kept falling over. She'd been at it for days, sometimes with a neighboring friend, sometimes on her own. When the walls fell over for the last time, cracking as they did, she burst into tears.

"You know what you need to make this work, Molls?" I said.

"What?"

"You need about sixty bricks."

"Yeah, but we don't have sixty bricks."

"But we could get them."

"Where?"

"The hardware store. Get your shoes on and hop in the car."

We drove the five or so miles to the hardware store and found the bricks. I started to load them, a few at a time, onto a big, flat cart. They were rough and heavy, and I realized that I had my work cut out for me. After being loaded onto the cart, they would need to be unloaded into the Jeep, and then unloaded yet again at the house.

"Oh, please, let me do that, Dad. Please!" Mollie begged.

If I let her, we'd be there forever. She would have to use two hands just to pick up one of them. I glanced at my watch and tried to keep my impatience in check.

"But sweetie, they're very heavy."

"Please, Dad, I really want to," she begged, moving quickly to the pile of bricks and hoisting one with both hands. She lugged it over to the cart and laid it next to the handful I'd placed there.

This was going to take all night.

Mollie walked back to the pile and carefully selected another brick. She took her time choosing.

Then I realized she wanted it to take all night.

It was rare for the two of us to have time like this alone together. This was the kind of impulsive thing her older brother Zach would usually get to do, past bedtime, just the two of us. Only with Zach, in maybe typically male fashion, I would see this as a task to finish quickly, so that we could go build the wall. Mollie wanted this moment to last.

I leaned back against one of the wood pallets and took a deep breath. Mollie, working steadily at the bricks, relaxed and became chatty, talking to me about what she'd build, and about school and her girlfriends and her upcoming horseback-riding lesson. And it dawned on me: Here we were buying bricks to make a wall, but in truth we were actually dismantling a wall, brick by brick—the wall that had threatened to divide me from my daughter.

Since then I've learned what her mother already knew: how to watch a TV show with Mollie even if it isn't a show I wanted to see; how to be with her without also reading a newspaper or magazine, to be fully present. Mollie doesn't want me for what I can give her, for where I can take her, or even for what we can do together. She wants me for me.

~Bill Shore
Chicken Soup for the Father's Soul

56

Given Away

There really is no use denying it. I've been given away. Sure I could attempt to hide it, make excuses for it, or just plain lie, but what's the use? The truth is, I am what is traditionally referred to as a "Daddy's girl."

Now, I know women today are supposed to be fiercely independent. We don't need validation from a man and are certainly more than capable of taking care of ourselves. We are supposed to be in complete charge of our own lives. And, although I might try to keep up a good feminist front, to be perfectly honest, my father has always been there to help take care of the major problems in my life.

As a child, I was a little shadow trailing behind the tall figure my father cast. I remained close to my father and even lived at home while I attended college. So when Mark and I discussed marriage, I must confess to being a little worried about my father's reaction. I knew losing the little girl he had so carefully protected all these years was not going to be easy for him.

I, too, was apprehensive. I loved my boyfriend, of course, but I found the idea of losing the most dependable person in my life a little bit unsettling. Getting married required me to leave his protective wing and face day-to-day life with Mark — with whose track record I was unfamiliar.

After our engagement was announced, long weeks of wedding plans followed. During this time, my father remained conspicuously quiet. Not that he was ever in the habit of discussing his feelings at great length. And anyway, it was a noisy, busy time with little opportunity to dwell on emotions.

When the wedding day finally came, I was in a state of panic. Until then, marriage was only theoretical—full of hopeful what-if and could-be scenarios. Now marriage was in the present and it was real.

What was I doing? Did I know how to be married? What if I was making a mistake? What if I couldn't handle all the things that marriage and married life threw at me? And how could I get through it all without my father to smooth out the edges?

Would my husband accept my attachment to my father? Would my father accept my attachment to my husband? Would there be rivalry between the two men in my life?

As we stood at the entrance to the church, I knew an entirely different life waited inside. I took deep breaths to calm my nerves. The Wedding March came on cue, infinitely appropriate. I was a soldier reporting for duty and the army had no idea I was too young and inexperienced to handle the battle.

I leaned over and whispered, "Dad, I'm scared."

He gently took my arm and escorted me into the church. We slowly walked the aisle together and he gave me away.

And it felt perfectly natural. My father had been there for all the major moments in my life, quietly guiding and leading me, knowing instinctively when to pull or when to push. His constant but gentle nudging had gotten me through every meaningful transition in my life.

At the reception, Mark and I made the rounds, greeting and thanking everyone in a whirlwind of smiles and hugs. When we started to drive away toward our new life, I realized I had forgotten something.

I turned to Mark. "I didn't get to say goodbye to Daddy."

My new husband instantly pushed on the brakes, turned off the car and got out. He yelled into the crowd and, after a few moments, my father stepped out from among the guests with a puzzled look on his face.

Mark opened the door so I could jump out and give Daddy a goodbye hug. At that moment I felt I had really been "given away." I realized my father had given me to my husband and, in turn, my husband had given my father back to me.

This, then, was the purpose of all those years of leading, nudging, pushing and pulling—to make me an adult who uses her heart generously. Who loves big and who loves in all directions. I finally understood what it meant to be truly given—to be loved yet never held back.

~Renata Waldrop
Chicken Soup for the Bride's Soul

57

The Gag Gift

Once a word has been allowed to escape, it cannot be recalled.
~Horace

It was our turn to open presents this particular Christmas morning. The living room was already covered with torn wrapping paper from the onslaught of the children's eagerness to unveil the hidden treasures that had tormented them for nearly a month. Now we adults sat around the room with our presents at our feet, slowly removing the paper while at the same time holding back the child within ourselves and maintaining our dignity in front of each other.

My wife, Brenda, and her family have a tradition of buying each other gag gifts. This always makes me a bit uneasy at Christmas or my birthday, never knowing what form of embarrassment lies waiting for me under the thin confines of the wrapping paper.

One of my daughters, Christy, who at the time was six years old, was standing directly in front of me. The excitement of the moment just beamed across her face. It was everything she could do to keep herself from helping me rip the paper from each present. Finally, I came to the last gift. With my natural Sherlock Holmes ability, I deduced that this had to be the gag gift, because with them it was never a question of if, it was a question of when you came to it. So, with everyone looking on, I decided to go ahead and get it over with — just let them have their laugh — and I ripped off the paper. And there it was... a toy airplane about two inches long. Our holiday guests started giggling to themselves as I looked up to my wife with a smirk on my face and blurted out, "A toy airplane, give me a break!"

Brenda gave me the look: that look that always tells me I have just put my foot in my mouth and am in the process of thoroughly chewing it. I had failed to look at the name tag before I opened the present to see who it was from. As I picked up the paper from the floor and read the name tag, my heart sank. On the tag were scribbled block letters that read, "To Dad, Love Christy." I have never felt as low at any time in my life as I did at that moment. One of the most agonizing experiences of my life was having to look down into my daughter's little face to find the joy that had once been there replaced with a look of total embarrassment and humiliation. The fear in her eyes spoke her thoughts of hoping no one would find out that the gift her father found so repulsive had come from her.

This loving child had taken her spending money that she could have spent on herself, but instead had chosen to buy her daddy a Christmas present. And it wasn't just any present. She knew from watching me play computer video flight-simulator games that I was fascinated with airplanes.

I quickly knelt down and grabbed her up in my arms and held her as tight as I possibly could, willing to give anything to be able to take back those words. I made a feeble attempt to explain that I thought it had come from Mom, but since I found out it came from her, that made it different. It was obvious that nothing I could say was going to change the hurt in her little heart. I had to find a way to prove I meant what I said.

And I did. I took that toy airplane in my hand and began making airplane noises. I taxied onto the runway, which was the counter, and throttled to full thrust and was soon airborne. My mission goal was to remove the hurt from my baby's face—that I had caused—and to continue until her smile returned. I played all day with that airplane. I put so much excitement into that airplane that the other children left their new Christmas toys and wanted a turn playing with my little two-inch airplane. And just like a little selfish kid I said, "No, this is mine!" It wasn't very long until Christy's face was beaming with a smile again. But I didn't stop there. That little plane became a treasure of great wealth to me, and still is, for I still have that little two-inch plane.

I keep that plane mainly because it came from my little girl's heart with love. But it's also a reminder to me of the power of words.

~George Parler
Chicken Soup for the Father's Soul

58

Only One

N orma Halstead was a slender fifteen-year-old in the summer of 1941. Her father, Grant, was the professional at the new Fresno Municipal Course located on the banks of the San Joaquin River. She and her parents lived on the second floor of the clubhouse, high on a hilltop overlooking the river and the first fairway. It was a simple time and Norma's life was filled with many things, but especially her love of golf.

Summer days in Fresno can be unmercifully hot. Norma would frequently rise before the sun, complete her chores, and then tote her canvas bag off to the first tee for a solitary nine. In the early morning a fine mist often rose off the river. The first hole, which plunged down the hillside from the clubhouse, appeared milky white. Norma was relatively new to the game, but her father's instruction was evident when she cracked a drive off the first tee and watched as it carried out and down into the mist over the fairway below. Norma loved the game and her life at the river's edge.

On one particular July morning Norma set out for her round with no more than the mere expectation of a good walk in the country. As she teed up one of the three Dunlop balls given to her by her father, she remembered his admonition, "a good golfer never loses a ball." Her father's word on matters of golf was gospel, and Norma dreaded the thought of ever asking him for more golf balls. But this morning her drive bore true through the mist and landed well down the first fairway.

Billy Bell designed the course. Grant Halstead convinced the city fathers that Bell was the man to draw up their first public course, and Bell's execution was flawless. It soon became known as the "big Muni" and was the site of many exciting city championships. The real challenge for Bell was in designing the first three holes in the limited space available. The first hole, a long par-4, stretched down the hill from the clubhouse and out along the riverbank. The second was a short, well-bunkered par-3 running up a hillside to a bowl-shaped green. The third hole paralleled the first, with its green chiseled into the steep embankment looming over the river. The design of these three holes, now obvious for its simplistic elegance, was considered impossible. But Bell's talent for the simple yet elegant solution was evident throughout the course.

As Norma approached her ball in the first fairway she could hear the distant whistle of an early morning freight train. The tracks ran the eastern length of the course and at the river's edge crossed a great trestle. Soon the train would be rumbling by the second hole, clattering north to Modesto, Stockton and Sacramento. It took Norma three strong shots to reach the first green, and she holed out with two putts for a personal par.

On the second tee she selected a long iron. Her father's simple wisdom told her never to fear any club. Swing them all the same. But most of all, he would say, "Trust your swing." As she took a practice swing, she thought only of mimicking her father's graceful style. He often said to her, "Imagine someone is taking your picture. Try to look pretty." It was easy for the young girl.

The train was just rumbling past the wooden fence posts lining the edge of the course. Norma's concentration was complete as she rocked into the ball. To her delight it soared swiftly on a line for the round green. Norma hoped for par on the short holes and tried extra hard to reach the putting surface. She was a good putter and could often get down in two. This looked like a good shot, landing at the front of the green, right on line with the flag. She picked up her bag and began climbing up the hill to the green.

On hot days players would often dawdle at the back of the second hole, where two big pine trees spread their limbs and offered momentary shade. The bowl-shaped green easily collected shots, but because it was a small green any tee shot more than ten degrees off line would ricochet off the hillside. Accuracy was rewarded. Norma knew the secret to this hole was to take plenty of club—and trust your swing.

As Norma reached the top of the hill she was unable to see her ball. The train, now well down the track and over the trestle, sounded three short hoots of its great whistle. Norma looked to the back of the green, expecting to see her ball nestled against the collar. It wasn't there. She laid down her bag and began looking closely at the ribbon of rough at the back of the green. Slightly exasperated, the realization began to sink in that she may have lost her first golf ball. She imagined her father's brow creased with wrinkles of incredulity, mouth gaping, dumbstruck by his only child's shameful loss.

It must be here somewhere, Norma thought. She began to walk to the front of the green on the chance the ball had not bounced forward as she had first thought. Then, as she walked past the hole, she looked down and there it was. A hole-in-one!

Though she was only a novice, she knew that a hole-in-one was a terrific golfing feat. She knew her father would be delighted. His broad smile and gleaming eyes filled her thoughts as she reached into the cup and extracted her ball. She wished her father had seen it. She wished her mother had seen it. She wished anyone had seen it.

She finished her round of nine and walked to the steps of the clubhouse, now washed with the warming rays of the morning sun. She looked up to the porch and saw the face of her mother. Not wanting to sound too excited, she said coyly, "Oh, Mom, I hit a really good shot today." Her mother, having been saturated with stories of golf from the time of her first meeting Grant, was prepared to patiently attend to yet another exploit on the field of glory.

Suitably braced to receive the laurels of her triumph, Norma announced, "Yes, on the second I hit a shot right into the hole."

Her mother scanned the horizon, looking out across the course as if she were taking inventory of the young trees sprouting along the fairways. Her mind was on the baking of pies, cakes and chili for the day's customers. While Grant ran the golf shop and taught lessons on the range, Norma's mother ran the coffee shop. Everything was fresh.

She turned and looked at Norma's shoulder-length brown curls, and noticed beads of sweat at her temples. Finally she said, "That's very good, dear. Be sure to tell your father. Now come inside and get out of the sun."

Norma was somewhat disappointed with her mother's reaction. Certainly there was meant to be something more to this. She must have announced it wrong. Trailing after her mother as they walked into the coffee shop, Norma said, "No, Mother, I mean I hit the ball into the hole with only one shot. A hole-in-one!"

Norma's mother put her arms across her young daughter's shoulders and guided her through the coffee shop, and then gently sent her off in the general direction of the golf shop. "Yes, dear, that's very good," she repeated. "Be sure you tell your father."

Norma's frustration only grew when she announced her triumph to her father. They stood alone in the golf shop. The slight fifteen-year-old was dwarfed by the muscled pro. Grant's most impressive features were his massive hands and bald head. His steady gaze could be stern, but most often his eyes sparkled with the spirit of Christmas.

In a solemn tone, Grant said to his child, "That's very good, Norma, but you have to understand something. It's not really sporting to say you've scored an ace while playing alone. You see, without a witness... well... we'd have jokers coming off the course every day claiming to have done one thing or another." Grant then wrapped his arms around his daughter, gave her a gentle hug, and said, "Just remember — trust your swing and you'll do fine."

In days to come, parents would ponder the psychological injury such a disappointing reception might inflict upon the young willow. But 1941 was a more realistic time, and in some ways parents were not so concerned with sheltering their children from the harshness of the world. They were more intent on preparing them to live in a world of both evil and good.

Norma thought little more of her triumph. She had learned that in addition to the Rules of Golf taught to her by her father, there were other rules. Rules that were only learned by experience.

Two weeks later a postcard, addressed only to "Head Pro," arrived at the clubhouse. Grant received the card and his thunderous laughter could be heard throughout the clubhouse. The card read simply, "Congratulations to that young lady who aced the second hole. What a beautiful shot." The card was signed, "J. C. Wade, Engineer, Southern Pacific Railroad."

When Norma heard the ruckus in the shop below, she came down the staircase from her bedroom and was greeted by her father and four members of the men's club. Her father's booming voice proclaimed his daughter's victory as Norma read and reread the postcard in disbelief. She smiled broadly, and with due modesty finally accepted the conqueror's wreath.

She was about to go back up to her room when her father spoke. "Now dear, fetch your piggy bank. You owe us all a drink."

Norma sensed she was about to learn one more of golf's unwritten rules.

~J. G. Nursall
Chicken Soup for the Golfer's Soul

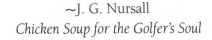

Simple Wooden Boxes

His courage is his legacy, our inheritance.
~Nita Sue Kent

I suppose everyone has a particular childhood Christmas that stands out more than any other. For me, it was the year that the Burlington factory in Scottsboro closed down. I was only a small child. I could not name for you the precise year; it is an insignificant blur in my mind, but the events of that Christmas will live forever in my heart.

My father, who had been employed at Burlington, never let on to us that we were having financial difficulties. After all, children live in a naive world in which money and jobs are nothing more than jabberwocky; and for us, the excitement of Christmas could never be squelched. We knew only that our daddy, who usually worked long, difficult hours, was now home more than we had ever remembered; each day seemed to be a holiday.

Mama, a homemaker, now sought work in the local textile mills, but jobs were scarce. Time after time, she was told no openings were available before Christmas, and it was on the way home from one such distressing interview that she wrecked our only car. Daddy's meager unemployment check would now be our family's only source of income. For my parents, the Christmas season brought mounds of worries, crowds of sighs and tears, and cascades of prayers.

I can only imagine what transpired between my parents during that time. I don't know for sure how they managed, but somehow they did. They made sure they scraped together enough money to buy each of us a Barbie doll. For the rest of our presents, they would rely on their talents, using scraps of materials they already had.

While dark, calloused hands sawed, hammered and painted, nimble fingers fed dress after dress after dress into the sewing machine. Barbie-sized bridal gowns, evening gowns... miniature clothes for every imaginable occasion pushed forward from the rattling old machine. Where we were while all of this was taking place, I have no idea. But somehow my parents found time to pour themselves into our gifts, and the excitement of Christmas was once again born for the entire family.

That Christmas Eve, the sun was just setting over the distant horizon when I heard the roar of an unexpected motor in the driveway. Looking outside, I could hardly believe my eyes. Aunt Charlene and Uncle Buck, Mama's sister and her husband, had driven all the way from Georgia to surprise us. Packed tightly in their car, as though no air was needed, sat my three cousins, my Aunt Dean, who refused to be called "Aunt," and both my grandparents. I also couldn't help but notice innumerable gifts for all of us, all neatly packaged and tied with beautiful bows. They had known that it would be a difficult Christmas, and they had come to help.

The next morning we awoke to more gifts than I ever could have imagined. And, though I don't have one specific memory of what any of the toys were, I know that there were mountains of them.

And it was there, amidst all that jubilation, that Daddy decided not to give us his gifts. With all the toys we had gotten, there was no reason to give us the dollhouses that he had made. They were rustic and simple red boxes, after all. Certainly not as good as the store-bought gifts that Mama's family had brought. The music of laughter filled the morning, and we never suspected that, hidden somewhere, we each had another gift.

When Mama asked Daddy about the gifts, he confided his feelings, but she insisted he give us our gifts. And so, late that afternoon, after all of the guests had gone, Daddy reluctantly brought his gifts of love to the living room.

Wooden boxes. Wooden boxes painted red, with hinged lids,

so that each side could be opened and used as a house. On either side was a compartment just big enough to store a Barbie doll, and all the way across, a rack on which to hang our Barbie clothes. On the outside was a handle, so that when it was closed, held by a magnet that looked remarkably like an equal sign, the house could be carried suitcase style. And, though I don't really remember any of the other gifts I got that day, those boxes are indelibly etched into my mind. I remember the texture of the wood, the exact shade of red paint, the way the pull of the magnet felt when I closed the lid, the time-darkened handles and hinges. I remember how the clothes hung delicately on the hangers inside, and how I had to be careful not to pull Barbie's hair when I closed the lid. I remember everything that is possibly rememberable, because we kept and cherished those boxes long after our Barbie doll days were over.

I have lived and loved twenty-nine Christmases, each new and fresh with an air of excitement all its own. Each filled with love and hope. Each bringing gifts, cherished and longed for. But few of those gifts compare with those simple wooden boxes. So it is no wonder that I get teary-eyed when I think of my father, standing there on that cold Christmas morning, wondering if his gift was good enough.

Love, Daddy, is always good enough.

~Martha Pendergrass Templeton
Chicken Soup for the Soul Christmas Treasury

60

Nonno Beppe's Gift

here I was, seven years old and back in Italy, the land of my birth. Uprooted from my life in America, I was bundled off to Europe in a rush by my mother so that she could recover and regroup after a traumatic divorce from my father. Being a war bride in America had been trying. She needed the support of her family and their simple way of life. She was sad and lonely in America. Now I was feeling the same way in Italy. I was living with my grandparents in their three-hundred-year-old farmhouse in a tiny village high in the mountains north of Florence. My mother, needing medical care and rest, was staying in the city.

I was used to an American way of life. Now, suddenly, I was in a place that had changed little since the eighteenth century, living with people I didn't know and struggling to understand a language I had never spoken. I was used to television, riding in cars, bright lights at the flip of a switch, and indoor plumbing—none of which existed in this village. Here, plows were pulled by oxen, water came in buckets drawn from a spring, and houses were lighted with kerosene lamps. My grandmother cooked in the open fireplace, our bread was baked in the ancient community stone oven. Clothes were washed in the river, and the toilet was a village outhouse.

I missed my father, my bedroom, and all the people and things I was familiar with. I was homesick, lonely and scared. I cried a lot those first few days. My grandparents and everyone else tried their best to ease the transition, but there was no TV to distract me—no toys, games, or books. Children played with nature's ornaments—stones, pebbles, sticks and the like. The people of the village were all subsistence farmers. Days were spent growing, harvesting, storing, preparing and eating food. The old farmhouses were furnished with only the barest necessities. Life was simple, uncomplicated, lived at the most basic level—but for me, it was, in a word, miserable.

One chilly fall day my grandfather, Nonno Beppe, announced that he was going to walk down the mountain (indeed he had no other way to go) and into the town of Baragazza, which had modern conveniences like electricity, running water and shops. I was made to understand that the purpose of his trip was to bring back a special gift for me. Perhaps I was starting to adjust to my new life just a little, because this stirred my interest and I felt a tinge of excitement. Although I didn't understand why, things suddenly didn't look quite so bleak and lonely. My seven-year-old mind began to hum with anticipation. What could this special gift be?

It was a long trudge down the mountain on a trail that was little more than a goat path. Because of the great distance and time involved, such trips were infrequent, never taken on the spur of the moment, and always had multiple purposes. But on this day, Nonno Beppe's trip was just for me. Nonno Beppe knew exactly which shop to visit. He had carried fresh vegetables down the mountain. These he traded for not one, but two, gifts—these he carefully placed in the inside pockets of his heavy wool coat, one on either side. Then he prepared for the long trek home.

Walking back up the mountain took more time than going down. Although the air was cold by now, Nonno Beppe was sweating and had to rest often, but he knew my gifts were safe in his inside pockets. It was after dark when he finally reached home, and the whole extended family—aunts, uncles and cousins—had gathered around the fireplace in anticipation of his return. When he burst through the door, he was flushed with excitement. I jumped up and down as he opened his coat, reached into his pockets and pulled out... two small, gooey sticks.

For a brief moment we looked at each other in surprise. I thought,

"What's special about these messy little sticks?" He must have thought, "They were ice cream when I put them in my pockets."

My uncles, who were a bit more familiar with twentieth-century delicacies, burst out laughing. They immediately understood that the ice cream had melted in the warmth of Nonno Beppe's pockets. My grandfather had never sampled ice cream in his whole life. His only thought was for me. He was certain that ice cream would make his little granddaughter, used to American luxuries, feel at home. As we started to grasp what had happened, everyone began laughing hysterically—including me.

I didn't get any ice cream, but somehow, it didn't matter. I couldn't explain it then, but at that moment, something wonderful happened. In all the hilarity, I was transformed. My inner turmoil was replaced by a feeling of peace. I understood that these people loved me more than I'd realized—really loved me and were there for me.

The real gift I got from Nonno Beppe that day was the knowledge that what we do for others is not as important as caring enough to try. The ice cream might have been eaten and forgotten, but because it melted in the loving warmth of my grandfather's coat, I've had Nonno Beppe's greater gift every day of my life.

~Susanna Palomares
Chicken Soup for the Soul Stories for a Better World

Dads & Daughters

Loss and Grieving

*When someone dies, you don't get over it by forgetting;
you get over it by remembering, and you are aware that no person
is ever truly lost or gone once they have been in our life and loved us,
as we have loved them.*
~Leslie Marmon Silko

61

A Surprise Gift for Mother

On Christmas Day, all the joys of close family relationships radiated throughout our parents' home. The smells of roasted turkey, Southern-baked ham and homemade bread hung in the air. Tables and chairs were set up everywhere to accommodate toddlers, teenagers, parents and grandparents. Every room was lavishly decorated. No family member had ever missed Christmas Day with our parents.

Only this year, things were different. Our father had passed away November 26, and this was our first Christmas without him. Mother was doing her best to be the gracious hostess, but I could tell this was especially hard for her. I felt a catch in my throat, and again I wondered if I should give her my planned Christmas gift, or if it had become inappropriate in my father's absence.

A few months earlier, I was putting the finishing touches on portraits I had painted of each of my parents. I'd planned to give them as Christmas gifts. This would be a surprise for everyone, as I had not studied art or tried serious painting. Yet there had been an undeniable urge that pushed me relentlessly to do this. The portraits did look like them, but I was still unsure of my painting skill.

While painting one day, I was surprised by a doorbell ring. Quickly putting all my painting materials out of sight, I opened the door. To my astonishment, my father ambled in alone, never before having visited me without my mother. Grinning, he said, "I've missed our early morning talks. You know, the ones we had before you decided to leave me for another man!" I hadn't been married long. Also, I was the only girl and the baby of the family.

Immediately I wanted to show him the paintings, but I was reluctant to ruin his Christmas surprise. Yet something urged me to share this moment with him. After swearing him to secrecy, I insisted he keep his eyes closed until I had the portraits set on easels. "Okay, Daddy. Now you can look!"

He appeared dazed but said nothing. Getting up, he walked closer to inspect them. Then he withdrew to eye them at a distance. I tried to control my stomach flip-flops. Finally, with a tear escaping down one cheek, he mumbled, "I don't believe it. The eyes are so real that they follow you everywhere—and look how beautiful your mother is. Will you let me have them framed?"

Thrilled with his response, I happily volunteered to drop them off the next day at the frame shop. Several weeks passed. Then one night in November the phone rang, and a cold chill numbed my body. I picked up the receiver to hear my husband, a doctor, say, "I'm in the emergency room. Your father has had a stroke. It's bad, but he is still alive."

Daddy lingered in a coma for several days. I went to see him in the hospital the day before he died. I slipped my hand in his and asked, "Do you know who I am, Daddy?"

He surprised everyone when he whispered, "You're my darling daughter." He died the next day, and it seemed all joy was drained from the lives of my mother and me.

I finally remembered to call about the portrait framing and thanked God my father had gotten a chance to see the pictures before he died. I was surprised when the shopkeeper told me my father had visited the shop, paid for the framing and had them gift wrapped. In our grief, I had no longer planned to give the portraits to my mother.

Even though we had lost the patriarch of our family, everyone assembled on Christmas Day—making an effort to be cheerful. As I looked into my mother's sad eyes and unsmiling face, I decided to give her Daddy's and my gift. As she stripped the paper from the box,

I saw her heart wasn't in it. There was a small card inside attached to the pictures.

After looking at the portraits and reading the card, her entire demeanor changed. She bounced out of her chair, handed the card to me and commissioned my brothers to hang the paintings facing each other over the fireplace. She stepped back and looked for a long while. With sparkling, tear-filled eyes and a wide smile, she quickly turned and said, "I knew Daddy would be with us on Christmas Day!"

I glanced at the gift card scrawled in my father's handwriting. "Mother—Our daughter reminded me why I am so blessed. I'll be looking at you always—Daddy."

~Sarah A. Rivers
Chicken Soup for the Grieving Soul

62

Budding Hope

*One of the most delightful things about a garden is
the anticipation it provides.*
~W.E. Johns, The Passing Show

"Will you hurry up?"

I don't actually say it, but I'm sure thinking it. Sitting here on the front steps of my parents' house, I'm waiting for my new husband, Jim, who's still inside packing a few last things. We've been married for a week and a day.

This morning, we're going to swing by the hospital to visit Dad, say our farewells, climb into our car and head to Colorado from New York. This is such a wonderfully exciting time for us. Everything is brand-new, and we've decided to begin our married lives in a new state where I've never been before.

But for the moment, I have to wait. My mind wanders.

I glance over at the rose bush my father gave my mother on their twenty-fifth wedding anniversary. It was a grandiose gesture then, but what a sad-looking bush it is now. It's scrawny with a few buds scattered across its branches. I have no idea what color it's designed to produce because it's never bloomed. It just keeps hanging on year after year, budding out but not going any further until the leaves fall off each autumn. It's such a stubborn plant, sticking it out, determined to live.

Stubborn.

Suddenly this rose bush reminds me of an argument Dad and I had about a month ago. We had both been so stubborn over something that seems, now, so petty.

A few weeks before the wedding, I brought my wedding gown home along with a beautiful veil I had found. The veil coordinated perfectly with the gown. Okay, I admit, buying it was a bit extravagant because the veil actually cost more than the dress.

Later that night, about 1:00 A.M., I woke up because I heard a noise downstairs. I walked down to the kitchen to find Dad sitting at the table holding my veil. Before I could even ask why he was awake, he began criticizing the cost of the veil.

"I can't believe you'd spend that much!" He slammed his fist on the table.

Startled by his unexpected outburst, I reacted with my own angry protest. "It's made for the dress. Don't you want me to look great on my wedding day?"

Then came my ultimate hit-below-the-belt comment. "But what do you care? You might not even be there!"

Whoa. That one hurt. Especially because we both knew it was true.

Seriously ill, Dad was scheduled to have open-heart surgery on the Thursday after my wedding. He was pretty weak by this time (although you couldn't tell by his yelling) and was supposed to be resting in preparation.

Dad would enter the hospital for two weeks of testing prior to the surgery—and my wedding fell right in the middle. We all hoped the surgeon would "let Dad out" to attend and give me away.

But the fear hung there: Dad might not be strong enough. And, as the yelling showed, it was a sensitive issue.

I had grown up feeling very close to Dad. Yet here we were, hollering at each other, neither of us willing to give in. I would wear this veil no matter what. After all, it was my wedding.

We stood in silence, fuming, glaring at each other because there was no more to say. I stomped upstairs to my bedroom and broke down.

But this time it wasn't about the veil. I was scared and so was Dad. Scared he really wouldn't be at the wedding. Scared he could die. Scared to admit how much we loved each other, knowing I would be moving 2,000 miles away to start a life he couldn't be part of every day.

I slipped back to the kitchen and gave him a hug, a wordless "I'm sorry" for both of us.

On the evening of my wedding, they released Dad from the hospital (with lots of "dos" and "don'ts") for four hours. While we sat in the brides' room for a few last moments together, he took my hands lovingly in his.

"Hello, Beautiful."

He was too weak to walk with me down the aisle, so my brother did the honor. But Dad waited up front by the minister and gently put my hand into the hand of my new husband.

Now, a week after our wedding, Dad has had his surgery and is in critical condition. But we'll head over to see him in just a few minutes... if Jim hurries up. After all, it's almost 10:45 A.M. and we have to get on the road to Colorado and our future.

I catch a whiff of something sweet. Like a rose. It is a rose.

That scrawny bush is blooming! I stare at it, hardly believing what I'm seeing. Right before my eyes, one of the buds bursts into a full white blossom—like a film in fast motion. Beautiful.

"Jim!" I call out. "You've got to come and see this."

"Just a second, I have to get the phone," he answers from inside the house.

I watch the rose, amazed, until he comes out. I feel him sit down next to me. I pull my gaze from the rose to his face because he isn't saying anything. A long pause.

"I'm so sorry, Elaine, but your dad passed away a few minutes ago."

Dad died that morning at 10:44 A.M.—the exact minute the rose bush bloomed. I'm sure it was his special goodbye to me.

Yet, in my mind, that rose is not about goodbyes. It's about hope. The hope a wedding brings. The hope loving parents leave with their children by giving their very best. And the hope that comes from knowing this new man will take me "from this day forward" to help me blend new memories with old ones.

~Elaine G. Dumler
Chicken Soup for the Bride's Soul

63

The Ride

It doesn't matter who my father was; it matters who I remember he was.
~Anne Sexton

Since both of my parents worked, Dad frequently shared in the parental duties of raising his daughters. It was often Dad who met us at the bus stop after school, ripped old Band-Aids off our skinned knees, and taught us how to ride our bikes without training wheels. He snuck quarters into our pockets when the tooth fairy forgot, made up funny stories, and attended school plays that I knew broke in to his work day. Often on his days off, he joined us in a game of hide-and-seek, finding creative and original places to hide my younger sister. I was certain the safest place in the world was being wrapped in my dad's strong arms. His hugs melted away all my fears.

Dad wrote notes on the back of my artwork and other school projects, saying such things as, "I love you more than you'll ever know," or "I'm so proud of you."

The summer I was fourteen, my father did something totally uncharacteristic of the other fathers in the neighborhood: he bought a motorcycle. We were amused at first, never realizing that owning a motorcycle was a lifelong dream of my dad's.

"I used to have a bike when I was in the Navy," he reminisced. "I've waited years for another." He beamed proudly at the bike parked by the side of the house, its chrome exterior flashing in the sunlight. My father drove it every chance he could, often taking my sister or me along for the ride. He bought us helmets and took time teaching us the rules of the road as they applied to motorcycle riding. I knew this was not just a passing phase with Dad, he truly enjoyed this motorcycle. The shiny bike and my father were a perfect fit. One day, while we were on a road trip, he confided in me that when his time came to die, he hoped he would be on his bike.

The following spring, my dad dusted the winter dirt off his bike and went for a ride. I never saw him alive again. He was killed instantly when a drunk driver collided with him. The grief and terror of the following days were a blur. Many nights I woke up and discovered my pillow wet with tears. I was inconsolable; I was convinced I would never feel joy again.

The grieving my family and I endured seemed endless, yet we mysteriously held each other up at the same time. On one difficult night, my mother shared with me a vision that consoled her: "I saw your father taking that last trip on his bike down a beautiful country road that lead straight into heaven."

That image was a healing balm for my aching heart. Whenever I felt insecure about losing my dad, I would retrieve that soothing image.

I was in my late twenties when I met John. He was in his early forties, the same age my father was when he died. John had warm eyes, a ponytail, a leather jacket, and—you guessed it—a motorcycle that he enjoyed as much as my father had enjoyed his. John and I became friends through our shared faith in God. I never told him the circumstances of my father's death, and I secretly prayed for his safety every time I saw him riding his bike. John frequently went on extended road trips, and I often didn't see him for months at a time.

One day, after an absence of several months, John caught up with me at a church gathering. He was excited about a recent road trip. He looked healthy and his eyes were sparkling.

"Come with me, I have something to show you." He took my hand and led me out the door. I had no idea what he was up to. We walked past the rows of cars and turned the corner of the building. There stood his huge, shiny new motorcycle.

The familiar sense of terror and grief returned.

"Come closer and take a look at this," he said, completely unaware of the emotions I was fighting.

I took a deep breath and walked up to the bike. The leather seat, paneled instruments and shiny chrome were all reminders of an innocent past. My heart began pounding loudly in my chest. Hidden memories of a cherished childhood surfaced in one bittersweet swell. How vividly I remembered traveling on that bike, my arms wrapped tightly around my father's waist, and my head buried in the back of his shoulder as the sharp wind snapped against us.

At John's urging, I walked closer to the bike and stopped. I couldn't believe my eyes.

"My son painted this," John said. His smile spread across his face.

The beautiful scene, skillfully hand-painted on the upper body of the bike, depicted a man riding a motorcycle down a beautiful country road leading into heaven. The clouds held an image of Jesus with arms outstretched, ready to meet the rider. It was an exact representation of the vision my mother had shared with me over a decade before.

"It's beautiful," I said to John.

The old grief and terror melted away, and peace filled my soul as I finally let my father ride into the waiting arms of Jesus.

~Michelle Beaupre Matt
Chicken Soup for the Christian Woman's Soul

64

The Smell of Grass

Death leaves a heartache no one can heal,
love leaves a memory no one can steal.
~From a headstone in Ireland

Oh, how cool and tranquil it was, lying in the freshly cut jade grass. The aroma of wet grass was enough to take Amber back to when she was four. Spread out in that grass, she gazed into the soft, blue heavens. She and her father would make clouds into animals, and her father would always say they looked like elephants. The cicadas would buzz, a sound of summer. Even though the heat was sweltering, the cool backyard grass was just the trick to refresh Amber and her father.

Every time she thought of her early childhood summers, she remembered grass, melon, Popsicles, plastic pools, sprinklers, blue skies, clear water and green, green grass. Amber snapped out of her memory and unlocked the front door. Lately, she had been thinking a lot about her backyard and those summers she spent with her dad.

Amber's father had died August 24, 1990, when she was five years old. He'd been diagnosed with cancer that summer but kept it a secret from Amber, not wanting to ruin their last few weeks together. She'd missed him a lot lately; last Tuesday he would have been forty-five years old. Even though she was so young when he died, she remembered everything about him. His big smile, tan complexion, his comforting laugh. She loved every second of the days she spent with him; she was definitely her father's daughter.

Amber plopped her stuff down on her mother's desk and started her history work. After twenty minutes had passed, she stretched and looked around. She needed a pencil sharpener. She fumbled through every drawer of the old oak desk. She came across a ragged blue book in a pile of others. Her hand trembled as she felt the leather cover. She took a deep breath. She opened it up and began to read the black scribbly writing:

July 26, 1990

I still haven't broken the news to my little angel. Every time I look into her sweet eyes, I can't find the words to put it lightly. I know I will miss her the most. If only I could stay to see her grow; we are so much alike. I pray to the Lord every day to keep her strong and beautiful, and I know I will watch over her, when I no longer exist in this world. I will desperately miss all of our fun times playing in the grass in our yard. I will be waiting for the day she comes to play with me up in heaven.

Amber put the book down. She did not need to read any more. She was already sobbing quietly—partly out of sadness, partly out of happiness, but mostly because four small blades of dried grass fell out of the book and into her hands.

~Adelaide Isaac
Chicken Soup for the Father's Soul

65

Both Sides Now

You can clutch the past so tightly to your chest that
it leaves your arms too full to embrace the present.
~Jan Glidewell

After my mother passed away, my dad tried even harder to stay healthy and active. Each morning, until the weather turned too cold, he swam in the turquoise pool in the complex where he lived. Each day—no matter how he felt—he swam one more lap than the previous day, just to prove there was always room for improvement. Every few days he reported the new number of laps to me, pride edging his voice. I would answer truthfully, "Golly, Dad, I don't know if I could still swim that many!"

By his late seventies, in spite of swimming and working six days a week, my dad had noticeably dwindled in strength and energy. By age eighty-one he was in poor health and had to retire. He pretended he didn't need to lean heavily on me for support as we walked slowly, and I pretended not to notice. His mind was clear, but congestive heart problems and disabling arthritis had worn him down. One day he said, "In case of an emergency I do not wish to be kept alive by any extraordinary means. I've signed an official paper to this effect." He smiled his wonderful, broad grin and said, "I've been blessed to have had your mother as my wife and you as my only child, and I'm ready to go."

Less than a month later he had a heart attack. In the emergency room, he again reminded his doctor and me of his wishes, but I couldn't imagine—in spite of this latest crisis—that he wouldn't always be saying, "Have I told you yet today that I adore you?"

He was miserable in intensive care; tubes seemed to come from every opening. But my dad still had his sense of humor, asking me, "Does this mean we can't keep our lunch date tomorrow?" His voice faltered.

"I'll be here to pick you up and we'll go someplace special." I answered, a lump in my throat.

Dad refused to look at me for the first time in his life and turned toward the blank green wall next to his hospital bed. There was a painful silence between us. He said, "I don't want you to remember me like this. Promise me you won't, darling! And please go now—I'm so miserable."

That night, back at the hospital with my husband, the attendants wouldn't let us in to see him. "He's having a little problem," one said. "Please wait in the visitors' lounge and we'll call you as soon as possible."

I sat holding my husband's hand for about ten minutes. Suddenly, a jolt shook me and I felt my heart stop beating. "Oh, honey," I said. "Daddy just died. I felt it!" I jumped up, rushed down the hall to intensive care and began knocking on the door. "Let me in to see him," I begged.

"He just died a moment ago," one of the nurses answered. "Please go back to the lounge and we'll come get you in a few minutes." They blocked the door so I couldn't rush in.

It had seemed to me that this beloved man could never die. He had been such a solid, loving presence in my life. In spite of what the nurse had said, my heart refused to believe he died so suddenly. I raged inside, believing I had let my dad down by not being at his side, holding his hand and telling him of my love as he had passed on. That's the way it should have been, my inner critic scolded. You should have told him how much you loved him, as he had always told you. You should have been there for him. It would have meant a lot to him. That's what you should have done! And I felt the relentless heaviness of guilt mingled with grief.

Knowing I'd been an attentive and loving daughter wasn't enough as the months and years wore on. Nothing made a dent in my stubborn conviction that I hadn't been there when he'd needed me the most.

Now a dream has set me free.

After a dozen years, my father came to visit me in a dream and tell me his side of the story:

You know I worked long past retirement age, and when my knees just couldn't carry me anymore, I felt disgraced by being so weak. Most of all, I never wanted you to see me as a helpless old man dying in a hospital bed. It would have hurt too much to have you there. So I'm telling you the truth, my darling daughter: I know you loved me as I loved you. And I did not want you there at my death, and I did not want you holding my hand when I died. That was what you wanted, not what I wanted. My death was perfect, just the way it was. There are two sides to every-thing—even death.

~Bobbie Probstein
Chicken Soup to Inspire the Body & Soul

66

Daddy's Garden

When I was little, I used to think my dad raked the maple leaves into a big pile so that we kids could dive into it and play. In those days, I thought the wheelbarrow that accompanied him to the back garden was meant for the rides he gave us back to the house. His flower garden at the side of the house was his special place of refuge—and it was there that his soul brushed mine to forever bond.

Daddy's garden was full of surprises. Rock paths led to goldfish ponds and little rooms made of evergreens and furnished with stone benches. Birdbaths stood in odd places, and a fountain surrounded by red geraniums and blue lobelia sent water music throughout the garden from an off-center mound in the lawn. As Daddy tended his garden, his gentleness and love radiated to the plants, which responded with luxuriant growth and color. Pulling weeds with him was never tedious, because his love radiated to me as well.

After I grew up and got married, I still spent many Sundays side by side with my dad—pruning, weeding, fertilizing, laughing, basking in the warmth of his unconditional caring. But as the years went by, I did more while he gradually did less.

Daddy's spirit stayed strong, but the feebleness of his eighties drove him to sell his property and move to a retirement community.

Before the new owner could bulldoze the garden, my dad helped me take samples of everything: the roses, the various perennials, the dahlias, the peonies, and even some of the rocks from the pathways. We took these—along with a birdbath, the fountain and a stone bench—and put them in my backyard where I made a miniature garden to echo my father's.

As I watched Daddy walk with his cane through our garden, I knew that every step was precious, every handful of earth he moved a gift, every rose he pruned a blessing.

At the retirement community, I tended my dad as he had tended his flowers. Every day, I had morning coffee with him, and in the afternoon I took him shopping. I organized his medicines and took him to piano concerts. In the spring, I drove him through the suburbs to look at other people's flower gardens or to my house to hear his own fountain singing with birds.

Two years into his new life, I held his hand as he passed away of pancreatic cancer. I felt his young, strong spirit with me, as if he was worried what his leaving would do. But his death could not break the bond between our souls, and I walked barefoot in the grass to receive comfort from the earth.

Now, years later, I still sense my dad beside me as I walk in my garden—the child of his garden. I can feel his enjoyment at the hummingbirds splashing in the birdbath. His laughter still echoes in my mind as I pull weeds from around the rosebushes. I carry his spirit in my heart, and with each flower that blooms, I know that he is with me.

~Linda Swartz Bakkar
Chicken Soup for the Nature Lover's Soul

67

Our Own Perfect Rainbow

Peace I leave you; my peace I give you.
Not as the world gives do I give it to you.
Do not let your hearts be troubled or afraid.
~John 14:27

Just when I thought there could be no way to comfort my two precious children, Robbie and Krista, only hours after burying their father, Davey, God delivered a special gift just for us.

The morning was cloudy and overcast with light drizzles, on and off. The funeral was behind us now. The only thought that raced through my mind was how to console my fragile children after all they had been through over the past few days.

My home was filled with close family and friends as we all tried to take care of each other at such an emotional time. Robbie and Krista were a priority for everyone in the house.

My father had taken the children to play in the backyard to give them a break from the chaos inside the house.

As each group of friends would leave, I would walk them to the front door to see them off. This particular time, we all walked out the front door to find the most amazing sight: The end of a rainbow was clearly in our front yard. We were astonished, to say the least.

Before I could catch my breath, my father and the children were calling from the backyard to come look at the beautiful rainbow in the backyard.

It couldn't be. I ran to the backyard to see that, indeed, the other end of the rainbow was in our backyard. I looked over the house to see the most perfect rainbow shooting its colors directly over our house—a complete, perfect rainbow right in front of our eyes.

There were no words to describe the warmth in my heart for what we were witnessing: a true gift from God. It was a sign to me that he was with us and that he was giving us his promise of the covenant between God and Earth.

As I tucked Robbie and Krista into their beds that night, Krista asked if her daddy sent that rainbow to her and Robbie. I couldn't help but think he had a little something to do with it.

We then thanked God for our own perfect rainbow.

~Liz Allison
Chicken Soup for the NASCAR Soul

68

My Dad

I think I was his favorite. My brothers and sister probably thought they were his favorite. He had the ability to make each of us feel special, even after we'd done something wrong. He didn't understand me as a teenager but knew enough not to try. He didn't offer advice unless I asked him and even then it was more of a soul-searching exercise with him. He knew I could figure things out on my own, without him, but I continued asking for his advice for as long as I could. My father and I shared a lot of similarities. We loved animals, liked the same movies, enjoyed the same adventures. We also shared the same commitment to our families—something that I learned from him.

My two brothers, my sister and I were raised in a very creative environment with many opportunities. Both my mother and my father were always there for us. They gave us the stability and the life that is so important for children. When I was about ten, I would try on my mother's wedding gown and my dad would run in from working in the yard, brush off his hands and play "The Wedding March" on the organ for me as I walked slowly down the stairs, believing my prince had come. We would do this over and over again until I got tired. He would never tell me he was too busy.

To see the way he treated other people and the helping hand he offered was a great gift to give a child. He forever wanted to stop and help people stranded on the highway. It was only because there were four tired kids in the car and my mother reassuring him that other people were stopping to help that my father could continue on. He also wanted to pick up hitchhikers, as he hated to see anyone needing something that he could give them. He felt it was our duty as citizens to help other people in need.

He was frugal but generous. He loved to have as many people as we could squish into our mountain cabin near Yosemite, and he was always baking. Pies were coming out of the oven as fast as anyone could eat them. He gave to many charities and sponsored children overseas. He was very proud of that and showed off the letters from those children whenever he could.

As I grew up, married and moved away from home, I realized the importance of having Dad in my life. He was still my rock—my stability, my security. The foundation that Dad provided for me had given me the opportunity to enjoy my marriage and my children. While many people cannot accept challenges or inconveniences in their lives, my dad taught me how to clear the hurdles that can cause complications in life.

And so it has happened. On the coldest day of the year in February 1996, my father passed away after battling cancer for almost a year. It's okay, though. After all, he wasn't thirty-five, forty-five or even fifty-five. He was a sixty-five-year-old man. His children were all happily married and living their own busy lives. He had eleven grandchildren and a great-grandchild on the way. Many people would say he had lived a full life. Which he had—but I still wasn't ready to let him go.

We worried about Mom going on without him. We worried that somehow our childhood chapter would close if he died. We worried that he would be in pain. He fought without complaining, and we now know he fought it for us. Battling lymphoma for ten months showed his four children the courage it takes to be a good father.

In his final days, we spent as much time with him as possible. In those few short months, I tried to pay him back for everything he had done for me in my thirty-six years. I wanted to do it all and could only do so little. Many days I just sat with him.

I believe he chose his night to die. All of us were in town. We had a big family dinner and I walked him to bed before I left that evening. I kissed him on his head and told him I would see him tomorrow. I know my brothers and sister left after me and went in to say goodnight also. They each had their moment: that last great moment. My mother had him in the end. As she walked him from the bathroom back to bed around 3:00 in the morning, he silently collapsed in her arms. She gently lowered him to the floor, put a pillow under his head and covered him with a blanket. That's how we saw him when we showed up minutes later, after my mother called us all together. My brother said that he heard it was the coldest day of the year, that day in February.

The days following his death just confirmed to me how important he was in my life and in the lives of my sister and brothers. Each of us has our special memories that are just of "me and Dad." As my life goes on he continues to help me make important decisions. Sometimes I can hear his voice. Standing in line to buy flowers for his grave one day, I could hear him so clearly saying, "Oh Brenda, don't buy those for me. Spend the money on yourself."

What's important for you to understand about me, Dad, is that in a way, I was spending money on myself. I've learned from you that doing things for other people is the best gift I can give to myself.

~Brenda Gallardo
A 5th Portion of Chicken Soup for the Soul

Dads & Daughters

The Power of Forgiveness

Only the brave know how to forgive;
it is the most refined and generous pitch of virtue
human nature can arrive at.
~Lawrence Sterne

69

Father Knows Best

Father!—to God himself we cannot give a holier name.
~William Wordsworth

I t went without question. I would take my walk down the aisle
alone.

As a young girl, I daydreamed that my natural father would
show up like "Wonderdad" on the day of my wedding, clad in a
tuxedo, ready to walk me down the aisle. In these naïve fantasies,
he'd have a justifiable excuse for not being in my life, and, of course,
I'd forgive him.

During my teenage years, the fantasy changed somewhat. Focus
on forgiveness for the father I'd never met was replaced by rebellion
toward the father I'd been given.

I had chosen to call my stepfather "Dad," and he had gladly
accepted that. But that decision was the only thing we ever agreed
on. In the perfect vision of hindsight, the road of disagreement
went both ways, but I only saw it as a one-way street—headed the
wrong way.

In the teenage daydream, l would stubbornly march myself
down the aisle, unescorted by anyone. It would be my proclamation:
I was an independent woman. I didn't need to be "Daddy's little girl."
Thankfully, I matured by the time I got engaged. "Revenge of the
Bride" was not the theme of the day. Our differences had faded over
the years, and we'd called an unspoken truce.

But the decision of anyone walking me down the aisle had
already been made for me, when shortly before my wedding, my dad

had his leg amputated. He used a walker, unable to endure the painful chafing and soreness that occurred from a prosthetic leg.

Our marriage ceremony took place at a park in our hometown where my fiancé, David, and I had played as children. It had a picturesque bridge over a shimmering lake with two swans swimming side-by-side, and the lush, green grass and weeping willows gave it romantic appeal.

Arriving in the limo, I tried to focus on the beauty around us. I made the bridal walk down the path, past my seated family and friends—alone. Until that moment, I hadn't realized I didn't want to walk alone anymore. True, my dad was never Wonderdad, and we never resolved the issues between us, but he was the only father I had. The path seemed to go on forever, but finally there I was, standing beside David, ready to become his wife.

When the judge asked the guests who gave this bride to be wed, I literally stopped breathing. We never did this during the rehearsal. Would my mom speak up? She and I never discussed it. I sent a quick prayer up to heaven, begging to avoid an embarrassing situation.

"Her mother and I do." I turned around and saw my dad, pulling himself up to a standing position despite the obvious discomfort and attention it drew. I searched his eyes, but they only stared straight ahead. Could it be he had thought of this moment before? Had he been disappointed in not walking me down the aisle?

For the first time in over twenty years, I considered the feelings of this man who I never thought of as a person. I'd made him out to be a monster. But he wasn't a monster. He may not have been the perfect daddy of my dreams, but he was the father I'd been given.

When I realized my dad wasn't going to meet my gaze, I turned to David and his reassuring smile, but I still felt a wave of guilt. I reminded myself there was no physical way my dad could have walked me down the aisle. But it was more than that. I should have seen him before as I did today.

As I stood at the base of the bridge, I noticed the sign across the lake: "Welcome to Lord's Park." The name hit me. We were in his park, in his hands. It was time to forgive both the father I'd been given and the father I'd never met. The Father in heaven knew what was best for me, even when I had no clue what that was.

I may have not been my daddy's little girl, but I had always been my Father's little girl. I hadn't made that walk down the aisle alone after all.

~Abigail R. Gutierrez
Chicken Soup for the Father & Daughter Soul

70

Chicken Soup for the Soul

The Miracle of Forgiveness

To forgive is to set a prisoner free and discover that the prisoner was you.
~Lewis B. Smedes,
"Forgiveness — The Power to Change the Past," Christianity Today

It was one of those hot, sweltering July days in Tennessee. I was going about my routine of laundry and housework, after putting on a pot of coffee, anticipating the usual Saturday morning visit from Dad.

Every morning, with the exception of Sundays, Dad drove from his house in town to my brother's farm, where he did daily chores. He had always loved farming, and staying active after his retirement was important to him. A few years earlier, I bought some property from my brother and built a house on his farm. It had become a Saturday ritual for Dad to stop by for a visit after finishing his chores.

Usually, Dad and I just sat and chatted about the latest family news while we sipped coffee. Sometimes he would give a little fatherly advice. I looked forward to our weekly visits. They had become a welcome source of comfort after my very painful divorce almost five years earlier. Mom and Dad were so wonderful during that difficult time. I don't know how I would have made it without the support of my entire family, who prayed for me and loved me unconditionally through all of my dark days. They stood by me even when I was wrong. I had been unable to forgive my dad for several years. I blamed him for everything that went wrong in my life. I reasoned that if he hadn't been so strict, so overbearing, so distant, so volatile, I would have turned out to be a better person. Maybe I would have made better choices as an adult if he had just taken the time to show me that he loved me. Maybe I would not have wanted to get married and leave home at such a young age.

After the divorce, I spent a lot of time with Mom and Dad. They were so different than I had remembered them twenty years earlier. They didn't judge me — they just loved me. I came to realize that my dad was only human, just like I was. I understood that he did the best he could as I was growing up, based on what he knew at the time. I also came to know that as an adult, I could no longer blame anyone but myself for the bad choices I made. Once I accepted all of that, the miracle of forgiveness occurred. Privately, I forgave my dad, and eventually, myself for making so many poor choices. I didn't have to make those mistakes anymore. I was able to move on with a new resolve in life.

As I looked out the kitchen window at my brother's cornfield, I breathed a prayer of thanks for all my family and special thanks for my fiancé, Dan. Our wedding was only a month away. I wondered what I had done to deserve so many blessings — a wonderful family, a fiancé who was everything I had ever dreamed of in a mate, a new house of my own. I loved my new life. Somehow, I didn't feel worthy, but God blessed me anyway.

With all these thoughts swirling in my head, my concentration was suddenly broken by the sound of a car door slamming in the driveway. Dad called out to me. I could tell there was something wrong by the sound of his voice. When I opened the garage door, there he was, staggering and breathless. His face was flushed and his eyes seemed unable to focus. He managed to say, "Something's not right... I'm not right...."

The doctors at the hospital in Nashville confirmed he was having a stroke. He underwent surgery to clean out a main artery in his neck to prevent another, possibly fatal, one. For the first several days, he required twenty-four hour attention. When the nurses told him not to get out of bed, he could not remember their instructions. His inclination to be active kicked in, and he repeatedly tried to get out of bed when the nurse left the room. It was like trying to put a jack-in-the-box back in the box. Each member of our family took shifts staying with Dad the entire time he was in the hospital to make sure he didn't fall and hurt himself.

During one of my shifts, I slept in a recliner next to his bed. He had to get up to go to the bathroom at least six times during the night. As I was helping him get back into bed for about the fourth time, he stopped and looked up at me with a helpless look in his eyes and said, "I'm so sorry you have to do this. I'm sorry for a lot of things." He stared into my eyes, as if to penetrate the message.

At that moment, I realized Dad didn't know I had forgiven him. My own father was uncertain about where he stood with me.

I said, "Dad, it's an honor and a privilege to take care of you." As I said those words, it seemed like it was someone else I knew who was so angry with him just a few years before.

Dad looked up heavenward and whispered, "Thank you, Jesus."

Then I knew that he had been praying for this miracle of forgiveness for years.

On my wedding day, tears streamed down my face when I saw Dad walk in the door of the church with his cane. God had granted us another miracle. At eighty-two, Dad was a survivor of the Great Depression, World War II, rheumatic fever, open-heart surgery, a stroke—and of raising me.

It was my turn to whisper, "Thank you, Jesus."

~Karen Davis Lees
Chicken Soup for the Caregiver's Soul

71

Never Too Late

The morning dawned sunny and warm; it was a perfect day for a wedding. All of the preparations had gone smoothly. My shining moment was near. My maid of honor had just begun her walk down the aisle, stepping in perfect time to the music. There I stood in a beautiful satin wedding gown my mother had so lovingly made for me. It was my turn. My heart filled with joy and anticipation as I stood ready to walk down the aisle toward my new life.

Then I saw my father, Ralph, stagger drunkenly toward me. I was sickened by the smell of alcohol on his breath. He nearly fell as he hooked his arm through mine. Within seconds, the "Wedding March" started playing—it was time to go.

So I did the same thing I had done so many times before—I faked it—just to keep up appearances. I glued on my best smile, mustered all my strength to hold my dad upright and then walked him down the aisle. Only when my dad was safely seated, and I stood at the altar holding my fiancé's hand, could I concentrate on the ceremony. For me, the most important part of my wedding had been ruined. I was angry, embarrassed and extremely hurt. I decided that day to never forgive my father.

My dad had been an alcoholic since I was a little girl. His drinking just snuck up on our family—starting quietly, but getting slowly worse each year. The escalating problem became very real for me one beautiful October day in 1963 when I was eight years old.

I sat on the back step of our home breathing in the fragrance of the autumn leaves and admiring the perfect blue sky. Then I saw my dad begin to load all of his belongings in the car. I looked up at him in disbelief and asked, "Daddy, where are you going?" With tears in his eyes, he answered, "I'm taking a job downtown and need to live there for a while. But I'll be back soon."

I held out a child's hope that he would return home one day. But his out-of-control drinking led to a divorce. He never moved back.

After that, I spent virtually every Saturday with my dad—all the way through my teen years. I wish I could say that those were happy days, but frequently they were spent waiting in the car while my dad went into the tavern to "make a few phone calls." My resentment toward him grew and continued to increase until that fateful wedding day.

My resolve never to forgive my father lasted for more than three years after my wedding. Then, something happened. On his seventy-first birthday, my dad visited a doctor to have a complete physical. Shocked at my dad's condition, the doctor told him, "Ralph, unless you quit drinking right now, you won't be alive to give your daughter away at her wedding." My sister's wedding was just six months from then.

Those words scared my father, so he checked himself into a thirty-day, inpatient alcoholic treatment center. Relieved he was finally getting the help he needed, my sister and brothers and I rallied around my dad to give him support. We attended family counseling sessions to learn more about the disease. Although I was supporting his attempt to get sober, I still felt a lot of anger toward him and was unable to forgive him for past hurts.

One day the physicians and counselors met with us and said, "Do not expect a miracle. Your dad is retired, lives alone and has been drinking for over forty years. He will relapse." So we didn't get our hopes up, but we did continue to pray for a miracle.

Then, one day, the miraculous happened. Dad called me and asked if he could meet with me. When we got together, the first thing he said was, "I'm sorry for all the pain I've caused you and the rest of the family. I know I don't have a lot of years left on this earth, but I want to live them sober." Dad took my hand, looked me in the eyes and asked, "Will you say the Lord's Prayer with me?"

Crying together, we held hands and prayed. As I recited the words of the prayer, I could feel the anger and hurt begin to melt away. The healing had begun. From that day on, Dad never took another drink. He read the Bible daily, joined Alcoholics Anonymous and became involved in a church. He frequently quoted scriptures to me and claimed only one thing was standing between him and alcohol: "Jesus." My own faith grew with each day of my dad's recovery. As my faith strengthened, my ability to forgive strengthened and I was finally able to let go of the past.

Dad remained sober for the next fourteen years and the miracle continued. At age seventy-two, he founded an alumni association for recovering alcoholics and typed an inspirational newsletter on an old typewriter, then mailed it out monthly to nearly one hundred people.

At age seventy-three, my dad helped organize an annual hospital event where hundreds of recovering alcoholics and their families gathered to celebrate their sobriety.

At seventy-six, he became a proud Red-Coat volunteer at a local hospital, delivering newspapers, flowers and encouragement to patients, and pushing the wheelchairs of new mothers holding new babies who were going home. Dad volunteered there until he was seventy-nine, when he became ill with prostate cancer and moved into a nursing home.

Instead of moping about his situation, however, he appointed himself "the ambassador" for the home. My father took newcomers under his wing, giving them tours of the place and showing them humor in every corner. On holidays, he occasionally called to say, "I'm going to be a little late today because some people here have no visitors—and I'm not leaving anyone alone on Christmas."

When my father died at eighty-five, my brothers, sister and I expected only a few people at his funeral, but over one hundred people came. Most were strangers to us, yet one by one, they shared their memories of my dad.

"Your dad is the reason my dad is sober today."

"Your dad is the reason my mom survived living in that nursing home."

"Your father is the glue that held our family together during our dad's drinking crisis."

Then seven men—all wearing red coats—quietly walked in to pay tribute to Dad for inspiring them to volunteer at the hospital. Many of them were over eighty years old.

Had I not removed the blinders of anger and resentment—had I not forgiven my dad—I'd never have witnessed the positive ways he had touched the world.

I know now that it's never too late to forgive.

~Debra J. Schmidt
Chicken Soup for the Christian Woman's Soul

The Haircut

Not everything that is faced can be changed,
but nothing can be changed until it is faced.
~James Baldwin

The ringing telephone pierced my peaceful silence as I relaxed in my living room. It was the admitting clerk at the hospital, calling to tell me that my mother was being taken there by ambulance.

When I arrived, they were wheeling Mom in on the stretcher. Her eyes were open in a blank, glazed stare; she could not move nor utter a single word. Mom had suffered a massive stroke. The doctor told us that any treatment would be futile and that death was imminent. As we watched in disbelief, she slipped from life to death in three hours. I was devastated and delirious with grief.

My parents had been married almost forty-two years. My mother had spent most of this time raising their ten children and trying to survive my father's alcoholism. Dad's problem had plagued our family. Mother's only solace was her faith in God and her commitment to her children.

Four years prior to my mother's death, my father retired, his drinking subsided, and their lives seemed less tumultuous. Somehow, after decades of abuse, there seemed to be more peace between the two of them and a lot less anger. It was as though she forgave him for the many years of sorrow and remorse.

But years of living with an alcoholic father had filled many of the ten of us siblings with anger and animosity toward him. We had not been blessed with the forgiving heart of our mother. Dad had been our cross to bear; Mom had been our savior. When we went to their house, it was to visit Mom; the fact that Dad lived there too was immaterial. When we called home, it was Mom we conversed with. We shared our hopes, dreams, future plans, sorrows, joys, heartaches and accomplishments with her. I guess we always knew she would relay all this information to Dad, but we never really sat down and had a meaningful conversation with him.

When Mom passed away, I was only twenty-two and living near my parents' home. It was difficult surviving without my vibrant mother. She had been the sun that could melt the winter snows, the electricity that could illuminate and enlighten my mind, the North Star as my guide to wherever life would lead me — and now she was gone.

Left here on Earth was my father. I had known for a long while that I was Dad's favorite. He was less harsh with me as a child than with my siblings. Perhaps it was because I was the youngest or maybe because I always tried to see a reason or find an explanation for the way he was. I prayed and trusted that God would make sense of a senseless situation. As I grew older, I learned to divide my father into two people: my sober father, whom I loved, and my alcoholic father, whom I treated as a stranger. This had become my key to survival.

One day not long after Mom died, I stopped by Dad's to see how he was doing. It was obvious that he was getting by, but not very well. He had learned to use the washing machine, vacuum, stove and microwave, but his menu included lots of hamburgers and hot dogs and barrels of coffee. It was also evident that he was in dire need of a haircut.

Mom had started cutting Dad's hair when they were first married. In forty-two years I don't believe he ever went to the barbershop. I spent hours watching her gently and lovingly cut and trim everyone's hair, with clippers, shears and comb in hand.

"Do you think you could cut my hair?" my father asked sheepishly.

Cowardly, I responded, "I've never cut hair."

"But you've watched your mother cut hair hundreds of times, so do you think you could try?" he pleaded.

I felt doomed. Why did it have to be me? Wasn't there anyone else who could fill these shoes? With grave reluctance I relinquished all my objections. I managed to utter only two words, "I'll try."

Dad retrieved the comb, scissors and clippers from the cupboard, and I began my feeble attempt. It occurred to me that I had never really "touched" my father, as we'd never been a hugging, touching family. I was even a bit embarrassed, not so much by my inept hair-cutting skills, but by my inability to cross the abyss that had always been present between my father and me.

Dad's graying hair was beautiful. Graceful waves gently covered up any mistakes I made. While I clipped away at his hair, carefully cutting around his ears and trimming with the clippers, we chatted about my son, my brothers and sisters, Mom, and the haircuts she had given over the years. This was truly the first real conversation I ever remember sharing with my father. As I finished, I trimmed his eyebrows and brushed the hair off his neck. He wet his hair and combed it — not a bad job after all.

Throughout the next few years, I became my father's barber. The job seemed to get easier with each attempt, and it was a ritual we both came to enjoy. Our conversations grew to include politics, religion, world affairs and what we would do if we won the lottery. He truly was a brilliant man and could talk for hours about the conflicts in the Middle East, China and Europe, giving insight into all the details and backgrounds of these events. He'd endured twenty presidential elections and subsequent administrations. His recollection of history and current world affairs was enviable.

Ten years passed. One day, when Dad was almost eighty, I visited him and cut his hair. When I had finished, he shyly asked if I might wash his hair in the kitchen sink. A bit embarrassed at first, I reluctantly agreed.

If I should live to be an old woman, I will never forget that day. It is forever imprinted in my mind. I can still see myself standing there at the kitchen sink, washing his beautiful gray curls, rinsing away all the many years of despair, anger and remorse. The washing, the touching, the healing, the forgiving between an old man and his loving daughter closed the abyss that had always been present between us. It would vanish that day like new snowfall on an early spring morning, to evaporate and disappear forever. The wounds that had festered for so long had finally healed; scars had been clipped, trimmed and washed away.

~Margaret J. Wasilewski
Chicken Soup for the Father & Daughter Soul

Behind the Mirror

Never does the human soul appear so strong as when it forgoes revenge,
and dares forgive an injury.
~E.H. Chapin

When I was a little girl, we lived in New York City just down the block from my grandparents. Every evening my grandfather would go for his "constitutional." During those summers of the mid-1960s I would join him for the walk, and he'd tell me how life was when he was a little boy.

As we walked past storefront windows reflecting the setting sun, he described a world of horses instead of cars, outhouses instead of flush toilets, letters instead of telephones, and candles instead of electric lights. As he pointed out all the hardships, my little mind wandered and I asked him, "Grandpa, what was the hardest thing you ever had to do in your life?"

I expected a tale of physical labor that those tough times demanded of him, but when Grandpa stopped walking and stared silently at the horizon I knew he was reliving an experience much harder than working long hours. He knelt down and took my hand. With tears in his eyes he began to speak.

"Grandma got very sick after your Aunt Mary was born. This was when your mom and your uncles were still little children. Well, Grandma had to go to a place called a sanitarium for a long time to get better. Since there was no one to take care of your mom and uncles, I had to send them to an orphanage where nuns could take care of them for me so I could work two and three jobs until your grandma got well. The hardest thing I ever had to do was put my babies in there. I went every week to see them, but the nuns wouldn't let me talk to them or hold them. I could only watch my children play from behind a one-way mirror. Sure, I brought them candy every week, but I could only hope they knew it was from me. I would keep both hands on the glass for the thirty minutes I was allowed to see them, hoping they would see me and come to touch my hand—but they never did. I endured a whole year without touching my children, but I know it was even harder for them. I'll never forgive myself for not making the nuns let me hold them. But they said I would do them more harm than good, and they would have even more trouble living there. So I listened."

I had never seen my grandfather cry before. He held me close, and I told him that I had the best grandfather ever and that I loved him. It was a strange and powerful reversal of roles, me reassuring him as he cried into my embrace.

We continued our walks for years until my family and grandparents moved to separate states. For fifteen years, that special walk with Grandpa remained our secret.

After my grandmother passed away, my grandfather began to suffer from memory lapses and bouts of depression. I tried to encourage my mother to let Grandpa come and live with us, but she and Grandpa had drifted apart.

One day, when I really harped on her to bring Grandpa back home, in a fit of rage she replied, "Why? He never cared about what happened to us!"

Little did she know, I knew precisely what she was talking about. "He has always cared and loved you," I said. "The hardest thing he ever did was put you and your brothers in the orphanage."

"You don't know what you're talking about!" my mother replied. "Who told you about that?" My mother had never discussed her days there with us.

"Mom, Grandpa told me that he came every week to see the three of you. He used to watch you play from behind the one-way glass. He used to bring you sweets every visit. He hated not being able to hold you for that year!"

"You're lying!" she snapped. "He was never there. No one ever came to see us."

"How could I know about the visits and the treats he brought if he didn't tell me?" I said. "He was there. He was always there. But the nuns wouldn't let him in the room with you because they said it would be too hard for you when he had to leave. Mom, Grandpa loves you and always has!"

I saw her eyes widen. She held her breath and then, suddenly, released it in a sigh that was almost a wail. Tears started to gather in the corners of her eyes. Suddenly, she realized that all along, years ago, Grandpa had stood behind that mirrored glass, hoping his children could somehow sense his presence, feel his love. The anger and sadness faded from her face. She could finally let the warmth and strength of his love get through the one-way glass.

Not long after, my grandfather came to live with us. At last my mom and Grandpa's love transcended the cold pane of glass that had remained between them for all those painful years.

~Laura Reilly
Chicken Soup for the Grandparent's Soul

Letter to a Stranger

If it were not for hopes, the heart would break.
~Thomas Fuller

"Y ou've got a letter from your dad." My husband's words stopped me on my way into the bedroom to change clothes. It was late in September, and we were already running late for the Friday night football game where our boys were marching with their high school band. We left the house a few minutes later, with the letter still sitting on the counter, unopened. I wanted to have a fun evening, yelling with the other band parents, not wondering and worrying about what the letter contained. And I did have fun—but I did wonder, and worry.

I had missed having my father in my life as a child. By all accounts, we had been extraordinarily close before the divorce. Most kids I knew in the sixties and early seventies had a dad, and being different was painful. Information regarding my father was always scarce. When Mom said anything about him, she just told me that he was a good dad. But the question always plagued me: If he was such a good dad, why didn't he want to see me? Whatever the reasons, I had seen my father a grand total of three times since second grade.

As the years went by, the emotions I felt about him ran the gamut: hurt, disappointment, anger, indifference. At one point, in my thirties, I wished secretly that he'd just die so that I wouldn't have to worry about him trying to come back into my life. I was doing well—a happy marriage, two children of whom I was extremely proud, a job that gave me satisfaction—why did I need a father?

But the years continued to pass, and though I still felt very angry at times, I found myself turning forty and wondering about him. Was he happy? Did he have other children? What had really happened between him and my mom? I asked a colleague who was visiting the town where I thought my father lived to check the phone book for his listing. She found his name and brought me his address. I carried it in my checkbook for six months.

A few months before my forty-first birthday, I wrote the letter I had been contemplating all summer. And rewrote it, and rewrote it. After all, the man was a stranger to me, and I to him. The finished product was short and matter-of-fact:

September 13, 1997

Dear Bill:

I apologize for calling you by your first name. I have no idea how to address you — everything I can come up with sounds too weird, so I hope "Bill" will be okay for now.

I don't have many questions, but they are the ones I need to ask. It may be that your ability to answer them is long gone — and if so, it's okay. You don't have to worry about starting something here that you might not want to finish. I really want nothing more from you than a few facts, but I'd particularly like to hear your side of things. But please, if you decide to answer, do it in writing. I don't think I'm ready for more than that right now.

It was a very self-protective letter, designed to minimize the hurt I felt sure was coming: no answer, or worse, a cool "thanks but no thanks."

That Friday night after the football game, I read:

Dearest Karen:

Wow, what a surprise to hear from you. Your question about why I did not keep in touch—I made a decision that it was better for you and your brother not to be sent back and forth between your mother and me. I now realize that was a wrong (underlined twice) decision. That was a long time ago. I miss you so very much, and only hope that someday I could be a part of your life again.

My love,
Your dad

There was more, of course, but I focused on those two parts; he was sorry he hadn't been a part of my life in the past, and he wanted to be a part of it in the future.

It took me a month to sort out my feelings enough to write again:

October 29, 1997

Dear Bill:

Truthfully, this father-daughter thing scares me to death. What if you're someone I don't like? Worse, what if I'm someone you don't like? What if we write a couple of letters and then you quit writing and it's like I'm five years old again? I guess it's about forgiveness. It requires no action on your part; I will be satisfied whether or not you ever respond again because I made the effort. I hope God will take the effort and make it into something good. I'm sorry if a writing relationship is less than you were hoping for. A year ago, even writing a letter would have freaked me out.

November 5, 1997

Hi Sweetheart:

The fact that you wrote back makes me feel so good, like the void in my life is starting to be filled. I do understand your feelings about me. All I can hope for is our starting to learn about each other will hopefully become a comfortable situation for us both.

His future letters were full of details about his happily married life and his past. In each one, he reiterated his love for me. Mine were a little more restrained, full of questions and misgivings:

November 13, 1997

Dear Dad: (I had progressed!)

I have to tell you that it was kind of uncomfortable for me to read that you love me. I mean, you don't really know me, so how can you know that you love me? But then, I thought about my children at five years old and knew that I would love them if I never saw them again. So it's a different kind of emotion for me; I can't say yet that I love you, or if I will. All I can say at this point is I, too, am full of emotions and want to continue to learn about you. I will leave the rest to God to work out.

We continued to write to each other, usually within a week of receiving the other's letter. We decided to meet after the holidays, and on Christmas Eve I spoke to my father on the phone for the first time in more than fifteen years. We both cried. On January 9, 1998, when I walked off the plane and saw his face filled with joy (and looking so much like mine), I knew God had indeed worked it out.

Now, I speak to my father almost every day, and our lives have become irrevocably entwined. Each conversation ends with "I love you," and now I believe that he means it, as I do. The anger I felt so often has mysteriously disappeared, and a wonderful sense of peace has taken its place. My life has been changed, in joyous ways I could never imagine, by that letter to a stranger.

~Karen L. Cooper
Chicken Soup for the Father & Daughter Soul

A Dance with Dad

A happy family is but an earlier heaven.
~Sir John Bowring

I am dancing with my father at my parents' fiftieth wedding anniversary. The band is playing an old-fashioned waltz as we move gracefully across the floor. His hand on my waist is as guiding as it always was, and he hums the tune to himself in a steady, youthful way. Around and around we go, laughing and nodding to the other dancers. We are the best dancers on the floor, they tell us. My father squeezes my hand and smiles at me.

As we continue to dip and sway, I remember a time when I was almost three and my father came home from work, swooped me into his arms and began to dance me around the table. My mother laughed at us, told us dinner would get cold. But my father said, "She's just caught the rhythm of the dance! Dinner can wait!" And then he sang out, "Roll out the barrel, we'll have a barrel of fun," and I sang back, "Let's get those blues on the run." That night, he taught me to polka, waltz and foxtrot while dinner waited.

We danced through the years. When I was five, my father taught me to "shuffle off to Buffalo." Later we won a dance contest at a Campfire Girls Round-Up. Then we learned to jitterbug at the USO place downtown. Once my father caught on to the steps, he danced with everyone in the hall—the women passing out doughnuts, even the GIs. We all laughed and clapped our hands for my father, the dancer.

One night when I was fifteen, lost in some painful, adolescent mood, my father put on a stack of records and teased me to dance with him. "C'mon," he said, "let's get those blues on the run." I turned away from him and hugged my pain closer than before. My father put his hand on my shoulder and I jumped out of the chair, screaming, "Don't touch me! Don't touch me! I am sick and tired of dancing with you!" The hurt on his face did not escape me, but the words were out, and I could not call them back. I ran to my room sobbing hysterically.

We did not dance together after that night. I found other partners, and my father waited up for me after dances, sitting in his favorite chair, clad in his flannel pajamas. Sometimes he would be asleep when I came in, and I would wake him, saying, "If you were so tired, you should have gone to bed."

"No, no," he'd say. "I was just waiting for you."

Then we'd lock up the house and go to bed.

My father waited up for me all through my high school and college years, while I danced my way out of his life.

One night, shortly after my first child was born, my mother called to tell me my father was ill. "A heart problem," she said. "Now, don't come. It's three hundred miles. Besides, it would upset your father. We'll just have to wait. I'll let you know."

My father's tests showed some stress, but a proper diet restored him to good health. Little things, then, for a while. A disc problem in the back, more heart trouble, a lens implant for cataracts. But the dancing did not stop. My mother wrote that they had joined a dance club. "You remember how your father loves to dance."

Yes, I remembered. My eyes filled up with remembering.

When my father retired, we mended our way back together again; hugs and kisses were common when we visited each other. But my father did not ask me to dance. He danced with the grandchildren; my daughters knew how to waltz before they could read.

"One, two, three and one, two, three," my father would count out, "won't you come and waltz with me?" Sometimes my heart ached to have him say those words to me. But I knew my father was waiting for an apology from me, and I could never find the right words.

As the time for my parents' fiftieth anniversary approached, my brothers and I met to plan the party. My older brother said, "Do you remember that night you wouldn't dance with him? Boy, was he mad! I couldn't believe he'd get so mad about a thing like that. I'll bet you haven't danced with him since."

I did not tell him he was right.

My younger brother promised to get the band.

"Make sure they can play waltzes and polkas," I told him.

"Dad can dance to anything," he said. "Don't you want to get down, get funky?" I did not tell him that all I wanted to do was dance once more with my father.

When the band began to play after dinner, my parents took the floor. They glided around the room, inviting the others to join them. The guests rose to their feet, applauding the golden couple. My father danced with his granddaughters, and then the band began to play the "Beer Barrel Polka."

"Roll out the barrel," I heard my father sing. Then I knew it was time. I knew the words I must say to my father before he would dance with me once more. I wound my way through a few couples and tapped my daughter on the shoulder.

"Excuse me," I said, almost choking on my words, "but I believe this is my dance."

My father stood rooted to the spot. Our eyes met and traveled back to that night when I was fifteen. In a trembling voice, I sang, "Let's get those blues on the run."

My father bowed and said, "Oh, yes. I've been waiting for you."

Then he started to laugh, and we moved into each other's arms, pausing for a moment so we could catch once more the rhythm of the dance.

~Jean Jeffrey Gietzen
A Second Chicken Soup for the Woman's Soul

Daddy's Story

The bitterest tears shed over graves
are for words left unsaid and for deeds left undone.
~Harriet Beecher Stowe, Little Foxes, 1865

Once, when we were children, my sister said, "Daddy will be home today."

"Who?" I questioned.

"Our father, silly. Remember, the man who's never here?"

"So what! I'll hardly see him anyway. How long will he not be here this time?" I said sarcastically.

"Who knows? You know Daddy," Bette replied.

And I thought to myself, No, I don't.

Noteworthy events of our lives are not the usual ones like birthdays and anniversaries. Sorrow sculpts us more than joy. Sorting through our lives we stumble upon the tough times — the times that teach us how to forgive.

My relationship with my father is one area of my life where I struggle to recall more than just a few happy times together. My sister, Bette, remembers good times with Dad. She was older, and I think he knew how to relate to an older child. He taught her how to play golf and gave her driving lessons. She thought he had something to do with hanging the moon. Their times together almost never included me, his other daughter. But the past can't be changed, just forgiven.

When I really needed a father's guiding hand during my teens, Mother and Dad divorced, and then he was gone for good. Eventually, he remarried, and a great person was added to our lives: his wife,

Elizabeth. Leave it to a woman to know how to rebuild a relationship with a man. And Liz did.

When he was diagnosed with cancer, I faced it knowing that the time left was precious. Deep within, I yearned to share some close, intimate time with my daddy before it was too late. I loved my father and knew, in his way, he loved me, too. But for both of us it was an undeclared love.

We asked Liz to tell us the best time for Bette and me to fly to California to see them. I definitely wanted to visit before it became a deathbed scene. Unfortunately, that happened sooner than I expected.

My heart was in my throat when I walked into Dad's living room and saw him sitting on the couch, frail, shaking and gray with weakness. The golfer, the World War II dollar-a-year man, the successful business tycoon, had been transfigured by illness. His strength was so depleted that Liz had to help him back to bed almost immediately upon our arrival.

On and off, all that weekend, we spent time at his bedside, discouraged. My plans for a one-on-one talk with Dad were fading fast, and I was sorely disappointed.

On our last evening there, Elizabeth came back from Dad's room and told us he was getting up, getting dressed and wanted to speak to us all together. I was unprepared for the man who, with good color and great strength, walked unaided down the hall toward us. His stride was sure and straight, as though some unseen power propelled him. It was hard to believe it was the same bedridden man I'd seen only hours before.

He took a deep breath, and when he spoke his voice was strong and steady. His eyes, no longer cloudy, were clear and direct as they fixed intently upon Bette and me.

Pausing cautiously between each sentence, he said, "Somewhere I've heard you can't change what you don't acknowledge. So here goes. I know I've fallen way short of being a good father to you. My own life and desires got in my way. I owe you an apology. So, before the man upstairs lets me go home, I need to say: I am so sorry. There are so many things I should have done that I didn't. I'd like to lay the blame on someone else—but there isn't anyone. The buck stops here. I can only hope you have enough love to indulge me and forgive your old man for all the times he's failed you. I know I don't deserve it, but I need your forgiveness." Then he paused, and for a minute tears choked his voice. "I've always loved you. It's a love you can take to the bank." Then he whispered, "I guess that's all."

We couldn't have taken more. Speechless and in tears, we hugged and patted him, mumbling our love. In the next minute, like flipping a switch, Dad again became the fragile, terminal patient. He was totally spent. I began helping him back to bed, almost carrying him down the hall, and for some reason Liz and Bette let me do it alone.

When we got back to his room, he sat on the edge of the bed as I knelt on the floor beside him. In a hushed voice he whispered, "Ruthie, did that help? Do you understand how much I love you?"

"Oh, Daddy, of course, I understand. I've never loved you more in my life." And for a little while we simply sat in the quiet. Finally, the child in me was holding tightly to her daddy's hand—an unforgettable moment.

Exhausted, he slept, and I lingered at his bedside, not wanting to break the newly found connection we'd made with each other. None of it completely answered my childhood questions about why he'd found the demands of fatherhood so difficult, but the adult daughter, mother and wife I'd become could understand what the child could not. His words had been like a medicine to me. I felt healed.

I'd had my longed-for special time with him. I wouldn't ask for more. There was forgiveness, and there was love. It was enough.

~Ruth A. Hancock
Chicken Soup for the Father & Daughter Soul

Dads & Daughters

Treasured Moments

*Certain is it that there is no kind of affection so purely angelic as of a
father to a daughter. In love to our wives there is desire;
to our sons, ambition; but to our daughters there is something
which there are no words to express.*
~Joseph Addison

77

I'm Daddy's Girl

I love my father as the stars—
he's a bright shining example and a happy twinkling in my heart.
~Adabella Radici

One evening not long ago, my husband stayed home with the children while I went to the grocery store. Shopping for a family of six when four of them are male takes a while, so it was late when I got home. When I walked back into the house, all was dark and unusually quiet. After setting down a bag of groceries, I tiptoed into the bedroom, lighted by the soft glow of the moon sifting through the window. Scott was lying there, his hands folded behind his head, staring at the ceiling. He seemed so pensive, I immediately thought something was bothering him.

"Hey," I said softly and sat down on the bed beside him. "What's the matter?"

"Aw, I was just thinking about my daughter," he grinned sheepishly. "And how much I love her."

Evidently, it had been a very good evening. "What happened with Rachel tonight?" I asked.

"Well," he sighed and searched for words to convey what he was feeling. "I had built a fire outside to burn some excess wood, and the telephone rang. It turned out to be a tough discussion with someone, and I was upset. So I went outside to unwind by the fire, and, before long, our little girl came out of the house and snuggled by my side.

"'Dad,' she told me, 'you look like you could use a hug.'" He paused briefly and breathed a contented sigh.

"She's my little sweetheart, you know."

"I know," I smiled as I rubbed the back of my husband's neck. "And I hope she always will be."

The next evening Scott came home from work and found me asleep on the couch. He woke me by tickling my nose with a long-stemmed red rose. Before I could properly gush over it, Rachel strolled in from her room, beaming from ear to ear, her strawberry-blond curls boing-yoinging happily as she plopped down on the sofa beside me. In her small, slender hands she held a lavender basket of fresh daisies and pink carnations. Tucked into the arrangement was a card in Scott's handwriting.

"Thanks for the hug," it read.

Rachel's brown eyes twinkled, and she smiled triumphantly in my direction. "You just got one flower. Daddy gave me a whole basket!"

~Becky Freeman
Chicken Soup for the Father's Soul

78

The Day I Met
The Splendid Splinter

My autographed Ted Williams baseball sat in my sock drawer for more than twenty years. It's not that I didn't want to display it. It was more like I was afraid someone might steal it or unwittingly throw it out as insignificant clutter. So I was quite unprepared for the day I opened my drawer and discovered that the prized possession had been defaced! There, in bright, bold indelible ink, my three adorable daughters, ages ten, eight and five respectively, had left their collective mark: "Carl Yastremskee Rules," "Your Pal Looe Tiant," "Babe Ruth Was Here," and other random scribbles.

It felt like someone had just pierced my heart. I was furious. If ever there were justification for punishment, surely defacing an autographed Ted Williams ball would qualify—especially with The Curse of the Bambino! As I tried to control my temper, I called for my daughters, and thought back to the day I met Teddy Ballgame....

I was just twelve years old in 1948, but remember the event like it was yesterday. My mother had just come home from the beauty parlor. She told me that Ted Williams' wife, Doris, had her hair done at the same salon. And miracle of miracles, she told my mother their home address. "He lives at Luceile Place," my mother casually mentioned, as if it was no big deal. How many kids in the world were lucky enough to have the greatest hitter of all time living less than two miles away!

Ted Williams was my idol. I followed his appearance in every game and could quote his daily batting averages and RBIs. I got into heated arguments with anyone who tried to tell me there was a better player, and even got into one playground fight with a kid who said that Johnny Mize was better. (In 1941, Ted Williams led the American League with a .400 batting average. He was given the chance to sit out the last two games of the season to preserve a mark that had not been equaled in over a decade. Of course, he refused, and in those games went six for eight at-bats, finishing the season for a .406 average. Even today, if it had not been for his call to duty in both World War II and Korea, I doubt that anyone could have eclipsed his record.)

In order to meet Mr. Williams, my timing had to be perfect. I had to make sure that the Red Sox team was in town and that he was home. So I chose a Saturday morning, grabbed a clean baseball and rode my J.C. Higgens bike uphill almost all the way. I told no other kids what I was doing. I knew that Mr. Williams could be difficult with the press and his critics, but I also knew that he liked kids. I hoped he wouldn't mind the intrusion.

I parked my bike outside his house, baseball in hand. As I stood at his front door and rang the bell, my knees were knocking. What would I say? Looking down, practicing my speech, I saw the door open. I looked up, up, up, and there he was, standing there, a giant of a man, smiling at me, a strange kid with a baseball in hand.

"P-p-pardon me, sir. I was wondering if you could sign my base-ball for me?" I stammered.

"Sure," he said. "Come on in!"

"Come on in!" He said, "Come on in!" I was in Ted Williams' hallway!

"Would you like a Coke?" he asked.

"No. No, thank you, sir," I managed to say. I was still in shock.

"How do you like the baby?" he asked, pointing to the adjacent baby carriage.

"Oh, he's alright I guess," I blurted out. (I later learned the "he" was, in fact, a "she.")

Mr. Williams laughed at my lack of gender sensitivity and signed my baseball. Then he walked me to the door and wished me good luck.

"Th-thank you, Mr. Williams," I said, still in shock.

The bike ride home that day was magical. When I reached my house I ran in to tell my parents about my adventure. They were hardly amused. Face red and arms waving, my father warned: "Don't you ever tell anyone what you did today, or they'll never give him any privacy. Do you understand me?"

"Yes sir," I said. And I kept my promise.

My mind returned to the present as I looked down at the now-colorful baseball in my hands, and up at the sheepish faces of my three artisan-daughters who stood before me. I realized that to them, Ted Williams was an unknown. In fact, the whole mystique of baseball was void in their world of Barbie dolls and fingernail polish.

I realized then that my girls needed a lesson about baseball: the joy you feel on opening day; the exhilaration you get when you hit another player home; and the kindness shown by a baseball idol who invited a kid in for an autograph.

"Want to know who the first person was to sign this ball?"

Months later, with my daughters' prodding, we organized a girls' softball team in our neighborhood. And while none of them ever made it to the major leagues, they learned a new respect for the game, and none of them has since defaced another baseball.

~Ted Janse
Chicken Soup for the Baseball Fan's Soul

A Musical Eye-Opener

Music is the art of the prophets, the only art that can calm the agitations of the soul; it is one of the most magnificent and delightful presents God has given us.
~Martin Luther

My father had been diagnosed with dementia and lived in a nursing home. He became ill enough to be admitted to the hospital so I stayed with him. He was confused and rarely spoke, but that didn't keep me from chatting away, trying to communicate with him.

One day I ran out of things to say, so I decided to sing. Unfortunately, I inherited my daddy's musical ability. Neither of us could carry a tune in a bucket. I crooned, "I love you. You love me. We're a great big family."

Daddy opened his eyes, turned, and looked at me. For the first time in days he spoke. "I love you too, honey," he said. "But you don't have to sing about it."

~Nancy B. Gibbs
Chicken Soup for the Caregiver's Soul

Daddy's Dance

I loaded the last of my retreat supplies in the back of my mini-van, then kissed my husband and son goodbye. Not only was I excited about the overnight ladies' retreat where I would be speaking, but I had mapped out a driving route that took me right through the town in which my parents lived. I planned to stop and spend a few hours with them, welcoming any opportunity to visit my mother and father, now eighty-three and eight-six years old. But often the visits were difficult.

Daddy was in the throes of Alzheimer's disease and his compre-hension and communication were severely impaired. The progres-sion of the illness was devastating, especially to my mother, his mate of sixty-six years. She was now more a caregiver than a wife, and often Daddy was unable to even recognize her face. I grieved for both of them as well as myself. I wasn't ready to let go of the father I had known forever... so full of life—smiling, singing, joking, laughing. Where had he gone? How did those "tangles" in the brain rob him of words, faces and places?

Many times Mama wanted to tell me of personal incidents, thinking I would understand, being the mother and caregiver of an adult son with special needs. But I didn't want to hear humiliating details of Daddy's debilitating disease. This was still my father; the man who held me on his lap and rocked me as a child; put me on my first horse to ride and taught me to drive in an old 1948 Ford pickup truck. This was the daddy who used to show up unexpectedly at my college dormitory to bring me home on weekends when he thought

I had stayed away too long. There was no way to divorce myself from those memories, nor did I want to. I held them close to my heart.

Once, when I presented him with a framed picture of me, Mama asked, "Do you know who's in that picture?" He smiled and pointed directly at my face and said, "That's my baby." Indeed, I would always be his baby girl.

But today, after arriving at my parents' home, Daddy gave me a quick hug then went to the bedroom to take a nap while I sat at the kitchen table with Mama. She spilled out her fears, resentment and pain. She had no idea how to cope with Daddy's anger when she didn't fulfill his requests. How could she possibly know what he wanted when she couldn't understand his words or gestures?

Because of my own son's lack of communication, I could identify with her frustration, but it seemed harder for my mother. This was her husband and it wasn't supposed to be this way. This was the time she had dreamed of traveling and relaxing after many years of hard work.

Daddy got up several times from his nap to make trips to the bathroom, always requiring Mama's help with snaps and zippers on his clothing. Neither of them liked this situation and both were argumentative and irritated with each other.

Finally, I left for the retreat, but my heart was heavy.

As I drove, I thought of the anger, fatigue and emotional pain that my parents were experiencing and wondered if they ever had a happy moment. I loved them and wanted to help, but had no idea what to do. As I guided the car along the highway I prayed for peace, harmony, love, health, and even joy in their lives.

The retreat provided a refreshing respite for my body and soul, and I was in great spirits as I headed back home. Again, I stopped for a visit with my parents, hoping things had improved.

I pulled into the driveway just ahead of my brother and we congregated in the living room with his guitar. Monte played and sang several songs; then Mama and Daddy joined in. By the time they hit the old hymn, "I Saw The Light," Daddy was singing every word from memory and smiling from ear to ear. I sat in awe as I watched his whole countenance change.

Suddenly, Daddy, who normally shuffled and slumped when he walked, jumped up from the couch and began to dance a jig to the music, his face alive with pure joy and fun. Then he put his hands out toward my mother. She stood up and together they two-stepped across the living room floor, both of them laughing and gliding like I remembered them doing when I was a child.

I sat clapping my hands in time to the music and wiping away tears. I had forgotten how much music had been a part of our family while growing up. I couldn't count how many times Mama and Daddy had stood beside our old upright piano and sung while I barely plunked out a melody. Daddy also led the singing at our little country church and even sang while he worked in the fields, often letting me ride on the horse's broad back while he guided the plow behind. My mind was flooded with wonderful memories. Good times and hard times, but happy times.

Soon Daddy plopped down on the couch, a smile still lighting up his face.

I left for home with a new peace and joy in my heart and again prayed for my parents while I drove, thanking God for allowing me to witness the love and happy times they still enjoy.

I know there will still be hard times in the future. But I'm thankful for this beautiful memory and reminder to celebrate every moment in life — perhaps, even dance in it.

~Louise Tucker Jones
Chicken Soup for the Caregiver's Soul

81

Turning Back the Clock

The bounce has been missing from my dad's step. Illness has invaded his body and spirit. He is eighty. Yet, this seems so sudden. Now I know the ache of the thought: If only I could turn back the clock, just for a day.

Besides his family, my dad has always loved a good joke, the San Francisco 49ers, playing cards and, "best of all," golf. His swing is one of his better jokes—a marvel of mistakes he makes work. "I really synchronized my jerks that time!" he says.

Searching through the misty barriers of age and gender, fathers and daughters sometimes catch only a glimpse of one another. Not us. The morning I quit piano lessons, my mother—the daughter of a music teacher—cried right into a box of Cheerios. She could only watch as I grew more like my father every day. Relatives say when I play cards I even tap my fingers on the table exactly as he does. When I was little, we had "our song." He would sing it, and we'd laugh ourselves silly:

We belong
To a mutuaaaalllll
Ad-mir-a-tion So-ci-e-ty,
My buddy and me.

Now we are a thousand miles apart in geography, politics and much else. But we are still buddies. We share the most enduring bond of all.

We are golf buddies.

A little more than a year ago, my dad experienced the first of many setbacks in his battle against cancer. All of us wondered if the end was near.

Shortly thereafter, I flew to San Francisco and talked him into a leisurely round at the Olympic Club. I thought just being out on the course would boost his spirits. And there was this other motive: I was playing the best golf of my life, breaking 90 the first time just two weeks earlier.

Once a steady 80s/90s player, Dad had never seen me play this well. I was wild to take his money and win his approval. With the same predatory DNA swirling in our cells, we always played for money. Over the years I'd lost nearly enough Nassaus to reimburse my college tuition. My dad says of this, "Want to earn forty thousand dollars the hard way?"

He delighted in being my mentor as well as my cutthroat opponent. I am convinced his parting words to me will be "Pull down with your left!"

That day at Olympic, I would have to give him strokes. What a proud day it would be for us both, I thought.

Well, he wasn't nearly as excited as I thought he'd be. Our golf date fell on his seventy-ninth birthday. But neither that, my new-found handicap nor a sunny San Francisco day could summon a smile. We began the round chatting sorrowfully about how his treatment sapped his strength, how he hated never breaking 100 anymore. Then it appeared to me he got down to business. He had 1-putt par on the first hole, while I gasped away with an 8. After that, he started holing out from everywhere. I'd never seen him putt better.

While my score was rising, his jerks were synchronizing. Time after time, he flailed his driver straight up in the air, his body shaking in every direction like Jell-O molds. Before I could even venture a laugh at the sight, THWACK, he'd look up and laugh at himself.

He began trotting back to the cart, urging me to do the same before I'd even completed my swing—just like when I was twelve. "Never up, never in!" he chirped for the hundred-millionth time as I dabbed a dainty putt four feet short. From some unknown place, a laugh rose up out of me.

With an all-too-familiar glow on his face, he totaled up the damage. A 96 for him; 114 for me.

It was exactly like twenty years ago.

Later, above the clouds on a plane to Seattle, I thought of my dad's deteriorating health. I wondered, for the first time, if I'd ever see him again. Then I recalled our game, how bizarre it was that he played so well—and I so poorly—and how much fun it had been. Suddenly, it was as clear as the sky in front of me. On the golf course, on his seventy-ninth birthday, we were given a magical gift. Someone let us turn back the clock, just for a day.

~Betty Cuniberti
Chicken Soup for the Golfer's Soul

82

Naming Worms

I think my dad wanted a son. Instead, he got three daughters. Seeing as how the son he anticipated was never forthcoming, Dad decided to improvise and I, being his youngest, won the privilege of being nurtured outdoors.

Being turned into a tomboy didn't bother me in the least. I loved putting on my plaid, flannel shirt and doing things outside with Dad, especially fishing. Whether we oared across a lake in a rowboat or hiked down a cliff with nothing more than a hook and some string, I could think of no better way for a dad and his little girl to spend the day.

I would marvel at how patient and focused Dad was when he fished. He would concentrate on his line for hours at a time. If he was any more calm, he would have slipped into a coma. This used to drive me bananas. Being seven years old, I craved more excitement. I imagined a huge fish, bigger than me, gulping down my bait and flapping ferociously in the water until I heroically hauled it into the rowboat. This never happened. Instead, I would spend my time watching Dad as he stared intently at his line. He never blinked, sometimes for the whole day. How could he be so patient?

One day Dad's patience was put to the test when my fascination shifted from the fish to the bait. While waiting for a nibble on my line, I peeked into the can of worms we had in the rowboat with us. I dug my little fingers into the moist soil and pulled a resisting worm from his burrow. I let him squirm (I decided it was a "he") across my hand. It tickled. I took another worm from the can. Then another. Then another. Soon, three or four worm heads popped out of the soil to see what all the commotion was about. I was in love.

I felt as though I had made a can-full of new friends who would keep me company during these long, uneventful fishing trips. Each worm was given a name according to his personality. When you are seven years old, worms have personalities. There was something endearing about my mucous-covered companions with no faces. I promised each of them that not one would be put on a hook and fed to the fish.

Then disaster struck. Dad pulled Hamilton out of the can. I gasped in horror as he attempted to manipulate his poor, writhing body onto a hook. There was a terrified look where Hamilton's face would have been, if he had a face.

"Daddy, No! Don't put Hamilton on the hook! He's my favorite!"

Dad raised an eyebrow. "You named the worm?" he asked in disbelief.

Exhaling and shaking his head, Dad pulled out another worm. It was Wigglesworth. He was the skittish one who was particularly worried about being used as bait. I had made a special promise to him and could not possibly allow the poor little guy to be hooked, for I was a woman of my word.

"That's Wigglesworth! Don't hurt him!"

Dad's frustration grew as he pulled more worms from the can. First Winthrop, the shy worm. Then Slimey, the friendly worm. And Marvin the show-off. Finally, Dad pulled out Maxwell, Sammy, O'Reilly, Buster and Doug. Dad groaned as I pleaded for him to not hurt my friends.

"Don't tell me you named all of the worms in this can."

With a sheepish nod, our fishing trip was suddenly over.

The next day, Dad drove into town and picked up a bucket of crawfish. When he brought them back to the cottage, I opened the lid and peeked in. I heard a despairing yelp emerge from his throat — I turned around to see him running frantically toward me, with his arms flailing and a look of terror on his face.

"No! You have to quit making friends with the bait!"

~Allison McWood
Chicken Soup for the Fisherman's Soul

Who Giveth?

The problem with children is that you have to put up with their parents.
~Charles DeLint

A cozy kitchen may not seem like the most romantic setting for a Christmas Eve proposal, but it didn't stop me from whispering "Yes" as Tom slipped a diamond ring on my finger.

But when he announced our engagement to my parents, the atmosphere in the living room was not quite as comfortable. After an interminably long silence, my father said, "I suppose she said 'yes.'" Tom, taken aback, nodded tentatively.

"Well, Tom," Dad said, "I think you should know I never give anything away cheerfully."

Although we realized his response had nothing to do with Tom but everything to do with a father's reluctance to part with his youngest offspring, it was definitely an uncomfortable moment. Mother broke the tension with expressions of joy.

Over the next months, Dad observed our wedding preparations from the sidelines. By May, he was fitted for his wedding attire, apparently reconciled to giving me away.

However, a month later, when our entire wedding party gathered in the kitchen for a late-night snack following the evening rehearsal, Dad was unusually quiet amid the chatter.

"I can't do it!" he finally burst out.

"Can't do what?" we all chorused. I caught my breath. Surely he wouldn't refuse to give me away at the last minute.

At long last, his voice broke the awful silence. "When the minister says, 'Who giveth this woman?' I can't say, 'I do.' I think I should say, 'Her mother and I do.'"

With deep sighs of relief, we assured him that he should say whatever felt right.

Our wedding day dawned bright and sunny. As we waited in the vestry of the old, gray stone church, the clear notes of my sister's final solo, "O Promise Me," rang out. When the organist struck the opening chords of the wedding march, I took Dad's arm. Together we walked down the center aisle.

Step, pause. Step, pause. A photograph of the moment shows me as a radiant bride; Dad was not smiling. All eyes were on us as we approached the altar and my handsome groom.

"Dearly beloved, we are gathered here..." the pastor began. Looking directly at Dad, he posed the question. "Who giveth this woman to be wedded to this man?"

Dad was ready. He never missed a beat.

In clear, measured tones, he replied, "Her mother."

With that, he placed my hand in Tom's, turned and took his place beside my astonished mother in the front pew.

Just as he'd vowed from the beginning, Dad didn't give me away cheerfully. Or—for that matter—at all!

~S. Maitland Schrecengost
Chicken Soup for the Father & Daughter Soul

84

The Anniversary

Watching your daughter being collected by her date feels like handing over a million dollar Stradivarius to a gorilla.
~Jim Bishop

My wife and I celebrated our seventeenth anniversary the other day. Not in commemoration of our wedding, but in recognition of our first date (we were high school sweethearts). And, as we were reminiscing, I admitted that our relationship almost never got off the ground.

"What do you mean?!" my wife demanded.

I smiled. "I was afraid of your dad."

The man was, and still is, huge. He was the proverbial father teenagers would look at and say, "I'M GOING TO DIE!"

"But you were brave, for me," my wife said sweetly. "What did you do when you knocked on my door? Did my dad answer?"

"All dads answer the door on first dates," I replied. "If I remember it right, my tongue swelled up in fear and I almost suffocated to death."

"Did my dad say anything to you?"

"No, he just stood there staring at me. I think he thought I was raising money door-to-door for the mute."

"Why do you think that?"

"He gave me a dollar."

"Well, apparently, you were okay—he let us go out, didn't he?"

"True," I replied. "But before we left, he looked at me, then he looked at you, and then he looked at my car."

"Why?"

"It was like he was telling me a little story through telepathy."

"What was the story about?"

"A horny high school student who now walks with a limp."

Her eyes flashed with a sudden realization. "Is that why you never held my hand in front of my dad?"

I nodded. "I was afraid he was going to say something."

"Like what?"

"Like, 'Hey, Romeo, do you want to keep that arm?'"

Of course, our first date was nothing like a week later when I went over to my future wife's house. It was the day before I was set to leave for spring vacation with my family. Her parents were gone, so, like high school kids do, we necked on the sofa.

Next thing I know, her parents are rolling into the driveway an hour earlier than planned. With my hair tousled about, I start going nuts, shouting "Our Father, who art in heaven," while my future wife was behind me spitting into her hand and smoothing down my cowlick.

Positioning myself on the couch to look as if I had been reading an interesting *National Geographic* article on apple maggots, her dad walks in and proceeds straight to the living room like a bounty hunter.

"Hi," I said, greeting him like a hoarse soprano. I would have also waved, but I got a paper cut from clutching the magazine like a life preserver, and I was trying to stop the bleeding with a linen doily.

Finally, as beads of sweat were rolling down my neck, the giant spoke in his deep, dark voice: "So, when are you leaving, Ken?"

"Right now," I answered, jumping up to go.

He looked at me for a moment, and then started laughing. "I meant on vacation."

"My dad still loves to talk about that," my wife remarked.

I can only hope to be half as scary when my daughter starts dating.

~Ken Swarner
Chicken Soup for the Romantic Soul

85

Secret Ingredients

I press "play" on the VCR and sit back to watch the ten-year-old video. On it was my kids' attempt to record my father's secret ingredients as he prepared our annual Christmas meat pies.

"Hi, Mom." I see myself looking out of the screen, gesturing for Lisa to aim the camera at her grandfather instead.

"Hi, Grandpa," she says next as the camera sweeps in his direction.

My dad nods in acknowledgement while he pries open the lid of a spice can.

"Mom, what are you doing now?" The camera swings back to me.

"The hard part, as usual." I make a production of stirring the meat in a large pot. "Dad, don't strain yourself shaking that spice can," I tease over my shoulder.

We're making meat pies—my family's holiday tradition.

As an adolescent, I was not particularly close to my father. After driving a delivery truck and unloading heavy packages all day to support our large family, he barely had energy left to talk to me, except to ask me to get him another beer from the fridge or go buy him a carton of cigarettes.

But one Christmas, he expressed a desire to make meat pies like his mother had. Although he could figure out the filling, he didn't have a clue about the crust. Then my junior high home ec teacher gave me a recipe for no-fail pastry.

Mustering my courage, I approached Dad and suggested we team up and experiment with the pies. Much to my delight, he agreed to give it a shot.

I began the pastry crust in the morning. Following the instructions precisely, I blended the dough while Dad sautéed the meat in a large pot—equal amounts of ground chuck and ground pork. He added onions and then debated on the spices.

They were the tricky part. Allspice, savory, sage, thyme, cloves, salt and pepper. He added them all on instinct, guessing at the amounts. The meat simmered and teased our noses.

Meanwhile, I successfully rolled out the crust and placed it in a greased and floured pie plate. I held the empty pie shell close to the pot while my father ladled in bubbling meat. When we judged it full enough, I positioned the top crust, crimped the edges with the tines of a fork, brushed it all with milk, and popped it into the oven. We put together several for dinner.

The aroma of baking pies was encouraging. By the time they were done, the whole family was salivating. But, would the meat pies taste as good as they smelled?

Dad placed a slice on each of our plates. The pastry flaked when our forks cut through it. Then the first taste: eyes closed, nostrils flared, smiles appeared and a unanimous "mmm... mm" resounded around the kitchen table.

"This is really good," Dad winked at me, "but I think the meat is the best part."

"Oh, really? I don't think so," I teased back. "The crust is delicious; the meat is a close second."

The bantering continued until we finally agreed that neither would be any good without the other. I glowed with pride. We had worked—side-by-side—to replicate the old family recipe, my dad and I.

That was the start of our Christmas tradition.

As he aged, it became more difficult for my dad to do his part. Some years we made as many as fifteen pies and stirring such a large pot of meat was not an easy task. Finally, I recruited my children, Brian and Lisa, as our kitchen assistants.

One year, Dad got pneumonia and never fully recovered. The Christmas after he died, I couldn't bear the thought of making meat pies. Besides, they wouldn't be the same without his secret seasonings. But Brian and Lisa insisted we continue the thirty-five-year-old holiday ritual.

Forcing my mind to the present, I focus again on the video, curious to see what he adds to the pot.

But Dad smiles now from the television screen while he scrapes the last of his savory meat into a pie shell. As I struggle to position the top crust on this final, skimpy pie, someone off-camera suggests it should be for Uncle Bruce, who's always first in line to get his.

"Here, let me spit on it." I wink. "I hope he's not watching this video." Everyone laughs and the screen goes white.

Silence.

It occurs to me that I hadn't noticed a single label on the spices Dad used in the video. Yet a huge grin sweeps across my face when I realize we'd captured the secret ingredients after all.

The secret wasn't in the seasonings. It was in the people. The teasing and joking. The laughing and loving. And I know it was the working together—side-by-side—that made our Christmas meat pies so special.

~Jane Zaffino
Chicken Soup for the Soul Christmas Virtues

One for the Books

July, 1972, promised to be a special time for my family. My husband Hank and I had recently moved to Maine and bought a home, and that summer we rented a cabin on a prime fishing lake. Best of all, my parents were flying up from Georgia to visit us.

We could hardly wait to take Dad fishing. He didn't believe me when I told him over the phone, "The fish up here just about jump in the boat and beg, 'Fry me!'"

Hank and I met Mama and Dad at the airport on one of those perfect Maine summer days. Dad and I talked about fishing all the way back. Mentally, we had our hooks baited by the time we reached the cabin. We had planned a big fish fry for that evening.

Suitcases unloaded and gear quickly stowed in the boat, Hank, Dad and I set out for my secret fishing spot. The fish didn't disappoint. Whooping and laughing, we were pulling in silver perch like no tomorrow.

"Didn't I tell you, Dad?"

"I've been trying to scratch for ten minutes," he said. "Can't 'cause there's always a fish on my line. Itchy nose. Must be somebody coming to visit."

There was!

I looked up to see a Maine State Game and Fisheries boat easing toward us. I felt sick. I hadn't thought to buy Dad a license. When the warden reached out to pull our boat closer to his, I felt as if I'd just been nabbed for bank robbery. Hank gave me the "don't panic" look.

"Sorry, Hank, but I always panic when I get my dad arrested!" I said.

The warden was pleasant, but firm. "Good spot you found here. Mind if I check your licenses?"

Hank whipped his out. The warden checked it, nodded, then turned to me. I shrugged.

"No pockets in this bathing suit. Mine is back at the cabin," I explained as I felt tears starting to well up. He was going to ask for my dad's next. My dad—high school principal, pillar of his community, deacon in his church—had unwittingly committed a crime, and I was to blame.

The warden's gaze shifted.

"Sorry, but I don't have one," Dad said. "Just got in from Georgia."

"Can't fish in Maine without a license. I'll have to write you a citation." The warden glanced at me, looking sorry for disrupting our day. "Toss 'em all back in the lake, then we'll go over to the cabin and check yours, ma'am."

Our perfect day was ruined. I couldn't have felt more miserable, more guilty. Once we were on our way back across the lake, Hank told me that Dad would have to pay a small fine, but no real harm was done. I believed him and got myself under control.

My feeling of momentary ease vanished the minute the warden said to my dad, "Your court appearance will be next Wednesday over in Bath."

On Wednesday, Dad and I arrived early at the historic courthouse. We were both nervous, but at last the time had come. Now we could get our legal problem over with and enjoy the rest of the summer—if Dad was not behind bars for the duration of his Maine vacation.

We sat through several other cases—a speeding motorcyclist, a deadbeat dad, a shoplifter. The white-haired judge was handing down stiff sentences. He took no guff from the offenders and seemed totally devoid of sympathy. Not a good sign. I figured the judge wouldn't see Dad's offense as simply fishing without a license. No, he would more likely brand Dad a "perch murderer."

Our game warden appeared to read the charge.

The judge said, "Mr. Lee, I want to hear what you have to say for yourself. Approach the bench." It didn't sound like a friendly invitation.

My dad was a talker. He could tell a story like no one I've ever heard. But as he stood before the judge, he remained silent. Not a word, not a whisper in his own defense.

Finally, the judge said, "Mr. Lee, I don't know how you people down in Georgia do things, but in the state of Maine fishing without a license is against the law."

Dad nodded meekly and replied, "I know that now, Your Honor."

"You didn't know it before?"

"No, Your Honor. In Georgia, senior citizens aren't required to buy a license to fish."

This seemed to interest the judge since he was a senior citizen himself. He almost smiled, I thought.

"Where exactly are you from in Georgia?"

"Brunswick, Your Honor. It's on the mainland, close to St. Simons, Jekyll, and Sea Island. You've probably heard of the place."

"Heard of it? I've been there. There's a restaurant right at the causeway to St. Simons. Best fried shrimp I ever ate."

Dad nodded and grinned. "Yes sir, I eat there often myself. Did you try their oyster stew?"

A lengthy discussion followed about the seafood restaurant, fishing techniques along Georgia's coast and the rights that all senior citizens should have. I could tell that Dad had forgotten he was in court. He had simply found in the judge a fellow fisherman.

Handing the judge one of his cards, Dad said, "The next time you're down our way, you give me a call. I'll buy you a shrimp dinner. I'll even take you out in my boat for some real fishing."

Someone came in and whispered into the judge's ear, obviously advising him to speed things along. He brought down his gavel for order, then said, "Mr. Lee, you being a senior citizen and a visitor to our fair state, I'm going to let you off with a warning and release you into the custody of that pretty daughter of yours. Now you get her to take you straight from this courtroom to buy a fishing license. And good luck on the lake this afternoon."

The crowded courtroom burst into applause. Even our game warden clapped. The judge motioned me forward to take custody of Dad.

For the rest of Dad's life, he told and retold the story of his one and only day in court. It turned out to be the highlight of his trip to Maine that long-ago summer.

As per the judge's instructions, we got that fishing license, headed for the lake and caught enough silver perch to have our fish fry that night.

~Becky Lee Weyrich
Chicken Soup for the Fisherman's Soul

We Are Dragon-Slayers

*I cannot think of any need in childhood as strong as
the need for a father's protection.*
~Sigmund Freud

Most knights wear chain mail and carry shields. Not me. My armor consists of boxer shorts and an old T-shirt with a hole under one arm. I am clumsy, not gallant.

I hear the princess scream, as I had dozens of times before — and always when I am sound asleep. Instinctively, I jump out of bed in the dark. It's only 2 A.M. My eyes don't focus. I put my arms in front of me to keep from walking into the door. I stub my toe and curse under my breath. My hand slides along the banister railing, guiding my path. I hear the princess scream again.

I quicken my pace and grope for the doorknob as I enter her room.

"Daddy, the dragon!" she cries.

I rub my eyes as I kneel down next to her bed, trying to focus on her small face.

"Is it the dragon from *Sleeping Beauty*?" I ask.

"Yes," she says with tears in her eyes. I hate this dragon more than the rest of the beasts that torment my daughter at night. While a crocodile or other monster may attack her now and again, the dragon from *Sleeping Beauty* torments her most often. Some of the lesser beasts flee as soon as I enter her room, but not this one. It towers above me and sneers. I smell its hot, stinking breath blowing down on me, but I realize it's my own breath I smell.

Empty-handed, I prepare for battle. No mace. No sword. No lance. I know what dragons fear most. I'd learned the art of dragon-slaying from my parents, both of whom were experts. I use many of their techniques. Dragons and other assorted monsters tormented me as a child. I trembled in bed and watched as my mom and dad quickly dispatched them.

Now I put my hand on the small of my daughter's back and slowly rub in circles that get larger and larger. Dragons hate backrubs. But what terrifies them most are happy thoughts.

"Think about Christmas and going to the beach," I say to her groggily. "Think about Easter and making snowmen. Think about eating ice cream."

I watch the dragon quake at my words. He is severely wounded but flees before I can finish him off. He always runs so that he can come back another night. And he will come back. He always does—sometimes in the same night. But, for the time being, he is gone, and my princess closes her eyes and falls back to sleep.

My personal record is six dragons in four hours. Between dragons four and five, I woke up on my daughter's bedroom floor. Either I'd fallen asleep while rubbing her back, or dragon four had landed a blow and knocked me out. I just remember feeling exhausted.

If you saw me on the street, you wouldn't guess that I am a knight. You'd probably think, There goes a balding, out-of-shape dad who's pushing forty. Perhaps you are a knight, too, in our secret society. We disguise our identities by working as accountants and factory workers during the day. We have jobs in offices and construction sites. We don't brag about our exploits. We are humble.

And, if, while dragging yourself out of bed after a night deprived of sleep, you become discouraged, repeat the refrain of the dragon-slayer: When the sleepless night seems endless, and you are exhausted and irritable, remember that your sacrifice is worth more than sleep. The tender care you give your daughter is not simply to help her rest in slumber. Your actions teach her to raise her own children—with unlimited patience and selfless love. You are raising the next generation of dragon-slayers.

Remember these words because it is often difficult to feel virtuous when you're standing in the dark in your pajamas.

And, each evening, as you go to bed, prepare for battle. When your princess cries, you will be ready. You are a dragon-slayer.

~Timothy P. Bete
Chicken Soup for the Father & Daughter Soul

Summer Memories

The sun was barely peeking above the mountains when we arrived at the harbor. Once we had gathered our gear, purchased fishing licenses and paid for the rental boat, the two of us headed for the dock. I couldn't help but notice the smile on Dad's face as we climbed into the aluminum vessel. After we settled into the small boat, Dad pulled the starter cord on the outboard motor and guided us into open water. Inside, my heart was jumping for joy. This was a rare opportunity for me to spend time alone with my hero. Opting to sleep in, Mom and my sister Rochelle declined the offer of going fishing at 5:30 A.M.

It has been our family's custom since my birth to go on a week-long summer trip every year. This year we had once again decided upon the beauty of Canada. Our fishing gear was brought along instinctively. Dad knew that his girls would want to catch some fish before the end of the week. Today was no exception, and I had been anxious to try Dad's new fishing pole since the day we arrived.

"Better hold on to your hat, Harmony. Otherwise the wind will take it away," he said, laughing above the roar of the boat.

"I'm trying!" I squealed, attempting to hang onto my hat and the edge of the boat simultaneously.

For the next twenty minutes, we glided across the lake's still surface in search of a choice place to fish. I began watching my father closely as if I were staring at a new man. A big grin stretched across his now peaceful face. In his eyes, I saw a rare sparkle. Maybe, I thought, this is his way of truly relaxing and winding down.

Dad was always a man who appreciated the outdoors and took

any opportunity, on trips such as these, to expose his family to the natural world. Yet, despite his enjoyment of nature, his job kept him busy and constantly out of state. At least every other month he'd leave on a business trip lasting anywhere from three days to a full week.

"When is Daddy coming home?" I often asked my mom. Every day I'd repeat my question, wishing that he would arrive soon and once again fill our house with his presence. Sometimes I would even secretly wonder if he would ever come back, but when he finally walked in the front door, the rest of that day was like Christmas for me.

"This looks like a good spot," Dad said, breaking the silence of my reflections.

Excitedly, I clamored to find a spot next to him as I watched him tie on the hooks and attach bait to them. I begged to use his new pole, and he let me try it out for a few casts.

"Dad," I asked, "when do you have to go back to work?" I watched carefully as he lifted his eyes to look at me. His carefree smile faded.

"A couple days after we get back, honey."

He suddenly looked much older.

"Why?" he inquired.

"I just wanted to know," I said, groping to find the right words. Suddenly, I felt the strongest need in my eleven years of life to be reassured by my father. I spoke the words that I had tried to say just moments before.

"Dad, do you miss us a lot when you go away?"

Concern now filled his handsome hazel eyes as he began to understand where I was headed. He shifted himself closer to me and took my hand in his as I set the fishing pole down.

"Harmony, I miss all of you very much when I have to travel," he said. "Even though you're asleep, I come into your rooms at night to kiss you and Rochelle before I leave. I call you as often as I can while I'm gone. I love you, Harmony. I want to spend more time with you, Rochelle and your mom. That's why I bring you guys on these vacations. I know I'm gone quite a bit, but you know that I would never leave you, right?" he questioned as he squeezed my hand.

"Yes, I know! I love you, Daddy," I said. Relief flooded through me as I threw my arms around him and laughed. "Thanks for bringing me out here today."

He hugged me back and squeezed tight as he gently replied, "I love you too, Harmony. Thank you for coming with me."

As my dad held me in his arms I could see the sun in the distance, rising above his shoulder and the mountains also, ever brightening the pristine sky. Thank you God, I said silently. What a beautiful day, and I have the greatest dad to share it with!

The rest of the morning we spent laughing as Dad poked fun at my inability to cast the line as gracefully as he could. I pointed out that he, as the more experienced fisherman, hadn't caught a single fish, so he was in no position to tease. When we finally decided to head back after three hours on the lake, we had only caught two pike, and both of us were thoroughly hungry. Yet that did not really matter to me as I pondered the time Dad and I had spent together, realizing suddenly that a deeper hunger had been filled. The man I loved most had shared a part of himself with me this day, and that I can never forget. Those nagging doubts that can fill a child's mind were now completely dispelled.

Now, more than six years later, that day still comes back to me as vividly as if I were still out upon the lake with him. Though Dad's busy work schedule has become more time-consuming, I am quite satisfied with the relationship we share. He still tells me he loves me, hugs me tight and is a continually supportive father and husband. We even talk about that day we spent together on the lake, recalling the things we had said and done.

"That was a good day, wasn't it, Harmony?" he says, as a glow fills his eyes again. I can't help but smile.

"It sure was, Dad. Our fishing experiences have always been good." As I near adulthood, in my heart I remember that summer day in 1996 as the best fishing memory Dad and I will ever share. No words need to be spoken for what the heart already knows.

~Harmony Zieman
Chicken Soup for the Fisherman's Soul

89

A Garden for Four

In San Francisco, where the houses rub shoulders and squat only steps from the street, we don't have gardens. We have backyards. And if you find a place to live with a backyard that has not been cemented over or gone to the dogs, you consider yourself lucky, indeed.

Four years ago, I found a new apartment. It had a backyard with a small concrete center patio, as so many of them do. A leaning fence corralled three sides of the yard. Between the patio and the fence, deep beds held a mishmash of bottlebrush and pine. The trees stood in weed patches and everything was tangled in climbing clematis that was busy strangling sweet-smelling jasmine.

This apartment happened to sit less than a block from my parents' big, but yardless, condo. They had just retired and were busy with bridge tournaments, guitar lessons and international travel. Dad was still a Hercules of a man, silly, creative and kind. Mom was The Planner. When they enthusiastically offered their gardening services, I was thrilled. I had no idea what would happen next.

It started innocently enough. For Christmas, they gave me one of those plastic green scooter seats—"to save your back," Mom said. For my birthday in February, Dad and my brother spent two entire weekends removing the top three inches of "bad dirt" and replacing it with Dad's "good dirt," a secret concoction of who-knows-what mixed with beer dregs. Mom and Dad got a set of keys to my place, "just in case" they felt like puttering in the garden while I was at work.

As spring warmed to summer, I began to feel as if leprechauns had moved in; each evening, I'd come home from work to find all sorts of garden mischief. A fragrant, fifty-pound bag of chicken manure materialized in the work shed. His and her watering cans stood at either side of the yard, to save steps and arguments about who last left what can where. And our gardening tool collection grew so fast that I suspected the shovels had married and started a family of little spades, hoes and picks.

Had I slept through moonlight work sessions? Window boxes changed their dresses nearly as often as I did. And each time the fog rolled in, rows of bumblebee wind whirligigs clattered in beds of purple petunias and pink impatiens.

I would wake up early on Sunday mornings, pull back the drapes and spit coffee at the sight of my parents' dungareed fannies pointing skyward, beginning another full day of planting and pulling. Mom developed a mania for combinations of orange and purple. She planted salvia, marigolds, poppies, golden aster and lavender. The jolts of color blanketing the yard made my eyes hurt. I took to reading my paper wearing sunglasses.

Dad, meanwhile, proclaimed himself paramedic to all sick and injured plantings — mainly because he stepped on them himself in his size-thirteen workboots. His gardening prescription? "Give it another week."

But my parents' gardening mania was short lived. Less than a year later, and just six weeks before I was to be married, Dad was in a hospice, dying of brain cancer. A ferocious biological weed had sent its tendrils deep into his memory, robbing him of speech and sight. Yet he insisted that whatever happened to him, we mustn't postpone the wedding. I promised him solemnly that we would honor his wish, and we did.

I had learned a lot watching my parents enjoy themselves, shaping that city garden in their precious last summer. Working, planning, bickering, experimenting and learning side by side, they built memories for all of us. I realized how much Mom treasured those months when she gave my husband and me a splendid patio set with a gigantic umbrella. "So you can enjoy your garden like your dad and I did," she said with a smile.

Recently, my husband—out of the blue—decided to plant a gigantic candy-colored bougainvillea. Nurserymen and neighbors galore warned him that bougainvillea roots are extremely sensitive and that they often get shocky, keeling over dead the minute they are put in the ground. Sure enough, two weekends later, it looked like a tumbleweed, no more than a collection of brittle twigs.

"Should we rip it out?" he asked me.

I remembered Dad's favorite gardening cure.

"Give it another week," I said.

Dad and I were right. I think that cheerful bougainvillea will be cresting our fence by this summer.

~Rayne Wolfe
Chicken Soup for the Gardener's Soul

90

What's Up with Dads and Pork Chop Sandwiches?

Since there is nothing so well worth having as friends,
never lose a chance to make them.
~Francesco Guicciardini

Mr. Delgado spreads two slices of white bread with mayonnaise. He looks over at his pork chop hissing in the frying pan and rubs his hands together like a fruit fly eyeing an overripe peach. His daughter, Elizabeth, and I sit at their kitchen table and watch him slice up an onion and hum a love song to his pork chop. We've watched him make pork chop sandwiches for the past twenty-five years. He always hums "Sólo tú," a Mexican corrido that would leave the toughest macho crying in his tequila, but Mr. Delgado is grinning from ear to ear at the pork chop turning crispy brown.

When the pork chop is "browner than me," as he likes to say, he'll gently place it on the bread he's prepared with mayonnaise, a lettuce leaf, a reel of onion and mmmmmm, the sandwich is good to go. Mr. Delgado sits down with us and smiles. Always smiles.

"Heaven," he says between bites and closed eyelids. This is all he needs, he says, and winks at me.

"Mi familia, good friends like your father, m'ija, and a good job where I can afford pork chop sandwiches whenever I want."

Heaven.

Before Elizabeth and I can make our escape from the table, Mr.

Delgado tells us, for the hundredth time, how he met my dad years ago in the '70s when "Mexican-Americans were Chicanos and not confused Hispanics," and if it wasn't for the almighty pork chop sandwich and a "crazy Chicano march in Califas," they never would have become such close friends. I don't really mind hearing the story over and over; in fact, I think it gets better every time Mr. Delgado tells it. He's always adding extra details never revealed before. Upon hearing a new or exaggerated bit, Elizabeth and I raise our eyebrows at each other. Once, Mr. Delgado added a love interest to the story, and another time a wild low-rider car chase, and later a confrontation with the ghost of Che Guevara.

My father's version always stays the same, ending with the same proud revelation:

"So you see, m'ija, I saved that damn Chicano's life."

Both men are from the same Kansas town, but didn't meet until they went to a Chicano civil-rights rally in California back in the '70s. At the rally, when an organizer asked if there were any Chicanos from Kansas present, both my father and Mr. Delgado raised their fists.

When Mr. Delgado tells the story, he says he didn't like my dad at first. He said my dad seemed like one of those goody-two-shoes, Catholic altar-boy types always trying to make peace, always trying to help out. My father had trimmed jet-black hair, black-rimmed glasses, and baggy khakis. He wore a crisp and clean white-collared shirt with a scapula of La Virgen around his neck. Mr. Delgado had a mop of curly black hair. He wore old jeans and leather sandals and some sort of fringed leather vest over a white undershirt stained with salsa verde.

After a four-hour march filled with speeches, singing and Aztec chants under a hot California sun, Mr. Delgado soon learned to appreciate my goody-two-shoes "Catholic boy" father. Hungry, thirsty, without a dime in his pocket — the night before he had spent all his bus and food money on a tattoo and too many cervezas — Mr. Delgado searched for my father to ask for a ride back to Wichita. About to give up his search for my father and hitchhike back to Kansas, my dad spotted him and waved him over. My dad pulled out two bottles of

Coca-Cola and a thick pork chop sandwich from a brown lunch sack and shared it with him.

Mr. Delgado says my father became like his right arm at that precise moment. (Elizabeth and I always giggle at that.) Mr. Delgado and my father returned from California with Che Guevara patches, Aztec war god tattoos on their backs and, more important, as compadres.

Compadres are inseparable once they meet. It becomes stronger than your last name and as casual as your first. If my father says, "Yeah, my compadre and I are going to look at that property tomorrow," everyone knows he is talking about Mr. Delgado. Compadres or comadres are the people you'd trust to watch your children. They are that close.

I love the relationship the two men have. Both complain about their backs, plan Fourth of July festivities during Christmas Mass and gripe that the priest puts them to sleep. On their days off, they gather at the driveway and shake their heads at my parked Chevy Corsica. My father and Mr. Delgado have tried to teach me how to change a flat tire for the last ten years.

"I've got AAA!" I wave my auto card at them. "I don't need to learn how."

My father crosses himself and asks the Holy Trinity and not AAA to bless me. Always sensing my father's concern, Mr. Delgado squats down near my right front tire and assures me he's going to show me again just in case AAA doesn't answer my call.

"I hate stupid tires! I can't ever get those darn lug nuts off," I answer back. "If I get a flat, I'll just wait for someone to stop and help."

My father crosses himself in the name of the Father, the Son and the Holy Spirit. The next day he buys me a new set of tires from Sears.

My father and Mr. Delgado have a friendship based on losing sleep over both their daughters' driving habits and the Chicano movement.

Elizabeth and I like to tease our fathers about their "rebellious Chicano past," the two of them trekking across Kansas, Colorado and

California for La Causa. Sometimes, together on the front porch, we will all thumb through photo albums where our fathers are leather-brown young men with goatees and baggy khakis. For every photo, there is a lecture about bilingual education, fair housing and resistance to total cultural assimilation. Elizabeth and I once counted over twenty photos of our fathers with their fingers gathered in a fist punched high against the Kansas sky—high and hard enough for God to feel and look down in wonderment. "There are Chicanos in Kansas?"

¡Sí, Señora! Mexicans, like my abuelo, who traveled from Jalisco to Kansas at the age of fourteen to work on the railroads. Mexicans, like my grandparents, who stayed and raised proud Mexican-Americans in Kansas towns like Hutchinson, Garden City, Newton, Wichita and Topeka. Kansas Chicanos, like our fathers, who were the first in their families to graduate from college and who brought home to their daughters books about César Chávez, Delores Huerta and Frida Kahlo. The same Chicanos whose brown fingers, now released from the fist, show me how to check my oil and put air in my tires. The same brown fingers that like to tear off a piece of pork chop while it's cooking in the skillet, and the same brown fingers that cross themselves when I tell them I'm considering another career change. Now they cross themselves with brown-callused fingers, but they still pray for their daughters, and they still pray for la raza.

If you ask my dad how he and Mr. Delgado became compadres, he will say it was the Chicano movement. If you ask Mr. Delgado, he will say it was the pork chop sandwich.

Either way, both men are right, and we are all the better for it!

~Angela Cervantes
Chicken Soup for the Latino Soul

91

Old Love Turned Brand New

Vicki gripped the steering wheel of her car, trying to control her anxious excitement. Twenty years was a long time—what would he look like? Would she recognize him? As she began her three-hour drive to the airport, it all came flooding back.

Vicki met David in 1975 at a campfire party in Georgia. They were sixteen and instantly fell in love. Not long after that, David's stepfather, who was in the military, received orders to move the family to Oklahoma. David asked Vicki to marry him and go with him, but she was simply not ready to leave home. Instead, her father retired, and she moved with her parents to Mississippi. Tearfully, the young lovers went their separate ways.

Soon after, Vicki discovered she was pregnant. Then she heard David had a new girlfriend. Not wanting to get in the way of what she perceived as his new happiness, Vicki decided not to call him. Rumors of a baby and pressures from their families frightened David as well. Broken-hearted, and in a desperate attempt to find himself and some sanity, he joined the Navy.

In January, Vicki gave birth to a baby girl and named her Tammy Lisa. By now, she and David had lost all contact. As more time passed, they both married other people. David became the father of two more daughters. Vicki had a son.

Six years passed, and Vicki worried that if something happened to her, Tammy would never know the real story of her father. So she wrote a letter explaining everything, included the only two pictures she had of David, and stored it all in a safe deposit box.

As the years passed, Vicki never forgot David and the love they shared. When Tammy turned sixteen, Vicki gave her the letter she had written ten years earlier.

After reading it, Tammy looked up. "Momma, it's time to find my daddy."

The search began. For the next three years they hunted for David Garcia. They tried agencies, libraries, police departments, even old military records, with no luck. After they placed an ad in the *Army Times*, the father of David's best friend saw the ad, and his son called Vicki. She learned David was now using his birth father's last name, Frizzell. A new search began, and twenty years after they had parted, Vicki held David's phone number in her hand.

With trembling fingers, she dialed. When David heard her voice, he was overwhelmed, shaken and—to her delight—thrilled. He told her he had longed to know how she was doing and yearned to see and know his daughter. Ten years earlier he had tried to find Vicki but with no success.

David was alive, well and happy to hear from her. He told her he would come to Mississippi to meet Tammy, the daughter he had wondered about all these years. Vicki shared with David what had been in her heart for so long.

"David, I promised myself that if I ever found you I'd tell you this no matter what. When we were kids, I loved you. All these years I've loved you. Even through my marriage, I loved you. Every man I've ever known, I compared to you, and not one ever measured up." Her words left him crying as he began to share his own, similar feelings. He had never forgotten her, never stopped loving her.

Tammy decided she wanted to greet her father privately, so she anxiously waited at her apartment while Vicki made the three-hour drive to pick him up—alone.

At the airport, Vicki's anxious excitement grew. Each minute seemed like an hour. She paced back and forth and touched up her make-up three times. David was also nervous. As the plane landed, his heart started pounding. Once on the ground, he was impatient to find Vicki, to see her again.

As David walked off the plane, they recognized each other instantly. Amazingly, they saw each other as if through a tunnel, and the rest of the airport went white and grew silent. With smiles of joy on their faces, they gazed at each other in wide-eyed amazement. David slowly drew her into his arms and kissed her. Time stood still as the past and the present collided in one dramatic moment.

The drive home passed in no time, as they talked about their lives and all that each had done. During short silences, they would glance at each other and whisper, "I can't believe it's really you."

When they arrived at Tammy's apartment, David immediately recognized the beautiful young woman waiting outside as his daughter. Sharing their first hugs, they began talking and laughing at the same time. That night, they watched home videos of Tammy growing up, and all three cried as the history of Tammy's life that David had missed rolled by on the screen.

Two days after arriving in Mississippi, David realized that the only place on Earth he wanted to be was with Vicki and Tammy. He proposed, and Vicki excitedly accepted.

"If I wasn't living it, I wouldn't believe it!" she exclaimed.

As they planned their wedding over the next few weeks, they easily rediscovered their love for each other. Vicki's parents were overjoyed to have David back in their lives, treating him as if he were a son who had finally come home.

The following June, Vicki's parents gave them a traditional southern wedding. The invitation showed a fairytale castle with the words "Dreams Come True." Tammy was maid of honor.

Arriving in a horse-drawn carriage, the bride wore the long white gown of her dreams. During the ceremony, David sang a song he wrote for Vicki that told the world the miracle of their love story: "Old Love Turned Brand New." At the end of the ceremony, David gazed at his daughter and sang a special song he'd written called "Daddy's Little Girl—Tammy's Song."

It took twenty years to fill the empty space they'd all had in their hearts. Now their family circle was finally complete.

~Vicki Frizzell as told to Janet Matthews
Chicken Soup for the Bride's Soul

Dads & Daughters

I Will Always Be There for You

What a man sows, that shall he and his relations reap.
~Clarissa Graves

92

Sand Castles

You know, fathers just have a way of putting everything together.
~Erika Cosby

She frantically piled sandpile on top of sandpile trying to build her dream sand castle independently, without her father's help. Finally, she gave up. With her silk pink ribbon hanging over one eye and sand building up inside her bathing suit, she ran over to her father.

"Daddy, I can't build my sand castle good enough. Help me!" she demanded.

Her dad scooped the sandy girl into his arms and, with a broad smile on his face, looked pleased that she wanted his help. He carried her over to a nice, flat spot of sand, and together they built a charming sand castle.

When they were finished, he took her tiny, sticky hand in his, and her puffy little fingers clung to his large firm hand. "I love you, Daddy," she said looking up at his face with large, expectant eyes.

"I love you very much, my little princess," he replied.

But then the huge majestic waves pulled at her feet like a rope tugging her into itself. She tried to break free from her father's protective hand so that she could play alongside the waves.

"Daddy, I want to go play in the ocean," she informed him.

"Okay, but I'll come with you to make sure the waves don't pull you away."

"No, Daddy. I want to go in by myself." And with that independent statement, she ran into the waves, which welcomed her with full force. They filled her senses with a pungent, salty smell, the foam blinded her eyes, and her active little body became one with the fast flowing water.

Twelve years later, the same girl, now a young woman, had lost her ribbons, but not her assertive independence. Her frilly, pink bathing suit had been reduced to a skimpy, green two-piece. Her long legs glided out of the harsh waves.

A young man with wavy golden hair flashed his magnetic smile at her, and her coy expression met his face. He wrapped her in a towel as he gazed into her deep, green eyes.

As they sat cuddling on the sandy beach, warming their feet in the thick pebbles, she asked him what he was thinking.

"Well, actually, I was just thinking that... never mind, it's deep. Let's just sit here," he said uneasily.

"Come on, what were you going to say?" she prodded him.

Her long, slim fingers had lost their puffy, childish features, and now they ran through his rough and wild hair as the wind played between the strands.

"It's kinda crazy. But, I think... I think... I love you," he replied.

Her eyes froze as she looked into his eyes. He looked down at the ground and nervously sifted the cold sand through his fingers.

"I don't know what to say," she truthfully told him.

"It's okay, you don't have to say anything."

A tear formed in her eye. She felt warm, and pleasure filled her heart.

Finally, they both got up, and she playfully kicked sand on his legs. He chased her down to the waves. As they landed on the cold, shifty ground, she said, "Let's make a sand castle like I used to do when I was little."

He looked at her with a funny expression on his face, but her enthusiasm enticed him to enter into his past. Together, they piled layers of sand on top of each other. But the waves kept claiming their fortress, blanketing the couple's efforts and stealing the sand back to its ocean floor.

Finally, the two of them lost interest in their failed efforts and walked back to the car, trudging their feet through the sinking sand.

After a few months, she came back to that same spot on the beach. This time, she was alone. Tears slept in her eyelids as resentment rested heavily in her heart. Her brain felt as though it had been filled with sand, and she could not think anymore. She felt dizzy and lonely. She thought of all the dances they had gone to, all the promises he pledged to her, and all the smiles she had thought were only flashed in her direction, although now she knew otherwise.

She collapsed her frail body on the hard and shifty sand. The pebbles were unusually cold as the clouds crawled along behind their mother sun. She desperately grabbed for the sand, for something to hold on to, but it seeped between her fingers. She began to unconsciously pile up sand. As a castle began to form, she decided it was a good idea to continue to build it; maybe it would take her mind off her sorrow.

Somehow, building the sand castle brought her a sense of peace. Something about it comforted her and began to make her feel like a child again. She felt innocent and lighthearted. The feeling of the sand in her hands and the strong scent of dried seaweed brought her back to a time when she was much younger, and life seemed simple.

She began to remember her failed attempt to build a sand castle when she was younger, her father's smile and his watery eyes filled with love as he helped her build her dream castle.

She struggled to push herself up from the suppressing sand and reached into her pocket for some change. She trudged to the pay phone as her toes wiggled in the wet sand that covered the concrete floor and made her feet unusually cold. Picking up the receiver, she dropped the coins into the slot and dialed the number she had known by heart since she was a little girl.

Her father picked up the phone almost immediately after the seventh digit had been pushed.

"Daddy...?"

"Honey, is that you?" his voice sounded relieved.

"Dad, I just wanted to say... I love you."

There was a pause.

"I love you, too, my little princess."

As she walked back down the sand to get her shoes, she spotted her sand castle. The waves had not touched it. It stood strong above the rest of the sand, while the waves crashed in the distance.

~Jennifer Reichert
Chicken Soup for the Teenage Soul on Love & Friendship

93

Just Between Us

It has been wisely said that we cannot really love anybody
at whom we never laugh.
~Agnes Repplier

I wish that I could have seen his face when he answered the phone. Even though I was married to Marty, I still called home when I needed him.

"Dad, my garage door broke..."

"Well, do you need me to pick up a new spring?"

"No. I think I kind of need you to come over. You see, I had places to go and people to see, so while I couldn't pull out like usual, I, um, tried to turn my van around."

"You did what?"

"I tried to turn my van around, you know, like a U-turn. I tried to turn the van and head out the other garage door!" I confessed while stifling my giggles.

For a moment there was silence. I could imagine my father sitting in his favorite chair trying to picture what his youngest daughter had attempted. While he thought, I assessed my situation and concluded there was no way I wanted my husband to come home from work and see my creative attempt to get to the mall.

Within moments, my father's thoughts broke into words. "Honey, did you make it out the other door? What exactly do you need for me to do?"

I took a deep breath and tried to find an appropriate way to break the news, yet nothing came to mind. As I had done my entire life, I swallowed hard and then presented my problem to my father.

"Dad, it's like this. My van is stuck in my garage."

"Stuck?"

"Yeah, stuck, sideways."

"Sideways?"

"Dad, I thought that I could turn it around. I simply began backing up and going forward, trying to maneuver my van around so that I could exit out of the second garage door. I had a full tank of gas and I was doing a good job of getting it out myself until now, and well, can you come over and get me out of this mess before Marty gets home from work?"

Within minutes my dad had left his chair and was standing in my garage surveying my dilemma. He scratched his head, placed his hands on his hips and assured me that he had "never seen such a thing." Then without saying a word, yet wearing a grin that hinted, "Now I've seen it all," he crawled into the driver's seat and began inching his way, slowly turning the van.

I crawled up on the workbench and watched. My dad caught my eye and gave me a wink. Holding my hand over my mouth, I tried to control my laughter as my father repeatedly drove my van three feet forward then three feet in reverse, while maneuvering the steering wheel. I thought of Marty surprising me, coming home early, finding his father-in-law "driving" in his garage and me cheering him on with passion!

Instantly, I flashed back to the many times my dad had come to my rescue, not questioning me as to the "how or why" of my predicament, but concentrating on the "what now" and the solution. It was no secret—my dad knew that I thought "outside the box." In fact, he'd been one to believe in my dreams, support my attempts and praise my accomplishments. I pondered his patience, wisdom and endless love for me. Today was no different. I knew for certain that, no matter what, I could always call on my dad.

An hour before Marty arrived home, my father beamed as he

drove the van out the second garage door and parked it in the driveway. I walked out to meet him, and he rolled down his window.

"Problem solved," he said.

"Just between us?" I asked, securing our secret.

"Between us," he nodded. "Yep, this one is 'just between us,' because no one would ever believe it!"

~Janet Lynn Mitchell
Chicken Soup for the Father & Daughter Soul

94

My Dad, My Source for Healing

Dear Editors of Chicken Soup,

I have been gobbling up your stories for years. I own all your books (and the game, too). I love what each story has to offer in its meaning and new perspective on life. I would like to take the opportunity to share what got me through a difficult breakup in high school—my dad.

When most of my friends were bickering with their fathers, I was looking to mine for guidance. He knows more about me than anyone, even myself at times. He travels for work and so he's gone a lot. Most people assume we have a distant relationship because he's not home very often. But we thrive under this situation because we talk every night by phone, and he makes his support known when he can't be present. One night my world just collapsed, and it was my dad who was able to pick up the pieces.

My first true love called from a party and broke my heart. He offered little explanation and this made the situation all the more difficult to accept. In that one quick phone call I lost my boyfriend and best friend, a comfort I had enjoyed for the past year and a half. I was sure I was the most miserable fifteen-year-old in the world—lost and lonely. It felt like everyone else's life could just continue on in its normal way, but mine couldn't. I would no longer spend hours on the phone with him each night, and his house would no longer be my home away from home.

I was forced to deal with my regular routine on Monday morning, as Mom went to work, Dad flew out on business and I went to school. Dad wouldn't return until Friday. I wasn't sure how I was going to be able to face everyone and their gossip at school. I was right: the questions and the whispering started around second period.

I returned home from school feeling completely defeated. All I wanted to do was crawl into bed and wallow in my own self-pity. I pulled back the covers on my bed and discovered a pile of cards left by my dad. I recognized the "calligraphy" instantly. Each card included an instruction that it was to be opened on a particular night that week. He was halfway across the country and still my dad was able to show he cared.

I made it through that week because of him. Each card seemed to say just what I needed to hear. Tuesday's card said, "The past is painful to think about and the future is impossible to envision. Don't try. Just take it one minute at a time." On Wednesday my mood lifted when I read, "What you are feeling now is natural and normal. It still feels lousy, but it is part of the healing process." Friday's card contained a poem he wrote. The last lines made me smile through my tears. "Whatever special challenges you face along life's way/May you trust that you will find the best in every day." I was instructed to open the last card after the party I went to on Saturday night. In it he sagely reminded me to laugh. "The world isn't so bad after a good laugh. The more you laugh, the more you heal." Each card was signed, "Love, Dad."

Even just flipping through the cards made me feel better in the weeks to come. I looked through them most days until I started to forget about them. It was then that I knew that I was healing.

Sincerely,

~Kelsey Cameron
Chicken Soup for the Teenage Soul Letters

95

I Love You, Pilgrim

Love has nothing to do with what you are expecting to get—only with what you are expecting to give—which is everything.
~Katharine Hepburn

"Howdy, Pilgrim! You aimin' to sleep the day away?"

I groaned and pulled my pillow over my head. I knew what today was without opening my eyes. It was a day of significance on the level of Christmas in our house. It was John Wayne movie marathon day. Apparently my father had already had a dose or two of the Duke before waking me up.

From my siblings' room next door I could hear him continue, "We got a can o' beans warmin' on the fire and black coffee to warm them bones." I assumed the thud that followed was Naomi's pillow hitting the door behind him while John groaned as I had.

My father had definite opinions about good entertainment. Movies must contain John Wayne or Jimmy Stewart. Music must be that of Handel, Mozart or Creedence Clearwater Revival.

Dad was also a bookworm, and our den showed the treasure of his collection. John, Naomi and I were an odd combination, inheriting a strong love for books from Dad, and a love of being on stage from Mom. Dad never quite understood this passion, but he always supported us.

During my middle school years, I joined the band. Dad was at each concert, reading a book until it began and reading again until it was time to give me a congratulatory hug. He always gave me a smile and replied, "Good work. You didn't forget any words."

In high school all of our interests turned to drama. During my senior year I reached the pinnacle—I was cast in our spring musical! I spent countless hours practicing. I'd run tap routines as I combed my hair and rehearse the songs as I set the table for dinner.

Opening night came. Pre-performance rose deliveries were made backstage. When handed my flower, my heart sank. Only Momma, John and Naomi had signed the card.

"What's wrong?" asked Stacie, my best friend and fellow "lady-in-waiting."

"I don't think my dad came."

"Of course he came," she reassured me.

"But he didn't sign the card."

"Maybe he was reading," she laughed.

"Maybe." But I was crushed. Even though he didn't understand my love of it, he had never missed a performance of anything.

The play began and ran beautifully. I danced and sang my heart out. I scanned the audience when I could, but never found my family. During intermission Stacie and I headed to the dressing room. She entered before me and was smiling as I came through the door. There, on top of my costume bag, was a single red rose. The card read, "Break a leg. I'm proud of you. Love, Dad." He had never sent me a rose from just him. He had also remembered the theater superstition of never saying "Good Luck." I was touched. During the second act I not only danced, I flew.

After curtain call I rushed to get back into my street clothes. I grabbed all of my stuff and raced out the door. I hugged Stacie's parents as I searched for Dad. Finally, over in a corner, I saw my family. Flying through the crowd, Mom grabbed me in a bear hug, bubbling over with how great we were.

Then I was face to face with Dad. Book tucked under his arm, he smiled and reached for a hug. "You did a good job," he whispered into my hair.

"I was afraid you didn't come," I said.

"I wouldn't have missed it for the world," he grinned at me.

As we turned to leave, I hooked my arm through his. He laughed and asked, "Tell me again why the boys wore tights. John Wayne would never wear tights."

~Aletheia Lee Butler
Chicken Soup for the Father & Daughter Soul

96

The Promise

There was a great deal of blood on the floor, and she just kept bleeding. Lamaze class never mentioned anything like this. Doc was cool as ice. A small-town obstetrician, he didn't care much for chitchat. Oh, he was friendly enough, just not in the way we, expatriates from New York City, had envisioned a rural doctor to be.

This delivery was different, even for Doc. I could tell by the way he kept talking. There was no sense of panic that anyone listening in could hear, but the nurses, who had been by his side for more than twenty years, well, they were practically hysterical at the sound of Doc's monotone voice just going on and on about how everything was all right.

Everything was not all right. I looked down at my wife, strapped into a torturous birthing position. All color had drained from her lips, lips I thought I knew so well after all these years. I cursed myself. After all, it was I who had begged to have a child. She looked at me with noncommittal eyes. These were not the eyes I saw flashing intense pain and a plea for help at me earlier, as our baby refused to come out, forcing her through eleven hours of labor.

With one final gasp and a terrifying scream that made me think the baby would come flying out of my wife's mouth, our daughter came into the world. Whenever I wonder why she's such a loud child, I think back to what she must have heard and gone through as she fought her mom, trying to ignore the eviction notice on her warm, quiet womb.

"Everything is going to be okay," the nurses kept telling me as I stood by my wife's side. Thinking it best not to lie to her as well, I told her jokes:

"Do eleven toes run in your side of the family?"

She forced a smile, trying to get me to calm down, seeing the near panic on my face; I was unable, as usual, to hide my emotions from her.

"Hey, be patient. They haven't taken the other one out yet. Didn't I tell you we were having twins?"

This wasn't far from the truth. A part of her placenta had remained inside, preventing her womb from sealing up properly, making for a spectacular mess. I had seen the placenta come out, and it seemed almost as big as our baby.

And what a baby she was. She didn't scream, but immediately she started making a stuttering sound. She arrived a month early, but showed no signs of being a preemie. Bluish-purple and covered with a fine white membrane that reminded me for some reason of chicken fat, she looked my way for the longest time before turning back to the nurse who was cleaning her and trying to record her size with a tape measure, only to have to gently take it away from Lina, who had managed to close her little fingers around it.

"We have to take her to the OR," said Doc. He finally stood up from the stool between my wife's legs and addressed us both, a faint smile crossing his face, which made me very nervous. I reached down and kissed Lizy, tears streaming down my face. I thought I had seen her in her finest hour during the birth of our daughter, showing courage and strength I hadn't imagined any human possessed.

I smiled as hard as I could. Her eyes came to life, eyes I had fallen so in love with years earlier and which lately I had begun to take for granted as we settled into the monotony of marriage. A soft glow returned to her for a moment as she reached up to caress my cheek, wiping the tears away and saying, "Don't worry, sweetie. Go have a long talk with our daughter."

As they wheeled her through the doors of the OR, I stood there paralyzed, the clean antiseptic smell of the place making me nauseous. I wanted more time with her. Just another minute to tell her the thousands of things I never got around to somehow, but I managed to yell out "I love you!" before she completely passed through the swinging doors. A nurse caught my arm and walked me over to the birthing room, where another nurse handed me my daughter, bundled up but stretching her neck and head back to get a better look at the world about her. Precious child. The nurse walked us to my wife's room, encouraging me as she continued to guide me by the arm until I couldn't hold it in any longer and broke down crying.

My daughter looked at me with intense black eyes—her mother's eyes—as I sat down in the room to wait. Wait. I laid Lina down in the hospital bassinet and sat on the bed next to her, leaning close as we talked in private for the first time in eight months. It was then I made her a promise—a promise to be kind and gentle to her, a promise to be strong like she was after having gone through so much to get here. We talked about her mom, and how she would be right back, and how there was no need to worry. This time, as I heard myself say it, I actually believed the words, and I watched and listened to my baby making her stuttering sounds, gripping my index finger tightly.

I made the same promise to her mother years ago. She looked long and hard at me after I proposed, leaving me there on the cool terra cotta floor of the rooftop bistro, waiting. She cocked her head ever so slightly, squinting hard, something she did when she was thinking with her heart, a heart that was patient and methodical from a life lived with disappointment.

"How will you treat me?" she asked quietly. It could have been her mom or grandmother asking as it seemed that the men ran out on all the women in her family.

"With kindness and gentle hands," I said.

It was enough for the moment.

Time stopped hounding me in that little hospital room as I held my daughter, rocking her back and forth as she yawned, closed her eyes and fell asleep, with one hand holding on to my finger.

The door opened and Doc walked in, smiling. I tried to get up, but he motioned me down.

"She's fine. Recovering well and should be back up in an hour. The bleeding has stopped, and it's just a matter of letting her regain her strength for a few days before she can go home."

I thanked him with such enthusiasm that the man blushed. He turned, hesitating a moment at the door as if he had forgotten to say something, but instead an enormous smile took over his face as he wished us a good night.

I felt a sudden release and draining of energy, as if my body would crumble, thinking of my family and how hard I would work to keep the promise that held up my world.

~Antonio Farias
Chicken Soup for the Latino Soul

97

Run for Gold

The interests of childhood and youth are the interests of mankind.
~Edmund Storer Janes

I was nine years old in 1967, the year of Canada's centennial celebration. I raced home from school on that bright spring day, bursting with excitement about a Canadian national fitness competition the teacher had told us about. "It's all running and jumping and sit-ups and stuff," I explained, "and I'm going to go for a gold medal just like in the Olympics!"

Around the dinner table that night, my older sister Nancy and I both explained to Mom and Dad about this fitness test. But I knew I wasn't very good at running long distance, so I asked my dad how I could get better at it.

"What about practicing?" Dad suggested. "We could go in the evenings to the track at the high school and do some training there."

"Can we start tonight?" I asked excitedly.

We left the house holding hands and talking. I had to almost run to keep up with my six-foot-two father's long stride. Soon the high school loomed ahead, and it seemed enormous compared to my own school building and playground. When we got there, we entered the gates onto a huge football field surrounded by an outdoor track.

"I have to run the whole way around this track, Dad, and the time it takes determines whether we score a gold, silver, bronze or participant medal. It seems so far!"

"Well, let's give it a try," smiled my dad. "You must be warmed up from the walk, so let's start right here." He chose a spot on the spectator side with a long, straight stretch to run first, and set us up to start running.

"On your mark, get set, GO!" he said, and I took off. Dad ran along beside me, and I was panting hard by the time we made the first turn.

About halfway around I stopped and cried out, "I'll never do it, Dad. We're not even halfway and I'm beat!"

"The problem is your timing. You have to learn to pace yourself if you're going to run the entire race. We'll try again, start off slowly, run more steadily through the middle section, and then sprint to the finish line. Let's see how that works," he explained as we returned to our starting place.

We began to run slowly, and my "coach" murmured encouragement like, "That's good, a bit faster now, keep breathing steadily." This time I got more than halfway around before I began to slow down. "Okay, push yourself now," cried Dad, and so I did. "We're almost there!" and sure enough, we completed the circle.

Every night for two weeks Dad and I walked to the high school and ran the track at least twice. I slowly grew stronger, and my pace began to improve. I loved having him running beside me.

Race day dawned sunny and warm, and since it was a Saturday, my whole family prepared to go to the track meet. My excitement had turned to nervousness, and I bounced around the house as everyone got ready.

"Let's get going, Dad. There will be a huge crowd," I called as I headed out the door.

The walk seemed short that day, and when we arrived at the track there were hundreds of people, loads of cars, and the air was filled with noise and excitement. The voice on the loudspeaker called out the race times, and it seemed only a few moments before my event was called.

"Line up behind the 'start' line," the voice instructed. My dad nudged me forward, steering me to an inside position. To me it seemed very strange to have the track lined with spectators and to have other friends lined up along with me. I looked over my left shoulder and saw my dad smiling. He said, "It's just like we've practiced. Start slowly and you'll be fine."

"On your mark, get set, BANG," and the race began. I started to run and watched many of my classmates sprint off ahead. I heard my father's voice in my head saying, "That's it, a nice smooth start. Now just run easy around this first curve and get into a rhythm and keep a steady pace." I ran steadily and soon began to pass many of the fast starters on the straight backstretch of the track. When I rounded the one curve, once again I heard Dad's voice in my head saying gently, "Now push, and pour it out over the finish line." I started to pick up speed and used my arms to pump extra energy into the last section of the race. As I ran across the finish line I heard the cheers, and I saw my mom and my sister on the sideline. As I ran a little further to slow down and cool off, once again I glanced over my left shoulder—and saw my dad! Suddenly I realized why he hadn't been on the sidelines with the rest of my family. What I had been hearing hadn't been a voice in my head at all! My dad had run the entire race on the grass along the inside of the track right beside me. When the winners were announced, and the medals were awarded, we both won gold that day.

~Ruth Barden
Chicken Soup for the Father & Daughter Soul

98

Arm-in-Arm

The family is one of nature's masterpieces.
~George Santayana

"Who will walk you down the aisle?" my mother worried.

My fiancé and I had been planning this wedding for months. I had taken care of the dress, the flowers, the hall, the catering and even the cake. Our invitations proclaimed, "Dreams do come true." But to my mother's question, I had no answer.

My father died about a year before I started dating Lou. I was haunted by the thought that Lou loved golf, my father's favorite pastime, but they never had a chance to play a single round. Sadly, they never even knew each other.

I thought about walking down the aisle alone. But I wanted it to be a happy occasion, not a reminder that I no longer had a dad. I didn't want people to feel sorry for me.

"What about David?" my mother suggested.

My brother? Maybe he could!

I sensed a glimpse of hope—until all the obstacles surfaced. He'd have to fly in early to rent a tux and make it to rehearsal, but because his work required him to be on call, it would be difficult for him to request time off. I was reluctant to ask.

"Mom, you know David is very busy."

"If you want him to do it, you should ask," my mother encouraged.

I knew I wanted my brother by my side during the most important time in my life. He always was in the past. Together we'd endured a traumatic accident, Dad's battle with lung cancer and, finally, his death. No matter what, David was there. It seemed only right for him to take my father's place. I decided to place the call.

When he answered the phone, I asked, "D-David? Do... do you think you could walk me down the aisle?"

"Yes," he said without hesitation. "It would be an honor."

"You mean it?" my voice escalated like a shy schoolgirl's. "You'd... you'd have to come a couple days early for a tux fitting and to make the rehearsal."

"Hmm," he said. "Now that's a problem. I'm not sure I can get more days off. I'll have to speak with my boss and get back to you."

"That's fine. If you can't, don't worry about it," I said in a rush, hoping my voice didn't betray my disappointment. I decided his response was a kindhearted excuse for "No." Maybe I was asking too much. My heart sank.

And the weeks passed without another word from David.

Four days before my wedding a strange car pulled up in the driveway. I went outside and saw my brother standing before me.

"Are you that blushing bride I've been hearing so much about?" he asked, with a proud grin on his face.

I ran and threw my arms around him. "But what about work?"

"I found a new job. This one pays better and gives me more free time."

Knowing my brother, I had a funny feeling that wasn't the only reason he'd switched jobs. "Really?"

"Yes!" He quickly changed the subject. "Now what size tux do you think I wear?"

The next few days passed quickly, leaving me little time to spend with him. But when the famous strains of "Here Comes the Bride" cued him, David knocked on my dressing room door.

"It's time."

I swung the door open and stood in front of him in bridal white.

"Wow!" he said, offering his arm. "You look beautiful!"

At that moment, I saw my father's pride beaming at me through David's eyes, the same shade of blue as my father's. I realized that in many ways Dad was with me on this important day. And so was the brother I had always relied on. David and I walked down the aisle, smiles gleaming and tears flowing, but most importantly, arm-in-arm.

~Michele Wallace Campanelli
Chicken Soup for the Bride's Soul

Secret Tears

"I know you don't believe this now, Nancy, but time will heal," my friend Jean said, as she hugged me a few minutes before my father's funeral. "It will get better. I promise."

During Daddy's funeral, tears fell freely down my face, but Jean's words continued to echo in my mind. During that hour of intense sorrow, I thought back to the days when I was a child. I remembered watching out the picture window, waiting for Daddy to come home from work. I thought of the times that I was sick and Daddy was with me, holding a cool cloth on my head. When I had problems as a young mother, I called on Daddy. What will I do now that he's gone? I wondered.

For the previous four years, my father had lived in a nursing home. Parkinson's disease destroyed his muscles, and dementia had taken away his mind. The ongoing stress of losing him had taken a toll on my health. I knew my blood pressure was high, but I didn't take the time to go to the doctor for treatment. I pushed myself to the limit and, suddenly, it was all over. Daddy was gone, and I would never see him again.

Each night when the house got quiet, tears filled my eyes and I cried myself to sleep. I tried to keep my secret tears bottled up inside of me. I wanted others to think I was in control of my emotions and that I was handling the grief.

One month later, I felt lightheaded and dizzy at work. I had my blood pressure checked and discovered that it was soaring well into the danger zone. My pulse was racing as well. I wondered if I had waited too long to seek medical attention. I went to the doctor immediately, and he placed me on a medication that would control my blood pressure and heart rate. He encouraged me to take additional measures to control the stress in my life.

I might be able to control the stress, I thought, but I cannot control the grief. The secret tears remained with me, night after night. Even the closest people to me were not aware of the number of tears I had shed. Many times I remembered Jean's words and wondered when and how the grief would end.

Nine months passed. With every special occasion, I grieved. My birthday was very difficult, but Daddy's birthday was even harder. Father's Day was pure torture. Even Memorial Day brought grief and gloom, since Daddy was a veteran honored in a special Memorial Day service.

One November night, I went to bed dreading Thanksgiving Day. What did I have to be thankful for? I was too sad to be thankful. I woke up at six o'clock that morning. I realized that I had been crying in my sleep. I was too tired to get up and eventually fell back asleep. During the next two hours I had a dream that turned my life around.

I was sitting alone in what appeared to be a waiting room. The walls were white as snow. Empty chairs lined the four walls. In my dream I wondered why I was waiting. Suddenly, the front door opened. A bell was hanging from the top of the door. As the door opened, the bell jingled. I knew that someone was coming inside. I looked up and saw my daddy. His body was perfect. He was no longer crippled. His white hair glowed. He smiled at me. He was wearing the suit that he was buried in.

I jumped up from my seat and ran and hugged him. He felt the same as he did when I was a little girl and I ran to meet him when he arrived home from work. I recognized his scent. He hugged me back and kissed me. For a few seconds, he held me tightly.

"Please don't ever leave me again, Daddy," I cried. "I have missed you so much. Please stay with me forever."

Daddy broke our embrace and looked into my eyes. I felt a peace that I hadn't felt since Daddy became ill some five years earlier. "I will be with you forever, Honey," he whispered. "I will be living right here in your heart," he said, as he gently touched my chest. "As long as you continue to love me and want me to be with you, I won't ever leave. But you must take care of yourself. Always remember that I love you."

Just as quickly as he had appeared, he was gone. I opened my eyes and even though there were tears on my pillow, I also felt a sense of peace that I hadn't felt in years. I jumped up to tell my husband what I had just experienced. I called my mother to give her the assurance of my dream, too. Seeing him, hearing him, smelling him, all proved that he had surely been there with me.

I don't understand exactly what happened that morning, but I do know that the secret tears are now gone. Since then, I have been able to cope with the loss of my father. When I think of him now, I don't remember his illness or the difficult days preceding his death. I think about the good times. I remember the glow of his white hair, the smile on his face and feel the love in my heart the last time that I saw him in my dream. My blood pressure is now under control; my cardiologist gave me a clean bill of health.

Occasionally, I think back to Jean's words. I realize that time does heal many wounds. In my heart, however, I know that the real healing came to me through a dream—and that my tears were not a secret after all.

~Nancy B. Gibbs
Chicken Soup for the Father & Daughter Soul

Promises Kept

There is no medicine like hope, no incentive so great,
and no tonic so powerful as expectation of something better tomorrow.
~Orison Marden

My father was not a sentimental man. I don't remember him ever "oohing" or "aahing" over anything I did as a child. Don't get me wrong; I knew that my dad loved me, but getting all mushy-eyed was not his thing. He showed me love in other ways.

I always believed that my parents had a good marriage, but just before I turned sixteen my belief was sorely tested. My father, who used to share in the chores around the house, gradually started becoming despondent. From the time he came home from his job at the factory to the time he went to bed, he hardly spoke a word to any of us. The strain on their relationship was obvious. However, I was not prepared for the day Mom told us kids that Dad had decided to leave. I was stunned. It was something I never thought possible. I went totally numb and pretended it wasn't happening until it actually came time for him to leave.

The night before my dad left, I stayed up in my room for a long time. I prayed and cried. I wrote him a long letter. I told him how much I loved him and how much I would miss him. As I folded my letter, I stuck in a picture of me with a saying I had heard: "Anyone can be a father, but it takes someone special to be a daddy." Early the next morning, before my dad left, I sneaked out to his car and slipped my letter into one of his bags.

Two weeks went by with hardly a word from him. Then one afternoon I came home from school to find my mom sitting at the dining room table. I could see she had been crying. She told me Dad had been over and that they had talked for a long time. They decided there were things they were willing to change—and they decided their marriage was worth saving. Then she looked at me.

"Kristi, Dad told me you wrote him a letter. Can I ask what you wrote to him?" I mumbled a few words and shrugged. Mom continued, "Well, he said that when he read your letter, it made him cry. It meant a lot to him. I've hardly ever seen your dad cry. After he read your letter, he called to ask if he could come over to talk. Whatever you said really made a difference to him."

A few days later my dad was back, this time to stay. We never talked about the letter.

Over the next sixteen years, my siblings and I witnessed one of the truly "great" marriages. Their love grew stronger every day, and my heart swelled with pride as I saw them grow closer together. When Mom and Dad received news that his heart was rapidly deteriorating, they were hand-in-hand throughout the ordeal.

After Dad's death, we had the unpleasant task of going through his things. I opted to run errands so I wouldn't have to be there while most of his things were divided and boxed up. When I got back my brother said, "Kristi, Mom said to give this to you. She said you would know what it meant." My brother was holding the picture I had given Dad that day. My unsentimental dad, who never let his emotions get the best of him, my dad, who almost never outwardly showed his love for me, had kept the one thing that meant so much to both of us. I sat down and the tears began to flow as I realized what I had meant to him. Mom told me Dad had kept both the picture and the letter his whole life.

I have a box in my house that I call the "Dad Box." In it are things that remind me of my dad. I pull that picture out every once in a while and remember. I remember a promise made many years ago between a young man and his bride on their wedding day, and

I remember the unspoken promise made between a father and his daughter — a promise kept.

~Kristi Powers
Chicken Soup for the Christian Teenage Soul

One More Cast

My daughter Chelsea stood knee-deep in the water, silhou-etted in the sunset's waning glow. It was so dark she could no longer see her fly on the water. But still she cast, grace-fully and confidently, hopeful for one last trout.

Kneeling on the nearby bank, I watched silently, proud yet a little sad. I willed a trout to take the fly, to provide sweet icing for this last outing before our lives would change forever.

But it was not to be.

"Time to go," I said.

"Just one more cast," she replied. "Just one more cast."

I smiled and recalled the first time she uttered those words. It was on our first fishing trip together, fifteen years ago.

Chelsea was just two and a half years old when we were invited to fish a stocked farm dugout. She helped me dig the worms in the garden, then eagerly pitched in to pack the gear. Bubbling with excitement as the rods were rigged up, Chelsea insisted on casting her own after I showed her how.

She shrieked with joy when the first trout hit her bait, almost wrenching the rod from her tiny hands. Her first fish.

An angler was born; I had a new fishing partner and a fresh outlook on a sport I had loved since childhood. The circle was complete.

When it came time to leave the dugout, Chelsea said—for the first of many times to come—those four magical words that are music to a father who fishes: "Just one more cast."

I packed up and still she sat, big brown eyes transfixed on the bobber floating on the pond's surface. When Chelsea finally, and reluctantly, got in the car, she recounted the outing all the way home, then provided her mom with a detailed narrative about each fish.

Over the next years, we fished together regularly, sharing conversations about fish and life, spectacular terrain, wildlife encounters, cold dunkings, sunsets, and other rich experiences that malls and video arcades can't provide. Mostly, we shared memories like the trio of swimming moose at that high alpine lake or the time we went fly-fishing and Chelsea caught and released three trout—before I even made my first cast.

When Chelsea's younger sister Sarah was old enough to join us on outings, Chelsea eagerly helped teach her how to fish. Together, they'd catch night crawlers by flashlight in the backyard the night before a walleye-fishing trip. They delighted in holding up writhing double handfuls of the slimy critters, then knocking on the window to get the attention of their mom, who hates anything that crawls.

Chelsea developed a deep concern for clean water, healthy habitats and fishing ethics. Her commitment to catch-and-release became so absolute she'd gently rebuke me for keeping the odd brook trout for lunch.

Three years and many trips to lakes, ponds and small creeks after her farm pond initiation, I thought that Chelsea was ready for a larger river. After setting up my five-year-old partner on the riverbank overlooking a deep hole full of promise, I started casting my own line a few yards away.

"Daddy," she said sweetly but firmly, "you're going to have to move. This is my spot."

While my daughter's skills and confidence grew, many of her questions tested my knowledge of fishing and the outdoors. I answered them as best I could, but knew many responses fell short.

Once, we reluctantly agreed not to bring fishing tackle on a group hike to a pretty set of waterfalls on a clear mountain stream. But the plan changed when we got there. Several brookies were rising to eat hatching insects. Chelsea insisted on breaking out flies, split shot and fishing line from the survival kit, then promptly landed a trout with the emergency tackle tied to a willow branch.

One spring, she caught a twenty-inch bull trout, the biggest I had seen. Chelsea gently cradled the fish in the water, reassuring it of its safety with soft, soothing words, until it regained enough strength to swim away.

A few years ago, I noticed Chelsea was changing. A little girl no more, she started fishing apart from me, politely but firmly declining advice about fly selection, where to cast and just about everything else.

This sense of independence grew stronger in everything she did, from schoolwork to social life and all things in between. A confident, self-motivated young woman had emerged, seemingly overnight.

When darkness finally chased Chelsea off the river the night of our final outing, she insisted on driving me home—the first time ever after a fishing trip. Silently, I wrestled with feelings of sadness, joy and pride.

As we travel this morning to the University of Lethbridge, where the biological sciences program should provide many answers I couldn't, I'll face similar emotions.

And I'll wish we'd shared just one more cast before she left.

~Bruce Masterman
Chicken Soup for the Nature Lover's Soul

Chicken Soup for the Soul

Share with Us

We would like to know how these stories affected you and which ones were your favorites. Please e-mail us and let us know.

We also would like to share your stories with future readers. You may be able to help another reader, and become a published author at the same time. Please send us your own stories and poems for our future books. Some of our past contributors have launched writing and speaking careers from the publication of their stories in our books!

Your stories have the best chance of being used if you submit them through our web site, at:

www.chickensoup.com

If you do not have access to the Internet, you may submit your stories by mail or by facsimile. Please do not send us any book manuscripts, unless through a literary agent, as these will be automatically discarded.

Chicken Soup for the Soul
P.O. Box 700
Cos Cob, CT 06807-0700
Fax 203-861-7194

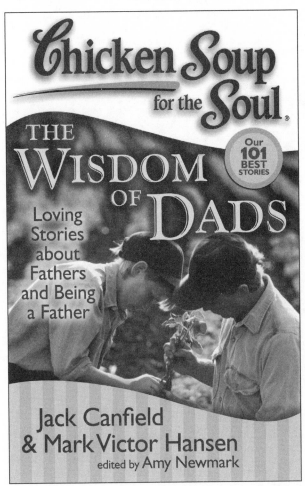

Children view their fathers with awe from the day they are born. Fathers are big and strong and seem to know everything, except for a few teenage years when fathers are perceived to know nothing! This book represents a new theme for Chicken Soup—101 stories selected from 35 past books, all stories focusing on the wisdom of dads. Stories are written by sons and daughters about their fathers, and by fathers relating stories about their children.

978-1-935096-18-4

More
Books for Dads!

Inside Basketball

Chicken Soup has a slam dunk with its first sports book in years, and its first on basketball, with the Orlando Magic's very own Pat Williams, well-known author and motivational speaker. Pat has drawn on his basketball industry connections to compile great stories from on and off the court. Fans will be inspired, surprised, and amused by inside stories from well-known coaches and players, fascinating looks behind the scenes, and anecdotes from the fans.

Tales of Golf & Sport

Golfers are a special breed. They endure bad weather, early wake up calls, great expense, and "interesting" clothing to engage in their favorite sport. This book contains Chicken Soup's 101 best stories about golfers, golfing, and other sports. Chicken Soup's approach to sports books has always been unique — professional and amateur athletes contribute stories from the heart, yielding a book about the human side of golf and other sports, not a how-to book.

The Golf Book

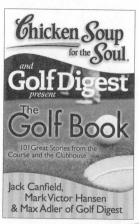

Chicken Soup and Golf Digest magazine's Max Adler and team have put together a great collection of personal stories that will inspire, amuse, and surprise golfers. Celebrity golfers, weekend golfers, beginners, and pros all share the best stories they've told at the 19th hole about good times on and off the course. Chicken Soup's golf books have always been very successful — with the addition of Golf Digest's industry connections, this book should hit a hole in one.

More Books for Men!

Moms Know Best

"Mom will know where it is...what to say...how to fix it." This Chicken Soup book focuses on the pervasive wisdom of mothers everywhere, and includes the best 101 stories from Chicken Soup's library on our perceptive, understanding, and insightful mothers. These stories celebrate the special bond between mothers and children, our mothers' unerring wisdom about everything from the mundane to the life-changing, and the hard work that goes into being a mother every day.

Like Mother, Like Daughter

Fathers, brothers, and friends sometimes shake their head in wonder as girls "turn into their mothers." This new collection from Chicken Soup represents the best 101 stories from Chicken Soup's library on the special bond between mothers and daughters, and the magical, mysterious similarities between them. Mothers and daughters of all ages will laugh, cry, and find inspiration in these stories that remind them how much they appreciate each other.

Moms & Sons

There is a special bond between mothers and their sons and it never goes away. This new book contains the 101 best stories and poems from Chicken Soup's library honoring that lifelong relationship between mothers and their male offspring. These heartfelt and loving stories written by mothers, grandmothers, and sons, about each other, span generations and show how the mother-son bond transcends time.

More Books for Women!

More books for Men

Chicken Soup for the Veteran's Soul 1-55874-937-3
Chicken Soup for the Baseball Fan's Soul 1-55874-965-9
Chicken Soup for the Gardener's Soul 1-55874-966-7
Chicken Soup for the Fisherman's Soul 0-7573-0145-2
Chicken Soup for the Golfer's Soul 1-55874-658-7
Chicken Soup for the Golfer's Soul,
The Second Round 1-55874-982-9
Chicken Soup for the NASCAR Soul 0-7573-0100-2
Chicken Soup for the Father's Soul 1-55874-894-6
Chicken Soup for the Grandparent's Soul 1-55874-974-8
Chicken Soup for the Father & Daughter Soul 0-7573-0252-1
Chicken Soup for the Single Parent's Soul 0-7573-0241-6

Books for Teens

Chicken Soup for the Soul: Preteens Talk
Inspiration and Support for Preteens from Kids Just Like Them
978-1-935096-00-9
Chicken Soup for the Soul: Teens Talk Growing Up
Stories about Growing Up, Meeting Challenges, and
Learning from Life 978-1-935096-01-6
Chicken Soup for the Soul: Teens Talk Tough Times
Stories about the Hardest Parts of Being a Teenager
978-1-935096-03-0
Chicken Soup for the Soul: Teens Talk Relationships
Stories about Family, Friends, and Love
978-1-935096-06-1
Chicken Soup for the Soul: Christian Teen Talk
Christian Teens Share Their Stories of Support, Inspiration and Growing Up
978-1-935096-12-2
Chicken Soup for the Soul: Christian Kids
Stories to Inspire, Amuse, and Warm the Hearts of Christian Kids and Their
Parents
978-1-935096-13-9

Books for Families

On Being a Parent

Inspirational, Humorous, and Heartwarming
Stories about Parenthood
978-1-935096-20-7

Parenting is the hardest and most rewarding job in the world. This upbeat and compelling new book includes the best selections on parenting from Chicken Soup's rich history, with 101 stories carefully selected to appeal to both mothers and fathers. This is a great book for couples to share, whether they are just embarking on their new adventure as parents or reflecting on their lifetime experience.

Grand and Great

Grandparents and Grandchildren Share Their
Stories of Love and Wisdom
978-1-935096-09-2

A parent becomes a new person the day the first grandchild is born. Formerly serious and responsible adults go on shopping sprees for toys and baby clothing, smile incessantly, pull out photo albums that they "just happen to have" with them, and proudly display baby seats in their cars. Grandparents dote on their grandchildren, and grandchildren love them back with all their hearts. This new book includes the best stories on being a grandparent from 34 past Chicken Soup books, representing a new reading experience for even the most devoted Chicken Soup fan.

About the Authors
&
Acknowledgments

Chicken Soup for the Soul

Who Is
Jack Canfield?

J ack Canfield is the co-creator and editor of the *Chicken Soup for the Soul* series, which *Time* magazine has called "the publishing phenomenon of the decade." Jack is also the co-author of eight other bestselling books including *The Success Principles™: How to Get from Where You Are to Where You Want to Be, Dare to Win, The Aladdin Factor, You've Got to Read This Book,* and *The Power of Focus: How to Hit Your Business and Personal and Financial Targets with Absolute Certainty*.

Jack has recently developed a telephone coaching program and an online coaching program based on his most recent book *The Success Principles*. He also offers a seven-day *Breakthrough to Success* seminar every summer, which attracts 400 people from fifteen countries around the world.

Jack is the CEO of the Canfield Training Group in Santa Barbara, California, and founder of the Foundation for Self-Esteem in Culver City, California. He has conducted intensive personal and professional development seminars on the principles of success for over a million people in twenty-three countries. Jack is a dynamic keynote speaker and he has spoken to hundreds of thousands of others at more than 1,000 corporations, universities, professional conferences and conventions, and has been seen by millions more on national television shows such as *The Today Show, Fox and Friends, Inside Edition, Hard Copy, CNN's Talk Back Live, 20/20, Eye to Eye,* and the *NBC Nightly News* and the *CBS Evening News*.

Jack is the recipient of many awards and honors, including three honorary doctorates and a *Guinness World Records Certificate* for having seven books from the *Chicken Soup for the Soul* series appearing on the *New York Times* bestseller list on May 24, 1998.

To write to Jack or for inquiries about Jack as a speaker, his coaching programs, trainings or seminars, use the following contact information:

Jack Canfield
The Canfield Companies
P.O. Box 30880 • Santa Barbara, CA 93130
phone: 805-563-2935 • fax: 805-563-2945
E-mail: info@jackcanfield.com
www.jackcanfield.com

Who Is
Mark Victor Hansen?

Mark Victor Hansen is the co-founder of *Chicken Soup for the Soul*, along with Jack Canfield. He is also a sought-after keynote speaker, bestselling author, and marketing maven.

For more than thirty years, Mark has focused solely on helping people from all walks of life reshape their personal vision of what's possible. His powerful messages of possibility, opportunity, and action have created powerful change in thousands of organizations and millions of individuals worldwide.

Mark's credentials include a lifetime of entrepreneurial success. He is a prolific writer with many bestselling books, such as *The One Minute Millionaire*, *Cracking the Millionaire Code*, *How to Make the Rest of Your Life the Best of Your Life*, *The Power of Focus*, *The Aladdin Factor*, and *Dare to Win*, in addition to the *Chicken Soup for the Soul* series. Mark has had a profound influence in the field of human potential through his library of audios, videos, and articles in the areas of big thinking, sales achievement, wealth building, publishing success, and personal and professional development.

Mark is the founder of the *MEGA Seminar Series*. *MEGA Book Marketing University* and *Building Your MEGA Speaking Empire* are annual conferences where Mark coaches and teaches new and aspiring authors, speakers, and experts on building lucrative publishing and speaking careers. Other MEGA events include *MEGA Info-Marketing* and *My MEGA Life*.

He has appeared on *Oprah*, *CNN*, and *The Today Show*. He has been quoted in *Time*, *U.S. News & World Report*, *USA Today*, *New York Times*, and *Entrepreneur* and has had countless radio interviews, assuring our planet's people that "You can easily create the life you deserve."

As a philanthropist and humanitarian, Mark works tirelessly for organizations such as Habitat for Humanity, American Red Cross, March of Dimes, Childhelp USA, and many others. He is the recipient of numerous awards that honor his entrepreneurial spirit, philanthropic heart, and business acumen. He is a lifetime member of the Horatio Alger Association of Distinguished Americans, an organization that honored Mark with the prestigious Horatio Alger Award for his extraordinary life achievements.

Mark Victor Hansen is an enthusiastic crusader of what's possible and is driven to make the world a better place.

Mark Victor Hansen & Associates, Inc.
P.O. Box 7665 • Newport Beach, CA 92658
phone: 949-764-2640 • fax: 949-722-6912
www.markvictorhansen.com

Who Is
Amy Newmark?

Amy Newmark was recently named publisher of Chicken Soup for the Soul, after a thirty-year career as a writer, speaker, financial analyst, and business executive in the worlds of finance and telecommunications.

Amy is a graduate of Harvard College, where she majored in Portuguese, minored in French, and traveled extensively. She is also the mother of two children in college and has two grown stepchildren.

After a long career writing books on telecommunications, voluminous financial reports, business plans, and corporate press releases, Chicken Soup for the Soul is a breath of fresh air for Amy. She has fallen in love with Chicken Soup for the Soul and its life-changing books, and found it a true pleasure to conceptualize, compile, and edit the "101 Best Stories" books for our readers.

The best way to contact Chicken Soup for the Soul is through our web site, at www.chickensoup.com. This will always get the fastest attention.

If you do not have access to the Internet, please contact us by mail or by facsimile.

Chicken Soup for the Soul
P.O. Box 700
Cos Cob, CT 06807-0700
Fax 203-861-7194

Chicken Soup for the Soul®

Thank You!

Our first thanks go to our loyal readers who have inspired the entire Chicken Soup team for the past fifteen years. Your appreciative letters and e-mails have reminded us why we work so hard on these books.

We owe huge thanks to all of our contributors as well. We know that you pour your hearts and souls into the stories and poems that you share with us, and ultimately with each other. We appreciate your willingness to open up your lives to other Chicken Soup readers.

We can only publish a small percentage of the stories that are submitted, but we read every single one and even the ones that do not appear in a book have an influence on us and on the final manuscripts.

As always, we would like to thank the entire staff of Chicken Soup for the Soul for their help on this project and the 101 Best series in general.

Among our California staff, we would especially like to single out the following people:

- D'ette Corona, who is the heart and soul of the Chicken Soup publishing operation, and who put together the first draft of this manuscript

- Barbara LoMonaco for invaluable assistance in obtaining the fabulous quotations that add depth and meaning to this book

- Patty Hansen for her extra special help with the permissions for these fabulous stories and for her amazing knowledge of the Chicken Soup library and Patti Clement for her help with permissions and other organizational matters.

In our Connecticut office, we would like to thank our able editorial assistants, Valerie Howlett and Madeline Clapps, for their assistance in setting up our new offices, editing, and helping us put together the best possible books.

We would also like to thank our master of design, Creative Director and book producer Brian Taylor at Pneuma Books, LLC, for his brilliant vision for our covers and interiors.

Finally, none of this would be possible without the business and creative leadership of our CEO, Bill Rouhana, and our president, Bob Jacobs.